ADULT FANTASY

searching for true maturity in an age of mortgages, marriages, and other adult milestones

BRIOHNY DOYLE

SCRIBE
Melbourne • London

Scribe Publications
18–20 Edward St, Brunswick, Victoria 3056, Australia
2 John St, Clerkenwell, London, WC1N 2ES, United Kingdom

First published by Scribe 2017

Typeset in Electra 11/15 pt by the publishers.
Printed and bound in the UK by CPI Group (UK) Ltd, Croydon CR0 4YY

Scribe Publications is committed to the sustainable use of natural resources and the use of paper products made responsibly from those resources.

9781925322163 (Australian edition)
9781911344285 (UK edition)
9781925548204 (e-book)

CIP records for this title are available from the British Library and the National Library of Australia

scribepublications.com.au
scribepublications.co.uk

For Annie,
and for Dad, who grew up with me.

PROLOGUE

For a long time I pretended turning thirty was no big deal. But looking back, it's clear I was bat-shit na-na for a good nine months either side of that birthday. I spent three weeks' pay renting a 1971 Dodge Challenger convertible in an original factory colour called plum crazy. I pictured myself at that auspicious anniversary, a wine-dark streak in a TV desert, ears too full of the summer wind to hear that ominous ticking in the sky: the sound of a cultural clock counting me out of youth.

The Dodge was the same model Mickey and Mallory Knox drove in the 1994 hyper-violent romance classic *Natural Born Killers*. It was a good car for rolling up to a Las Vegas drive-through chapel – important, because I'd decided that thirty was wedding age, regardless of how troubling my partner and I found the idea of marriage. For months I'd been pausing significantly outside jewellers. For months I'd been locked in an internet search loop that oscillated between white dresses, unaffordable houses in towns I'd never been to, career aptitude tests, and pop-psychology articles on obsessive compulsive disorder and rare degenerative brain diseases, all of which seemed to explain the patterns of behaviour that were rapidly becoming my life. I tried to tear my attention away from these seemingly pressing matters back to my terminal degree — a doctoral dissertation on the apocalypse — but only seemed able to focus on wastelands in literature for mere seconds before the literal wasteland of listicles, think pieces, and advertorials ensnared me once again.

Thirty Things You Should Know by Thirty, screamed my Facebook feed, drawing me into a tunnel from which I would emerge hours later, screen-shocked and disconnected.

Around me, friends were marrying, having babies, and buying houses, or gliding gracefully along a path of career advancement — at least, it seemed that way. What was wrong with me — why was I failing to come of age? Why was my life on the cusp of thirty so similar to what it had been at twenty-five, or even seventeen? And why did I care so much?

When my birthday finally came around, I got so pre-emptively drunk that I couldn't drive the Dodge and spent most of it holed up in a family motel popping generic-brand valium and watching *The Big Bang Theory*.

'It's okay,' my boyfriend, Serge, assured me. 'We have the car for another twenty-four hours. We can pretend that tomorrow is your birthday.'

I nodded palely, though I knew this pretence would not suffice. Some crucial illusion had been broken.

A week later, I had to fly home suddenly to put my dog to sleep.

A month later, I thought, *I can't get fucking married, are you serious?*

Six months later, oxygen streamed back into my lungs as if I'd surfaced from thirty continuous laps of the pool.

'What just happened?' I spluttered, the sky suddenly too bright, the past year coming into sharp relief against this vicious spread of blue.

1
SUDDEN AGE FORWARD

When the movie *Big* came out, I watched it with my parents. I was small then, and my parents were still together. We lived in a house in the country, and occasionally we did things like drive into town to see a movie as a family. Thinking back, that time itself seems movie-tinted now: edited and filtered through the cinematic gaze of memory.

As I remember it, my parents liked *Big*. They laughed at things that did not seem funny to me at all.

Big is a sudden-age-forward comedy, a popular subgenre of the body swap wherein a young person is thrown into the life of an adult. The plot is simple: a boy wishes to be big enough to fulfil his dream of accompanying a cute girl on a carnival ride and subsequently wakes up to discover he is Tom Hanks. Naturally, he's appalled. His jeans don't fit. He is hairy all over. This is not how he pictured adulthood. Forced to fend for himself, he finds the world beyond suburban picket fences garish and confusing. Being a grown-up looked like a sweet alternative to sharing a room with a baby, but in 1980s New York there are examples of urban lives gone awry muttering and staggering through the smeary neon of Times Square. Also, adults, it turns out, are subject to all kinds of ignoble oppressions. The senseless queues. The horrors of bureaucracy. The necessity of work.

Most of us have a moment of adult reckoning. It can come at any age, at any time. You suddenly become acutely aware that you are a cliché; you don't like what you do every day; your job title and pay packet aren't much different than when you first started in the workforce; you are becoming your mother or your father – or you are failing to. You come to the realisation that life is just not what you thought it would be when you were a child filled with fantasies of becoming an adult. Unlike Tom Hanks, though, you can't play or whimsy your way to adult success.

My adult reckoning came at thirty.

In the second decade of the twenty-first century, I turned thirty amid a mediascape littered with the details of my generation's inadequacy. Millennials – those born roughly between 1980 and 2000 – are dubbed the 'Peter Pan generation' on account of our unwillingness to give up childish things such as high-tech toys and our childhood bedrooms. We are accused of adolescent spending habits. We like smartphones more than cars (don't we ever want to actually go anywhere?). We are recalcitrant brats who refuse to take up responsible roles in the community. We are all a bunch of thoroughly bad adults.

These editorials came in thick and fast, a regular dose of hyperbole and panic to accompany my tea and toast each morning. They sell papers, these accusations. They also fuel the outrage machine. I did my best to swallow breakfast and move on, but some days the headlines swarmed the internet like locusts.

Worse yet, despite the sensationalising, and the general tone of paternal disapproval, this portrait of the Generation Y post-adolescent malingerer was not wholly without resonance. I could laugh, though just barely, at Daniel Clowes' *New Yorker* cartoon of a man hanging up his doctoral certificate in his childhood bedroom, above the rock posters and high-school trophies. I could brush off the descriptions of kidults who were more interested in entertainment than in exercising their right to vote. Intergenerational sledging was an age-old pastime, I knew. Yet the descriptions lingered, leaving their oily trace on my self-assessment.

As I approached my thirtieth year, in circumstance my life was not very different from when I was twenty. I was still living in rental accommodation. I was still studying; working part-time in unchallenging, minimum-wage jobs; and pursuing various creative endeavours. All this felt fine – most often, more than fine. Nevertheless, with each new statistic, with each damning indictment, the sense of having missed some crucial memo on how to grow up got stronger.

This feeling was exacerbated by those around me, who did not fit the stereotype. One by one, my close friends all seemed to be breaking into grown-up society. Was it possible that I knew the only responsible, career-building, baby-making, mortgage-signing millennials in the world? Were those newspaper editorials aimed solely at me? As thirty approached, I became fascinated by other people's decisions, making a pest of myself, like a toddler who can't stop asking why. Mostly, my friends just shrugged. The consensus was that, eventually, marriage, babies, and mortgages is just what you do. This idea — so far from the vision of adulthood I imagined for myself, from how I saw my life — made me feel like an unwanted guest who accidentally stays too long at the party.

My family had been starting to have similar concerns about my life direction. I fought with my dad on census night.

'Marital status?' he said, in his best deadpan parody of a bureaucrat.

'Never married.'

'But you're practically married,' he protested. 'It's the same thing.'

'No, it's not,' I said, tapping between the lines. 'Never married.'

He raised an eyebrow, a skill I did not inherit. Dad is a journalist of the old school, and I was reminded, in his need to spin my life, of one of his maxims: 'Give me a fact and I'll invent you a story.' He continued through the form, recording my lack of religion, my education level, my lack of a second language. Nothing tangibly adult, though. Nothing quantifiable.

This agitated Dad. He poured another glass of plonk. He wanted to record a milestone or two on that census night. And he held the pen. He was the scribe, the arbiter of fact;

a role he had occupied since I was a kid. My relationship to him, 'daughter', in block letters, gleamed like an order on the muted orange form. There was duty in that word, centuries of paternalism drawn tight around it. Perhaps it was this (or perhaps the half bottle of wine) that got my hackles up. The editorials began ringing in my ears: I felt as if I'd been drawn into the ring to fight for my cohort once more. I was in the Y corner. Why, why, why?

Dad hesitated at 'occupation'. I'd been working casual shifts at a greengrocer for years, while studying and writing. My income from all sources was just above the poverty line, with nothing distinguishing itself as a career through earning capacity. When he was my age, Dad was on his first mortgage, his second wife, his third city, his eighth car. He was busy building a house and planning a family with my mother. He was a heavy drinker and questionable decision-maker with a penchant for poor bets on the ponies, sure, but on paper he had locked things in – and for his generation he was a late bloomer. 'I suppose you are a…'

'Full-time student,' I supplied.

'Really?'

'You know this, Dad.'

'I think you're more like a freelance researcher.'

'I don't know what that is.'

'You can't be a student,' he said. 'You're almost thirty.'

And there it was. In the middle distance, a man wearing Brylcreem and suspenders rang the bell. Round one: Dad.

In a twist of fate, in *Big* it's precisely the protagonist's childlike qualities that make him a successful adult. He's innocent – he doesn't understand sexual innuendo. He does not kowtow to the manners and mores of the stuffy grown-up milieu. He is imaginative, creative. He wears appalling shirts and plays pinball. He looks at the world with an intoxicating sense of wonder. Here's some adult stuff he doesn't have: doubt, hatred, ambition, intellect, lack. He plays chopsticks on a giant piano with his feet. He embodies our culture's reverence for childhood.

People did not always have such a solid distinction between child and adult, nor did they always revere childhood. Historian Philippe Ariès famously declared that in the medieval world 'the idea of childhood did not exist'. Before the seventeenth century, high infant mortality rates meant babies were often given the names of deceased siblings so as not to tax the parental memory. Renaissance paintings show children as stern little adults; babies suckle at luminous breasts, their tiny faces sculpted into grimaces of mature distain. Improvements in healthcare laid the foundations for a more sentimental view of children, but even so, childhood as we know it was popularised after the Industrial Revolution. Before this, a thirteen-year-old going to work was no joke, and it wasn't their creativity and innocence that was valued, but their small stature and smaller demands. When jobs became scarce, adult labour was prioritised. Let out of the engine bays and crawl spaces of labour, Tom Sawyer went fishing and Pip asked for more. Whimsical childhood as a protected space was birthed from these literary worlds, rather than from the wombs of actual women.

Now, far from enduring or distaining childhood, we think it is where we left our authentic selves. Childhood has come to dominate our cultural narratives. I remember my mother giggling at the scene where a grown woman suggests a sleepover with Tom Hanks, and he shows her his bunk bed. Now that I'm a grown woman myself, I find this film more hauntingly prophetic than funny. A man behaving like a boy is certainly no novelty in the dating scene. Play as the antidote to stuffy corporate culture is less of a joke in the age of Google campuses and advertising agencies with intra-office slides. But if the message of *Big* was to find our inner child, in the second decade of the twenty-first century, we got it.

Given that childhood is now more prized than independence, it's no wonder that its temporality has become stretchy. If we can assert our right to longer childhoods, when and how does adulthood begin? Looking for a sociological basis for the latest lagging generation, Jeffery Jensen Arnett coined the term 'emerging adult' to refer to the elastic, transitional period between adolescence and adulthood. He argues that this has recently become a socially entrenched developmental stage, in which people are granted a 'moratorium' from the responsibilities of adult life. Arnett's research was inspired by his work with college students, and a series of interviews conducted in the 1990s that often began with the question 'Do you feel like you have reached adulthood?' Perhaps unsurprisingly, people's responses tended to be 'yes and no'. In developed countries, during your twenties, while you might be more independent than you were during high school, it's likely you still have more in common with a seventeen-year-old than most forty-five-year-olds.

What Arnett refers to as emerging adulthood is called different things in the international media, but the pattern is the same largely throughout the Western world, and in some other countries too. In Korea, the sampo generation (*sampo* translates as 'abandon three') are a cohort said to have given up on dating, marriage, and procreation. The Japanese corollary is the satori generation, a kinder term referring to a cohort who seem to have transcended desire (*satori* means enlightenment in Japan). The satori generation work in undemanding jobs. They don't often date. They don't share the national passion for shopping, but neither do they save money for the future. They aim to have less stressful lives, to live within their means, says the press.

In North America, the terrible term 'twixta' was dreamed up to refer to those caught between adolescence and adulthood, typified by college graduates who can't find work and continue to live at home long past the age they should be moving out. In the Middle East and North Africa, young adults are said to be experiencing a 'waithood', a new developmental period after the end of education where young people feel as though they are simply waiting for adult life to begin. Interestingly, this final formula has become an international relations issue: the prevalence of the waithood is described as part of the 'youth crisis' in the Middle East, which interests international organisations and the United States particularly in their consideration and representation of radicalisation.

While there are cultural nuances in each of these characterisations that make writing about, say, millennials in Argentina a project out of my depth, the fact that there are indications of a globally relevant trend is fascinating. Because that's the catch for people of my age. Many societies have come to revere childhood, but they also haven't let go of the idea of an adult as a productive citizen and an agent of the economy. Whereas once routes were more firmly mapped out, options more limited, today young people develop under a confusing imperative to simultaneously perform their age-appropriate roles and maintain their youthfulness: to be both Tom Hanks the CEO and the boy he once was.

As my thirtieth year approached, I felt simultaneously resistant to normative standards for adulthood and plagued by the fear that this obstinacy was a symptom of my own immaturity. I loathed previous generations for having what seemed an easier transition to adulthood, richer people for having an easier everything. Then I loathed myself for not feeling lucky, grateful, privileged. It was a hideous spiral fed by the media. I was conflicted, confused, and irrational. I found myself browsing realestate.com despite the fact that I had no money and no idea what city I wanted to live in. On Saturday-night dates with my sweetheart, I paused significantly in front of jewellers' windows to gaze at the diamond rings (Diamonds! Appalling!) all the while incredulous at myself, my inner critic's brow raised, Dad-like, as if to say 'Are you serious?'

I wanted a clue as to how to approach the new decade of life I was about to enter, but I couldn't stop mentally rehearsing the Mickey Rourke speech from *Barfly* — Mickey in bar-fight makeup before bad choices messed up his face for real, before he found the redeeming love of god and rescue chihuahuas; Mickey channelling Bukowski in the blue-lit bar: 'I get so tired thinking about all the things I don't want to do. All the things I don't want to be.'

'You're not supposed to think about it,' says the barkeep. 'I think the whole trick is not to think about it.'

On a cultural analysis, it's no surprise I freaked out at thirty. According to the dictates of popular culture I grew up with, twenties = youth and thirty = adult. More insidious than this, twenties are the 'aspirational age', a marketing term for a demographic that those on either side aspire to be. This is the college years of American teen soap operas, the smudged, salt-licked utopia of capitalist coming-of-age. Contemporary cultural messages on adulthood are fairly unambiguous: if you are middle class it's acceptable, if not wholly commendable, to blaze up your twenties in 'a holocaust of desire'. Experiment. Travel. Think and talk about yourself — a lot. Get a job and save some money, sure, but this doesn't have to be the centre of your life. It's okay, when you are working out who you are, not to have a handle on your social position yet. Advertising and much of popular culture suggests using this time to exorcise your inner wild child, to take risks and wear gaudy sneakers. Just remember, all this behaviour has an endpoint, and it's called thirty. Jeffrey Arnett terms it 'the age thirty deadline'.

A cynical take on Arnett's idea of emerging adulthood is that, like 'pre-teen' and 'teenager', it consolidates a market. While the freewheeling teen with money to burn on records and pizza drag-raced out of the post-war economic boom of the 1950s, the emerging adult as we know it today seems to have slumbered through the birth of Christ, the tough times of the Dark Ages, and the extremes of the Renaissance and the Enlightenment, to finally slouch forth from 1970s counterculture, bolstered by birth control, changed attitudes to premarital sex, and gender roles, along with a heightened emphasis on education as the way to get ahead in life. It is an important demographic development, and the idea of self-involved youth has been cultivated to sell popstars and sneakers, cigarettes and meal-replacement milkshakes.

Of course, the idea of blazing up your twenties is not a universal. If we believe the shows on television, almost every twenty-something is a middle-class, English-speaking white person living in a developed country, and, while Arnett claims that the emerging adult will be a more-or-less globally apparent phenomenon by the end of the twenty-first century, it's important not to erase the very real social relations of class with those of generations. Yet much of our popular culture, rooted in a woebegone sense of nostalgia, is inured to these differences of class and life experience, and is aimed at selling this period of life to teenagers and mid-lifers.

At thirteen, my best friend Annie and I longed to be twenty-something. We sat on the roof of the school library listening to the sound of bands playing in the bar across the street, focusing our longing. Life was only just over there, and yet it was so intolerably far. Something had to be done. We decided to use the method favoured by impatient teenagers ever since the distinction between teen and adult was officiated over by bureaucrats behind plexiglass: we got fake IDs.

We walked into the roads and traffic authority as children and walked out as adults. (Well, not quite adults; Annie's lips were cut from the effort of smiling for the camera without revealing her braces.) We were both anxious to get back to school by fifth period. And yet things were different when we returned. Bureaucratic magic had bestowed us with many powers. Now we could buy cigarettes and beer, see rock shows and violent films. We stepped forth into our dreams, a bright age of fake majority. We were free.

It was the 1990s, the beginning of what would soon be declared as 'the death of the adult' in popular culture. In one of my favourite films, a teenage Winona Ryder described the future as a place where 'we just grow up, be adults and die'. It was a perfect time to experience the freedoms of adulthood in tandem with the irresponsibility and security of adolescence spent under our parents' roofs.

When my dad – rifling through my schoolbag looking for cigarettes to bum – found my ID, he made me hand it over. Dad was in his fifties, but he wanted to be twenty-five as much as we did. He understood, he said. He would keep the ID and I could borrow it from him to see rock shows, on the proviso that he knew where I was. For six months, he was reliably up the back at every show, one eye on us and one, aspirationally, on some actual twenty-something woman. He never gave us up, though, and eventually – when our age caught up with the fantasy – we realised that an aspirational age is not a real period of life. It is an illusion we could reach for eternally. Cigarettes and beer do not taste as sweet when you also have to buy your own food, when you are suddenly responsible for your life rather than simply perpetuating a splendid pantomime of it.

My actual twenties was a messy, dark, and difficult period. Sometimes I felt I was scrambling to get a foothold in some kind of sustainable life plan; other times I was still trying to muster the energy and certainty of that strawberry youth. It was a decade of contradictions, anxieties alternately crippling and energising, insurmountable limitations coupled with the broader cultural insistence that I would never be so free. During my twenties I worked crappy jobs, I studied and shoplifted, I wrote and danced and took a lot of long drives. And then I was thirty. This is the point when the moratorium ends, according to Arnett.

'I'm past the point where I can just have fun,' says Rachel from *Friends* in the episode 'The One Where They All Turn Thirty'.

In the 1970s, youth culture was cause for celebration and panic. In the 1990s, twenty-something nihilism became a top-selling posture. Teen angst was the best way to sell records. Urtexts such as the film *Reality Bites* and the novel *Generation X* set the tone for a whole genre. The messages of these texts still resonate. But a world without the internet, without constant conversation and comparison, is not the world in which I and most other millennials dwell. And, while the twenty-something is still a lucrative market demographic if you can just tell them how they are feeling (or better yet, let them tell you) and secure the rights to a hip soundtrack, youth itself is now currency in a far more competitive and complicated network of exchange. As Malcolm Harris notes in *Kids These Days*, where once corporate entities co-opted youth culture and repackaged it for mass consumption, now it's the job of young people to design personal brand strategies and sell themselves to one another and to corporate backers. In the twenty-first century, most young people are painfully aware their youth as a finite resource, and many are anxious to leverage it for more durable forms of capital, whether cash, cache, or fame.

We all collaborate on the fiction of the aspirational age — young and old. We yearn for shared narratives, but this desire leads to the collapse of difference and the emergence of a false cohesion that makes us, above all, easier to market to.

In 2014, prime-time television in Australia was dominated by an advertisement for a mid-price family car known as a Sportage. The ad begins with a thirty-something mother reversing down her suburban driveway. Her mincing, worrywart husband and his reminders about milk shrink to a speck in her rearview. The Sportage (long, classy *a* sound) turns a mundane family errand into a vital space of rebellion and escape. The stereo powers up, conjuring 1990s rap superstars Salt-N-Pepa into the cabin, where they accompany the woman in a karaoke rendition of their hit 'Push It'. From the car's plush yet practical interior, the suburban mother postures with adolescent attitude. She's sassy, making gang signs out the window and casting threatening glances across the hedges of her middle-class white neighbourhood. The advertisement closes with the slogan 'Grow up, not old', both a command and a promise.

This commercial is clever because it manages to parody the idea of aspirational age — what's more embarrassing than a rapping mum? — while selling its vehicle via this very premise (rap, generic suburban mum; you are as young as you feel!) It presents youth as a series of stylised gestures and slogans. And yet the woman has the cultural trifecta of adulthood: a family, a house in the suburbs, an expensive car.

Texts such as the Sportage ad campaign and the film *Big* are reliant on the tension between two cultural narratives about ageing. The first, progress, insists that ageing and development is an accumulation of skills, assets, and status. This is the narrative we learn as children, when we are graded by age and expected to behave and achieve accordingly — a pressure we will likely continue to feel until we die. The second narrative, decline, insists that ageing is a slow process of inevitable decay. Your physical appearance degenerates. Breasts and scrotums sag. Hair thins. Brows furrow and crease. Memory becomes unreliable; even intellect and personality warp and crumble. Each narrative can be exploited for commercial gains. Our booming plastic surgery industry profits from narratives of decline, as do tech, fashion, and pharmacology. Purchasing power can stand in for progress in a pinch, meaning if you don't feel as though you are getting somewhere, you can always buy a ticket.

Progress and decline are not mutually exclusive, though. In *Aged by Culture*, cultural theorist Margaret Gullette insists that our narratives about ageing help us to internalise the imperative of advancing, improving, and keeping up 'while simultaneously never getting any older (because being young is the single best promise of being able to succeed in the future)'. For those who, despite having adult responsibilities such as babies and mortgages, still feel juvenile: *Don't worry*, the ad says, *drive a Sport-ahh-ge*. The youthful consumer upgrades, they keep shopping; they stay frivolous and young at heart. It's a desperate, anxious imperative.

At thirty, I didn't own a car. I didn't feel frivolous, but my life wasn't consequential, either. I walked that tension between the narratives of ageing like a tightrope. We live in a culture that idealises childhood and youth, and reduces adulthood to career and family, so naturally the move between the two can be a bit traumatic. Particularly if, at that point when you can no longer ignore your adult status, career and family are nowhere around.

At the grocery shop where I have worked since I was twenty-five, most of us have regrettable tattoos. I have a set of skeletal conjoined twins on my left shoulder. (Annie and I got the same image together on my twenty-first birthday. Having had access to cigarettes, beer, and violent films for almost a decade, we really had to turn it up a notch.) I also have the word *Vegas* tattooed across my wrist like a watch. That's right. It's always Vegas time. When someone asks me about this, I comfort myself in the only way I can muster: by remembering all the tattoos I do not have. I don't have The Dead Kennedys logo on my forearm. I don't have a spine tattooed on the skin over my own spine. And, most importantly, I don't have a pixie sitting in the shade of a toadstool, making a wish on a dandelion, just above my butt crack.

One of my co-workers has the advertising-slogan-worthy sentiment 'Growing up is giving up' scrawled across her thigh. 'Of course the person with this tattoo would end up at law school,' she said with a laugh when I noticed it.

But this tattoo is almost totemic. It shows how, in our imagining of youth, and in the way we describe and police the roles of adults, maturity has become something to fear and loathe, and youth something to guard against losing. It seems impossible to even begin addressing the question of how to construct a meaningful adulthood if one is totally consumed with the colossal task of measuring losses against gains and freaking out about the deficit. This is what I was doing when I lingered outside the jewellers, sent futile emails to realtors, and booked ridiculous holidays. I was trying to acquire an adult identity all at once. I didn't go so far as to buy a Sportage. My adult fantasy was a rental, and it was plum crazy.

Statistics tell us we are more likely to chuck a tantrum or make a rash decision before our major birthdays, with thirty featuring large. In my thirtieth year, despite my resolve not to declare some minor apocalypse, a statistically predicted significant event found me. A week after my birthday, my dog died.

Cassady, my splendid ridgeback cross, had cancer. Like any death preceded by a long illness, the circumstances were sad and difficult.

I felt numb as I drove her to the vet in a borrowed car, stopping en route at the park for a final moment together. We leant against each other, both on all fours in a patch of winter sunlight. The moisture from the grass seeped into my jeans. Cassady leaned into me slightly and sighed. I offered her a treat, but she just closed her eyes.

I tried to hold on to the moment, to draw it out so as to be sure to remember it vividly, but all I could feel was her pain, my desperation. Resigned, we staggered back to the car, and I helped her slump onto the passenger seat. I turned the key in the ignition, and the engine choked. I tried again: only splutter.

I opened the car door. It was cold outside. A lone jogger lapped the park's perimeter.

I got out my phone and scrolled through the names of the people in my life. There was not one I could call. Everyone would be busy: at work, or juggling life while looking after children, or moved away, or not close enough to me to be here in this sad moment. I turned to Cassady but she was sleeping — dying, really. The numbness broke and I wept, staring tearily out the windscreen at a pair of teenage goths sharing a set of headphones and a cigarette on a park bench. Why was I so alone, so disconnected from the lives of those around me? Where was my community, my family? My car?

More than a decade ago, Cassady had crawled out from under a caravan in Humpty Doo, a tiny town in Australia's Northern Territory, and locked her strong jaw on my life. I loved her and our life together. She was my first real responsibility.

We were inseparable for eleven years, as I watched her grow in dog years from a puppy to an adolescent to a reliable matron. I have never been so sure of what I wanted from life as I was the day I picked up that tiny brown puppy.

The common wisdom is that you don't know what you want when you are a teenager. I felt as if I was experiencing the opposite: I knew less the longer I lived. Possibilities broadened, but my perspective lost its rigidity, and my will, once certain and uncompromising, was becoming reedy. My understanding of the world and my place in it was less certain. It struck me, in the weeks after Cassady's death, that she had aged and died without my making another big life decision.

I decided to speak to someone, choosing a psychologist who specialised in helping people deal with grief. Miraculously, she also turned out to be a dog tragic who referred to her standard poodle as a person.

'Cassady was at the centre of my life,' I sobbed in her office, crumbling under my first crucial dose of sympathy. 'And now, right when I need one, it feels like my life has no core.'

My psychologist talked about identity foreclosure and recommended a book by an Auschwitz survivor that made me feel like a total arsehole. Then she drew block diagrams representing the stages of life. They were, I found out later, Abraham Maslow's famed Hierarchy of Needs. 'In your twenties,' she said, 'you spend most of your time on the fundamentals: working out how to feed yourself, have clean sheets, and turn up to things on time. If you get this far, you might start to exercise. You might work out that if you drink too much you get sad, and if you behave poorly, people stop inviting you over for dinner. These are basic things, but they aren't easy. Some people don't work this stuff out until well into their fifties – I see men particularly who become widowers and realise they don't know how to feed themselves. It's nearly impossible to attain higher meaning in life unless you have mastered the basics.'

'I have clean sheets!' I protested. My sheets had been at least moderately clean for seven years. I'd been exercising and flossing my teeth. I could cook and drive and meet deadlines. My needs were less basic and more existential.

'It's a difficult time to become an adult,' she admitted. 'I see a lot of young people, especially women, between the ages of twenty-eight and thirty-two, who are having trouble deriving satisfaction from their lives.' She blamed helicopter parenting and underemphasising resilience in childhood. She blamed popular culture and advertising. She blamed the changing nature of work and the vapidity of social media. She said we were all too busy comparing ourselves to one another, and that status updates and photos of fancy holidays and babies exacerbated the feeling of falling behind the pack.

She was right, of course. But it was impossible not to make comparisons. We all know the pain of envy and fear-of-missing-out that stabs us when we scroll through the reams of cute baby, new house, island getaway, great haircut on Facebook and Instagram.

Instead of collecting those things, I had spent my late twenties in various bedroom-cum-offices writing a complicated dystopian novel and a dissertation on the apocalypse in contemporary film and literature. 'Those are very depressing choices,' my Dad had observed, more than once, seguing into nervous suggestions about courses in photography or HTML.

I never found the apocalypse, world destruction fantasies, or virtually impenetrable books of theory depressing, though. Anyway, if all those devastating waves, exploding skylines, and vociferating adverbs did get too much, I would simply grab the lead and walk it off. Cassady and I rambled through the suburban scrublands and across the dirty streams of Melbourne. We swam and dug up the beaches of Sydney. We curled up together in a caravan in Darwin. After she died, I realised how important 'walking the dog' had become to my day. It had become praxis; a method of engagement.

Each morning, I pulled myself reluctantly from dreams of dogs, ignoring the pitter-patter of ghost feet downstairs. I made tea and sat down in front of my screen. 'Fin-de-siècle Apocalypse' read the heading of a new chapter. I sighed, looked over my notes. Hours passed. Downstairs, the ghost dog got restless. Outside, the rain fell. I paced the house, made endless cups of tea. Ghost dogs walk themselves. In the city where I live, when it rains it hails.

Melbourne winter. Endless and unfair.

'It's a cliché,' the psychologist had said, 'but everything is very abstracted at the moment.'

I'd nodded. A dog is very helpful in an abstracted life. I told her about reading Baudrillard during my undergraduate degree when a filthy stick dropped on the pages and I looked up to see Cassady, panting and drooling as if to say, *You wanna know what's real? Dirty stick. That's what's real.*

'You would probably get that feeling from having a baby,' she said.

I screwed up my face. 'But I don't want a baby.' I didn't want a baby for a lot of reasons, but mostly because I could not spend the next fifteen years teaching someone how to get along in a social organisation that I felt extremely dubious about.

'That's fair enough,' my psychologist said. 'But you're right, then: you need to work out what's important to you.'

It's hard to beat your own path through the scrub, and seemingly ill-advised, too, when there is a well-lit road that runs straight past it. How do you structure an adult life that resists normative definition without finding yourself shut out in the cold?

It got me thinking about the possibilities for alternative conceptions of what it means to be an adult today, and how we can start a conversation about them.

Sociologists talk about five adult milestones: completing school, leaving home, becoming financially independent, marrying, and having a child. While it's easy to conceive of reasons a person might not want or be able to hit these markers — and we all know someone who can tick all the boxes and yet behaves like a toddler with Benjamin Button disease — milestones are the foundation for how we constitute and describe adult life at this point in history.

I wondered, was it such a radical thought to ask if they should? Does our tenacious need to measure adulthood on a standardised scale work to conceal all the ways in which the world is changing? Given the relatively brief existence of the adult as we currently understand it, how can we be shocked that these key moves are executed later, or with less ardour, or in the wrong order, or not at all?

My father and his parents immigrated to Australia in the 1950s. He was raised in boarding houses and apartment towers in inner-city Sydney, schooled as a choirboy at St Mary's. He received a scholarship to teachers' college in the late 1960s but dropped out because life felt pressing and vital. He became a journalist. By thirty, he had the adult game stitched up. It's not surprising, then, that he wondered what I was doing with my time. Our fight on census night came about because the differences between parent and progeny alarmed him. They produced anxiety about my progress. He worried — I worried — about my place in the world.

He might well have been imagining the census form flying off express to a room of judgemental aunties who would cluck disapprovingly over the details, and was trying to save me the ignominy. He might have been trying to jam the statistics to keep the national profile on track. But there was another possibility, too. My life might just hint at a discreet challenge to my father's decisions. If a child's choices are different from their parents', could they also suggest that what constitutes a 'good life', a meaningful adult existence, *can* be different? What are the possibilities for alternative forms of adult life today, and how can we start a conversation about them that doesn't end in misunderstanding, disappointment, and intergenerational sledging?

It is a truism that economic and social conditions shape people. Could it be possible that, unlike my father's baby-boomer cohort, many of whom took their malcontent to the street and cried out to transform society via revolution, my generation are embracing a different method of change? Perhaps in a moment of entrenched capitalism, in which markets have the uncanny ability to co-opt cultural moments as soon as they cohere, social structures come under challenge by way of shifting behaviours within them. Resistance, by this model, could be as simple and as unromantic as not owning a car, not signing a mortgage, because the future is too slippery to bond with our calculations of it. Is there a way to understand recalcitrance as an act of agency rather than a symptom of laziness and selfishness? If so, the so-called Peter Pan generation might be thought of as taking the first baby steps towards different forms of social organisation. Instead of asking why Gen Y are not replicating the models of adulthood we in the West have known for the last century, we could ask different kinds of questions. For instance, what would a society that doesn't centre on traditional gender roles, the couple, and the family look like? So, too, what would it mean to advance higher education to embolden curiosity rather than aspiration?

In researching this book, I have started to believe that adulthood, as measured through markers such as marriage and mortgage, is no longer a very useful term. The goalposts of a traditional adult life are getting further away the longer you run at them. It's exhausting. And while sometimes I think I'd take the shot, at other times it seems more sensible to sprawl out in the grass and watch the clouds stretch and blur across the sky.

There is a great moment in Jonathan Franzen's *Freedom*, a thoroughly adult book. Towards the end of a chapter, some neighbours are sitting around gossiping, as neighbours do, passing judgment on the lives of the protagonists. 'I don't think they've figured out yet how to live,' says one neighbour to another, smugly.

Like all nosey neighbours, or readers of dense texts, the idea that you can work out how to live, as if it is a complex stratagem to be decoded, appeals to me.

I can see problems with this plan, of course. But the promise is still enough to leave me hanging over the fence, peering into the world beyond and speculating how it came to be like that and why. How, I wonder, does anyone ever get along within it?

The possibility that I can work out the answers is my own adult fantasy.

2
DREAM BOARD

My friend Olivia is in possession of what I consider to be the all-time greatest dating anecdote. In this story, Olivia is a twenty-something art student. She's dating an older man, a guy in his forties who is either in art school too, or has connections to the art-school crowd in their small city — the details are lost to time. It's morning and she is at his house alone. He's gone to work or to school and she's making coffee and languidly snooping around, the way new lovers do when they are in the space of the beloved.

There is a chilly breeze coming in off the lake. She shivers and moves to pull down the window, but it's stiff — one of those old wooden window frames suspended on a rope that has been painted over by lazy renovators so many times it will always stick and bang. It does just that when she tries to close it, sliding suddenly down the rope that's crunchy with paint and slamming against the sill.

This disturbance causes a chain reaction. Maybe a broom that was leaning against the window tips sideways, snaking a collection of vintage wooden trains across the mantle. The trains collide with a cactus, which in turn upends a large sketchpad that has been placed open, displaying some charcoal or watercolour. I like to imagine an unspeakably banal still life fluttering as it falls to the floor.

'Seriously, Doyle,' Olivia said, half hysterical, calling from the boyfriend's backyard just minutes after the fact. 'It was like something out of a 1950s sitcom.'

Olivia tries to tidy up; she stubs her toe, swears, feels guilty, as if she has been busted, and then suddenly she sees it. A thing previously concealed by the placement of the sketchpad. A thing both marvellous and totally gross.

'A dream board.'

'What the hell is a dream board?'

'Have you heard of the New Age self-help program called The Secret?'

I gasped: I had. I knew the book. The cover was cheap-looking: a ye olde–style map, like one a pirate might use to find treasure in a videogame, the title scrawled in blood red, the S stamped in digital wax as though sealing some pseudo-ancient communication.

'A dream board is part of The Secret. You're supposed to write your goals on it. Like, your ultimate goals, the things your life will move towards,' Olivia confirmed.

'How awful!'

'I know,' she said. 'And do you want to know what my forty-year-old boyfriend wrote on his dream board?'

'Oh my god, yes.'

'Get ready,' she said, giggling. 'He wrote that he wants to be a famous artist.'

'No!'

'Wait. He also wants a million dollars, a Porsche, and a hot young wife.'

'No!' I said again.

'Yes. A million dollars.'

'Not a penny less, plus Porsche!'

'Wife both young and hot!'

We yelped with amusement. We guffawed, chortled, and choked. We mocked his secret until we were exhausted. Then Olivia became serious.

'I don't know what to do, Doyle,' she said. 'I really like him, but I think he might believe in angels.'

I love imagining this man sitting down to the task of dream-board creation. I picture him racking his brain and then, selecting the gold pen, writing his goals in careful, broad letters: FAME. MILLION DOLLARS. PORCHE. HOT YOUNG WIFE. He's decorating these words accordingly. Did he use a ruler? As an art-school alumnus — or student — he probably has a natural sense of design. He places it on the mantle and stands back to admire his work. He is filled with hope but also, what? Shame. The shame gets stronger. Is this his moment of adult reckoning?

He places the sketchpad in front of the dream board. He barricades it with the cactus. He doesn't rip it up and throw it out, though. In fact, on star-bright, wistful nights alone, he removes the sketchpad and, standing reverently before his goals (naked, I imagine) – their promises of riches, speed, and succour respectively glittering in candlelight – he repeats his mantra, or does his power yoga, or whatever The Secret tells him to do when invoking the divine. Maybe he summons his fucking angel.

It makes me laugh, this story. It also highlights a uniquely contemporary confusion people have about what a successful life is and how a person can get one. We live in a world where forty-year-olds are making dream boards. It's clear I'm not the only one having trouble working out what to structure my life around.

Adulthood was not always seen as a state of being, a characteristic that you acquire. For centuries, short life expectancy meant making it to thirty was a reasonable achievement. Tellingly, many cultures do not even have a word for adult, as distinct from woman and man. According to sociologist James E. Côté, 'adult' only appeared in the *Oxford English Dictionary* for the first time in 1657; 'adulthood' remained at large until 1870. The term marks a stage of life that is understood as more than just physical maturity, but when I thought about it, I realised that I viewed the idea of an adult as if through a paper telescope. There was an image there, but it was severed of context. I could pick out the features – the haircuts and 'real jobs', the things owned and things cared for, the eyes set forward with a look of commitment and forbearance. But I could not place this image in its environment, and, as soon as I tried to animate it, the image dropped out of frame entirely.

Where did it go? Where did it come from?

The image is slippery because adulthood is not a naturally determined state but a cultural artefact. In Ancient Rome, adolescence lasted until thirty among the nobles. This was the youngest a man could be admitted to public office. In 56 BC, Cicero famously defended a former student charged with political violence by deploying what critics have called a 'boys will be boys' defence: Cicero insisted that no one could expect a twenty-nine-year-old to take responsibility for his actions because such a youth possesses neither foresight nor wisdom. He was not yet a man. In Ancient Greece, you were a man so long as you had a good family name and a beard, but if you were rich, it was fair enough to stay in school until your late thirties, like Aristotle. In other places and times, people were adults as soon as they were old enough to work and procreate, and for most, there was no way to delay or control either. Right through the ancient and classical periods and well into the eighteenth century, free men and women worked from home growing food, making what they could, and trading for everything else.

The border between adulthood and childhood is not just developmentally but also legally and economically defined. It's hard to discuss adulthood without emphasising that, for much of Western history, slavery endured in agrarian, industrial, and domestic labour and so only the minority were constructed as adults in a way we can recognise today – that is, in full possession of their bodies and futures, and empowered to make choices about what to do with them. For centuries, coming of age has occurred in economic systems in which people have been bought and sold as property. It's telling that in the Americas, slaves were considered adult children. This structural injustice endures today in many ways, in many places. Age-based laws, meanwhile, that prevent people from working, or having sex, or voting, tie the term 'adult' to a discourse about rights and responsibilities. For instance, attitudes about the age of consent changed at the end of the nineteenth century. In England, a thirteen-year-old girl could reasonably take on the very grown-up roles of wife, mother, or sex worker until 1885, when the age of consent was legally enshrined at sixteen. In the United States, early feminists managed to get the age of consent raised to sixteen in most states by 1920 (it had been as low as seven in Delaware just twenty-five years earlier).

The more I looked, the more I found that what constitutes a 'normal' adult life at any moment in history depended almost entirely on what was required economically in the period one came of age. The modern concept of adulthood has its roots in the Industrial Revolution: more men began to leave the home for work, and consequently, women were expected to stay and labour unpaid – and so the idea of motherhood as a calling emerged, as did the necessity of infant–mother bonding. During the late nineteenth century, young people did not necessarily leave home, achieve financial independence, marry, and procreate in that order, or in a timely manner. Middle-class life trajectories were more flexibly defined and, according to historian Steven Mintz, 'tended to swing between periods of relative independence and phases of dependence when they returned to the parental home'. This description caught my eye: boomerang kids, more than a century before they had a name!

The move to different kinds of manufacturing, and the emergence of new ways to bank, travel, and communicate led to the beginning of our modern idea of a self-selected career. In North America, when the labour movement grew in the late 1800s, the system of prescribed apprenticeships for young people, whereby one shipped children off to become butchers or soldiers or smiths, deteriorated. Partly as a consequence, many middle-class white children were able to pursue a longer and more comprehensive education, and this perhaps was the first hint of a world where young people were expected to scout their own opportunities and decide on the shape of their futures.

Today, though, despite all our rights and choices, social historians argue that adult lives in rich countries are more uniform than at any previous point in history. This, Mintz points out, is thanks in part to institutional innovations such as mortgages and income insurance, which smooth the transition from family of origin to a particular kind of family of reproduction. Looking at a comparative sample of Americans from 1880 and 1970, researchers at the University of Pennsylvania concluded that in many ways 'growing up, as a process, has become briefer, more normful and bounded' over the century.

Normful and bounded. They aren't words that we typically use to describe modern life. And yet wasn't this the very thing

I experienced at my moment of adult reckoning? I was unable to see alternative ways of being and so became focused on the things I had not yet acquired.

In the final years of the last millennium, when I was working to finish high school, local newspapers ran editorials accusing Gen X women of forgetting to have kids. They were too busy with their careers, said the media. They were short-sighted and selfish. They were narcissists, and now we were paying for it. Gen X women in their late thirties and early forties were clogging the waiting rooms of fertility clinics, listening to Pavement on their Discman, clutching copies of *Infinite Jest*. Wastoids. Looking back, these stories managed to combine generational sledging and a patronising anti-feminist agenda. Working hard in a depressed economy, women, a segment of the workforce with statistically less opportunity to attain seniority, are unlikely to 'forget' that for many centuries their main social function has been having babies.

Generational portraiture is always political. In 2013, the year I turned thirty, after *Time* ran a cover story dubbing millennials the 'Me Me Me Generation', Elspeth Reeve of *The Atlantic* pointed out that the magazine had made these claims before — in 1990, when analysing the defects and challenges that characterised Generation X.

Laziness, entitlement, apathy, and narcissism have been the best way to describe every generation since such observations were first declared a story. An article from a 1907 edition of *The Atlanta Monthly* cites the 'worship of the brazen calf of the self' as the reason American marriages fail. In 1976, gonzo journalist Tom Wolfe used the cover of *New York* magazine to declare 'The Me Decade', hilariously citing everything from LSD, post-war prosperity, changing gender roles, and haemorrhoid-reducing meditation practices to back his charges. In this era of the third awakening, Wolfe cried, we 'begin with the most delicious look inward; with considerable narcissism'.

This look was so far inward that it coalesced on the haemorrhoidal rectum as a mystical and spiritual centre. Wolfe conjured the image of a convention centre full of New Age devotees, a closed feedback loop in which energy is reabsorbed as quickly as it is generated: a whole epoch meditating fiercely on the importance of their own arseholes.

The way we describe people matters. The way we frame adulthood in both private and public discourse matters – because it works to include and exclude people from social engagement. As in class conflict, acrimony between young and old divides people, allows them to blame one another for inequality, and facilitates wilful blindness to the broader social context.

James E. Côté argues that the adult of the contemporary moment is linked with the rise of the individual, whose freedoms are seemingly greater than ever, as the primary economic agent (as opposed to families, villages, tribes, and other groups). The popularisation of adulthood as something one sets out to achieve coincides with the modern idea of the middle class, a group of people whose potential is manifest in their possession of a great deal of human capital. Theoretically, a middle-class individual has freedom, and a range of choices grounded by their economic responsibility; but what if the definition and attendant privileges of the middle class is changing as populations grow? Our understanding of adulthood is linked to the growth of capitalism, and can consequently be deployed in its service. Does this mean that definitions of adulthood can be deployed to induce people to fill social and economic roles on an ad-hoc basis?

This is probably why passions run so high in generational sledging matches. *Time*'s 2013 article purports to give the 'cold, hard data': 'The incidence of narcissistic personality disorder is nearly three times as high for people in their 20s as for the generation that's now 65 or older.' The spate of editorials from older people characterising my generation as selfish whingers has been met with equally vehement accusations of parsimoniousness and greed aimed at my father's generation. Younger people in Australia, wrote one millennial critic in *The Monthly*, 'have been locked out of the housing market, locked out of affordable education, locked out of the welfare system and secure employment'. They have seen 'their political power and real wealth shrivel' at the hands of baby boomers, who have 'been the drivers of economic policy for decades'.

Reading these kinds of editorials really gets the blood pumping. I can jump up from my desk and left-hook the sky, but the anger or the thrill is cheap and short – surely the economic and social reality we are currently living in can't simply be reduced to the behaviour of one group, old or young?

Tracking the accusations, it's clear the media can and does cite anything as a harbinger of generational inadequacy. Recessions are as big a culprit as boom times. Spirituality. Nihilism. Too much happiness or too little. Too much responsibility, leading to a politically conservative generation, or too little, creating a *Jersey Shore*–level spoiled brat. Every generation is more self-centred and lazy than the one before. At this rate, by the end of the century we will only be capable of squatting in front of our screens, pleasuring ourselves to home movies that depict us squatting in front of our screens pleasuring ourselves…

My anus itches just thinking about it.

I pop one of the vitamins from the assortment of glass and plastic bottles that line my desk. Energy. Stress. Women's balance. Memory. Hair, skin, nails, eyesight. Stabilised probiotics, because the gut is the new mind. Birth control, because I do not have time for menstruation. Herbs – I don't know what the fuck, my naturopath gave them to me and now I'm scared to stop. Flower essences based on my flower taro. Don't ask me what that is. It can't hurt, that's all I know. I don't want to spend my life inefficiently, delinquent and lacking in some vital force only to find out at sixty that I have a rhododendron deficiency.

I decided to put aside the comparisons as they appeared in the media and attempt my own small-scale comparison of the last few generations. Had my cohort really dropped the ball? I suspected not, but I could not back my suspicions at an intergenerational dinner party. This was a severe handicap, given that my opponents could always point out that they understood this progression more fully, simply because they were older. And they had years on me when it came to holding dinner parties, too.

In his book *The Greatest Generation*, American journalist Tom Brokaw recalls his parents' cohort, those who came of age during the Depression of the 1930s and lived through two world wars. He describes their lives as a collective 'towering achievement'. 'Looking back,' he writes, 'I can recall that the grown-ups all seemed to have a sense of purpose that was evident even to someone as young as four, five, or six.'

This was my grandparents' generation, and in many ways it is the generation to which each subsequent cohort has been compared. It was a point in history where media was relatively centralised, and an adult in the United States, the United Kingdom, Australia, and parts of Europe was depicted as someone who could make do, and pitch in – not for a war so much, but the war effort. Rose Bonavita Hickey embodies the ideal adult in the United States (which influences so much of Western culture) for this period. She was one of the many Rosies that inspired the propagandist figure Rosie the Riveter.

Born in 1921, Bonavita grew up hard. At eighteen, she worked in a laundry. At twenty-one, on an assembly line building Grumman TBF Avenger torpedo bombers, she and a friend set a new work record, drilling 900 holes and driving 3,300 rivets in their six-hour shift.

I knew Rosie from the feminist student collective badges that were handed out at uni, but I didn't know that she married her high-school sweetheart during a break in his service to the US Navy. She was twenty-five and pregnant by the time he was redeployed. She left the workforce after the war and raised three children, becoming a housewife in Long Island. Her parents lived upstairs, and her in-laws next door. She went to Mass every day and baked a fresh apple pie for her children to come home to after school. Has there ever been an adult life in which one person is required to fill and abandon so many different roles?

My maternal grandmother stepped up like a good Rosie. The photographs of her during World War II are of a strong, vivacious young woman with a purpose. By the time I met her, she was a reserved, sharp-tongued sixty-something with an appallingly racist worldview.

'She had a good war,' Dad liked to say to me when, as a child, I complained about my grandmother's heavy-handed, strict discipline and intolerance of noise or precociousness.

It took me decades to understand that 'a good war' was code for a brief form of female becoming that opened up in that historical moment and then closed again, ushering women back into the home, whether they were suited to it, as Rosie B. seemed to be, or immensely irritated, as my grandmother surely was.

In the conventional picture of generations, the next generation is the baby boomers. Yet a description in the introduction to Renata Adler's essay collection *After the Tall Timber* interrupted this continuity for me: Adler writes about belonging to a generation 'unnoticed even as we spread clear across what people call the generation gap' — that is, the gap between the world of my parents and grandparents. Those who were born at the end of the Great Depression were children during World War II and looked on, as Brokaw did, at their parents pitching in and making do.

'We grew up separately,' Adler writes, 'without a rhetoric, drawing our ideas from age and cultural groups already formed, as we were not.'

This description resonated with me as though it were written yesterday. Perhaps there is something specific in being born at the very beginning of a generational cohort, as I am. You operate in a transitional space, paving the way for some future change of which you can't quite take ownership. I wondered, too, as I read more descriptions of generations, what the impulse is to write in such a mode. We all know this kind of writing demands stereotype, is reductive to the point of being class- and colour-blind. And yet there is a connection between people born within a decade or two of one another. There is an understanding that moves through other social categories. Generations certainly exist. Is the desire to write about them always a desire to defend and explain one's self to one's parents? Or is it about writing history, not in terms of events, but in terms of the everyday — the ways that history produces our psyches before we even know it? I feel this impulse strongly, but I can't quite decode it.

My parents were the children of adults from the so-called greatest generation, and so their experience includes an insider perspective. My mother was dropped off at boarding school early, and held at an emotional and physical distance for much of her childhood. My dad describes the absence and frustration of his own father, who fought in World War II and who demonstrated the necessity of 'staying out of combat if you can' (this, along with 'stay away from factories if you can', were the earliest, most sensible pieces of life advice Dad imparted). My parents' experiences of childhood, and the other, similar descriptions that litter the biographies of members of their cohort, go some way to providing a counter-narrative to the one woven by wartime propaganda, and the nostalgic descriptions of great optimism and social connectedness amid a climate of sadness and terror. Interestingly, in Australia we have an alternate name for the greatest generation — we call them the silent generation, a haunting epithet that evokes the trauma that so many brought home from war.

Before the media began its campaign to caricature my generation, I received private coaching in intergenerational sledging from my dad.

'Rhythm and blues?' Dad scoffed in 1993, as I danced around the living room. 'That's not rhythm and blues.'

Nor was rap 'music', and Cat Stevens should have sued Ugly Kid Joe. As a kid I had loved my parents' records, and Dad's mythologising, nostalgic stories. But as I grew into a teenager, I hated how there always seemed to be a boomer around to tell me that the music I was listening to was derivative or mislabelled, or to make smug comments when I read or watched something from the '70s, or brought home vintage finds from the op shop. Parents wanted to own everything, yet were always telling you to share. It wasn't fair.

Now I realise that the sudden assumption of expert opinions on the young might, in fact, be a true milestone of adulthood. I catch myself, at dreaded toddler's birthday parties, or in the waiting room at the doctor's, judging tiny humans quite harshly. *They are totally hooked on that iPad*, I think. *They don't seem to be able to tolerate boredom at all! It can't be good for their imaginations. What will become of them? What will become of our future?*

Nevertheless, I carried my resentment against boomers effortlessly into my twenties, and rarely bothered to subject it to critical scrutiny. I wasn't alone. I don't know what it felt like to protest in the countercultural heyday of the 1960s and 1970s, but in the late 1990s and early 2000s, whatever we protested, it felt as if we were also protesting our parents' generation, *their* greed and *their* policies. University intakes and fees were increased, and hadn't classes been capped and free for our parents? Joining the union was voluntary, and didn't casual work enslave the young? MV *Tampa* was refused entry to Australian waters, but didn't my own parents both come here by boat?

'It's totally ridiculous, though,' an activist friend pointed out. 'This is a generation that instigated women's shelters and legalised homosexuality, and we're going to hold them to account for not being able to stop neoliberalism? Tell them, "We hate you because you didn't protect us from our own failure to organise in defence of our own rights?" It's like if, when I'm old, my kids are like, "I can't believe that there was fresh water when you were a kid, and there were all these islands in the Pacific Ocean."'

He was right. Yet we sought, rightly or wrongly, to weaponise our sense of alienation in a battle against our parents.

Both my parents are first-line baby boomers born into that fabled post-war prosperity. They were middle class, if at opposite ends of that spectrum. My mother went to university in South Africa. She did not acquire any student debt, but was expected to graduate into marriage rather than a career. Like so many of her peers, she defied expectations and forged a legacy for the next generation of young women. After university, she immigrated to Australia and a workforce in which new professional career paths were appearing every day. She took a job that did not yet have a clear entry requirement, becoming a psychologist with a Bachelor of Arts with honours and a combined major in Theatre Studies. In her late twenties she met my father, a journalist and rogue about town. They got a small loan, bought a block of land, and built a house with a minimum of fuss. They had their only child relatively late (at thirty-five) and were separated by their early forties. They followed different paths to their parents, but this was pioneering, not malingering.

'I belong to that generation of American and European women who, having come of age in the 1960s, discovered that so great a gap existed between our mothers and ourselves that we had almost nothing in common,' wrote Sigrid Nunez, considering the 'generation gap' and her own adult fantasies.

I know that my mother felt this way as she moved far from her family of origin and their expectations for her life. Perhaps this feeling would make adult life easier. If you have nothing in common with your parents, you would never expect them to know you. Today, though, we communicate far too much to be able to claim not to understand each other. If anything, in the rhetoric between boomers and their children, generations X and Y, there is too much understanding going on. It is comprehension as a form of violence.

I have a lot in common with my parents, and this might be true even at the level of the generational cohort. Like baby boomers, millennials are exceptional. We are seduced by utopias. We are pop-culture-obsessed. We hate capitalism but love Beyoncé (or Bob Dylan) and being our own boss. We desire change yet crave security. The world, unconcerned with our similarities, has altered. Free or low-cost tertiary education, new opportunities in the jobs market, relative affordability of housing, new media technologies, and the fierce energy emanating from the women's movement and civil rights struggles combined to produce a unique world for my parents to matriculate into. The world I get is unique too, but its logic is not the same.

To counterpoint the various sledging battles that have dominated the media, another narrative has emerged recently in which millennials and baby boomers are asked to empathise with one another. *The Guardian* recently published an article where a representative woman of each generation 'swaps lives', à la *Freaky Friday*, in order to write about the relative challenges of the other. Rhiannon, twenty-eight, can't help envying seventy-two-year-old Michelle's North London flat and free education. After looking at how the other side lives, she wonders if the time she spends online affects the amount of time she can spend 'out and about', noting how Michelle, ironically, appears to be so much more socially connected. Michelle has dinner parties with her friends, who talk about art and politics rather than work and relationship stress. They 'seem much more comfortable in their own skins and at home with their eccentricities than me and my friends', Rhiannon observes, with a trace of longing. Other than her distrust of social media and smartphones, Michelle defies stereotypes and has nothing but sympathy for Rhiannon's student loan and unfathomable rent. In the London of the 1960s, she says, they had 'appalling racism, homophobia, slums', but landlords couldn't be quite as greedy. 'My friends and I were terrified witless of nuclear war, but we didn't have to panic about finding a home or work.'

My mother resembles the sympathetic boomer delegate from this article. She bemoaned the proposed increase to the retirement age in Australia. 'Now, hang on!' she yelled at the TV news in her best whistleblower shrill. 'When are we going to let young people work?'

Mum abhors tax breaks and refuses to invest in negatively geared rental property because 'it's just wrong' (and I agree), though it also means she has far less for retirement, which is a burden I worry we will share.

Mum doesn't think it's my fault that I haven't set my life up yet, but she is worried about me, and I suspect she still doesn't quite see me as an adult. As a psychologist, Mum is professionally trained to measure development and worry about it.

She is on the front line of an industry that popularised the understanding of life as a developmental project — psychology was instrumental in establishing normative descriptions of adulthood and in popularising anxiety-inducing imperatives such as fulfilment. Adulthood and its problems are in some crucial sense a product of psychology, and my own adult problems, doubly so.

As a child, I had already learned that adult life was a manifestation of all the dreams and talents I was cultivating. The messages I received from my storybooks, from my mother's love, from the way I was spoken to and about all through my childhood in the 1980s and 1990s, reflected the dominant line for middle-class kids at the end of the twentieth century: YOU are special and YOU can do anything!

Everybody agreed on this — or, rather, if anyone disagreed they'd have my mother to answer to. My Grade Three teacher dared to suggest that fountain pens should be a privilege reserved for peers with better penship than me. Mum paid her a visit to remind her how special I was, how important it was that I was given every opportunity to learn. My teacher didn't look me in the eye for the rest of the term. I left inky fingerprints all over the classroom.

My mother was big on extracurricular activities. I took creative dance. I was a junior forest ranger. I set the kitchen bench on cold blue fire with my chemistry set. I was a junior scientist with the CSIRO, enlisted in a study that involved collecting local earthworms and killing them by immersion in methylated spirits. I learned to play awkward sonatas on the piano, joyless jazz on the saxophone, plaintiff waltzes on the clarinet. I wore homemade dresses. I didn't know how to talk to other children. During dinner parties, I sat at the table with the grown-up guests. I had a sherry glass full of riesling.

During lulls in the adult conversation, I amused the guests by reciting the titles of self-help books from my mother's shelves.

'Fat is a Feminist Issue,' I interjected. 'I'm Okay, You're Okay.'

(At the time, all I felt was the glory of a successful performance. Looking back, I can imagine the kinds of comments those liquored-up, nut-loaf-stuffed diners made about the fate of psychologists' children as they reversed their cars up our long, unpaved driveway.)

I spent afternoons marvelling over the covers of those books, with their bold capitals and artwork of flowers, leashed tigers, smiley faces, and sunsets. *The Road Less Travelled. Women Who Run with the Wolves. The Man Who Mistook His Wife for a Hat.* The future was blue skies, bright and full of adventure: a man rolling out a highway like a rug.

Mum frequently diagnoses her friends' grown children and their failure to launch in ways that transfer seamlessly to me. 'I get the sense that he is very restless,' she said pointedly of one of her favourite cases, a guy whose degree has stretched on for half a decade and spanned several disciplines and departments. 'He's a bit stuck. I don't know what his relationship status is, but certainly in terms of his work, the lack of commitment has really hindered his progress.'

On a good day, I half-listen to these analyses. On a bad day, I can't let it stand. 'What if accumulating things isn't the goal? What if the lack of commitment comes from the general shittiness of what you are trying to commit to?'

'I suppose,' said Mum. She never blocks my input. It is not her professional or parental style.

'I just think sometimes we worry about people because we are comparing them to an impossible or redundant standard.'

'Yes,' Mum said. 'That could be true.'

Dad is more hardline. 'Yeah, yeah,' he says, flapping his hand in a beak-like motion as I decry the state of my rented home, or the insecurity of my casual job. 'Get on with it. The trouble with your lot is . . .'

Dad thinks that most of the obstacles I cite are in my head and that a good bit of determination and resourcefulness would put me on the fast track to the right kind of life.

Late capitalism, so it goes, is all about choices. We can be whoever we want to be. Our lives are a canvas (or a dream board) for us to fill, and so on. This is the contemporary line, and it comes with a cunning reversal: we are solely responsible for the kind of life we have. If Olivia's ex doesn't get that Porsche, it's probably because he wasn't dreaming hard enough, or he chose the wrong colour pen or called up some slacker angel. If the current crop of young people have not hit their adult milestones on time, it's probably because we are lazy and deficient.

But what is this normative description of adulthood wielded in aid of now? What Rosie the Riveter–type roles are we being enlisted for? Is our equivalent of war-time nationalism the effort to bolster the illusion that our global economy and environment are fine and that human enterprise over the next century will look the same as it did in the last?

If so, is it any wonder we are stressed out and pissy? If this is our task, a dream board seems as realistic an approach as any.

I never said any of this to Dad. I know how he would have replied. And anyway, on reflection, a win in this round wouldn't have helped with the adult problem that weighed on me the heaviest: Dad was right to doubt me. Though I possessed some of the qualities that adults at various times have had, I did not seem to possess the right ones for now, and, worse still, I didn't feel grown up at all.

'I need something substantial to structure my life around,' I told Serge a few months after Cassady's death, parroting the wisdom of my psychologist.

But what was that thing? How do people build a meaningful centre for their lives? I scrolled through the volunteer databases. I began and abandoned roles that I hoped would catapult me into the community. The aged-care facility was far away and left me sad; the after-school homework-helpers, too maths-intensive. I asked around, but many of the volunteer positions my friends had required long, intensive training followed by year-long commitments, something I wasn't prepared to make. Eventually, I called a local animal rescue agency and signed up as a foster carer.

'We really need someone for large and difficult dogs,' said the woman on the phone. 'We need someone to teach them how to live sensibly in the city.'

I almost laughed. I was counting on the dog to help teach me.

I drove to Melbourne's Lort Smith animal hospital to pick up a dog called Mishka, a kelpie cross, blonde with fierce eyeliner and a white tip on her anxiously wagging tail. Her beleaguered carer looked at me with relief.

'She's too much of a handful,' she said, apologetically. 'My first priority has to be to my family.'

'I have no family.' I smiled at her.

I loaded Mishka into the back of my van. On the radio, some classic rocker sang it out: '*Oh yeah, life goes on. Long after the thrill of livin' is gone.*'

Mishka and I yowled along as we lurched through the grey streets of Melbourne. There was solidity in our chorus, tuneless as it was.

3
EDUCATIONAL PRODUCTS

It's story time. I'm cross-legged on the floor of my local library. I have borrowed Olivia's three-year-old so that I could get into this exclusive club, membership attained through connections in the small world.

The storyteller is a gigantic woman clad head-to-toe in green, with green tinsel in her hair. She has that over-enunciated, hyperbolic way of talking that kids seem to love. The children – some cautious, some gung-ho – gather at her ebullient forest-green skirt. They range in age from infant to five-ish. The expressions on their faces are ungovernable, a turgid flow of emotions.

My own charge, Maria, set out intrepidly for this excursion.

'Dr Doyle is taking us to the library,' her mother explained.

'Ooooooh!' said Maria. She beamed up at me, apple-cheeked and ready.

Now, though, she states plainly that this whole scene is scary.

Olivia did warn me. 'Sometimes Maria doesn't like to participate,' she said as we left the house. 'Sometimes she prefers to just scream over the top of everyone and then leave.'

I could relate.

After a welcome from the tinselled storyteller, the kids get up for a very noisy stomping-around song. Maria flops down, howling.

The children are instructed to become 'big stomping bears' and then 'quiet little bunnies'. When the metamorphosis is complete, the storyteller begins. 'Does anyone know a song about a frog to start off our story?' she asks.

'Yes,' the kids drone in monotone, assuming the position for 'Galumph Went the Little Green Frog'.

'I don't like this sooooong,' moans the boy next to me, throwing down on the grey carpet like a soldier anticipating fire.

Galumph went the little green frog one day...

The child spasms. I didn't know that children this young had such developed aesthetics. Where do they come from?

The other kids *galumph* in staggered unison.

'This is scary,' Maria repeats.

The storyteller begins the tale of a frog who is desperate to go to the stars. He's unsatisfied and agitated, this frog, soliciting all kinds of favours from interspecies neighbours in his cosmic quest. Fortunately, he has an epiphany, and realises he is happiest swimming in the stars as they are reflected in the pond of his birth.

Fairytales, myths, and fables have been instruments for shaping children's imaginations forever. For the adults who write and share these stories, they can become, as Rebecca Solnit observes, 'shorthand for an aspect of the human condition' – a yearning for justice or recognition or adventure, disappointment when desire is thwarted or reconfigured. We tell these stories to prepare our children for their adult lives, but we also tell them to understand our realities, to reinforce our ideals, and to perpetuate the order our lives have had. I assess the room: it's true that these kids are absorbing ideological messages, but something more complex is going on, too. Something in their nerves and blood that can't be written adequately, or illustrated and read aloud. It's a chaos of desire in here. A small redhead starts shrieking for no discernible reason. Another girl stands up and points at her, expressionless, like a twin from *The Shining*. A boy takes off into the latter Dewey Decimals; it's only a matter of moments before he breaks into the disordered world beyond. This, then, is where the social foundations are laid; here is where the wild are asked to sit and listen.

Maria stamps impatiently, beckoning to the street.

Jean-Jacques Rousseau, in *Emile*, one of the first books about childhood education, attempted to provide a comprehensive list of methods (from breastfeeding to bushwalking) to avoid the denaturing of children's wild instincts. For Rousseau, children should learn to think unhindered by adult prejudice. Rousseau would probably have been unhappy with storytime at the library; he would have preferred to take the children to the pond and ask them what they thought the frog was saying.

What Rousseau understood implicitly is that children are important to the kind of adult social world we make. If a society wants to aim to rid the future of discrimination, dissatisfaction, superficiality, and fear, as Rousseau professed to, they need to begin this mission with the education of children. Conversely, if you want to know the dominant values of a moment in history, look at what the children are being taught.

My oldest friend, Lyndal, recently had to dress her six-year-old daughter up for Future Day at her primary school.

'Future Day?' I asked, impressed, imagining a classroom full of rockets and holograms — or, more likely, alien overlords and post-apocalyptic zombie children, hungry for brains.

'They dress up as their future selves,' Lyndal explained.

Unfortunately, little January was ill-prepared for this task of quotidian imagination. 'Can I be a hairdresser like you?' she asked her mother, who no doubt baulked at both the reduction of her complex managerial job and the alarming image of her child brandishing scissors over the heads of classmates.

'Let's think of something just for you,' Lyndal countered.

This was not an easy task. After all, what exactly is it adults do? Not for the first time, I marvelled at Lyndal's fortitude. We met when we were just eleven, and preceded to misspend our future days cutting class to hang out in the gym change rooms and light toilet paper on fire. Now she was a totally functional adult with a husband, two children, and a fancy job, but she still had to find a way to explain this to her daughter.

Finally, January decided to go as a teacher. Specifically, her own preparatory teacher. This was, after all, the only adult other than her parents and grandparents that she got to see on a regular basis. Lyndal showed me the photo of her, grinning beside her teacher in matching hair and clothes, a tiny single white female. The teacher was smiling in that false way that belies existential discomfort.

'She only let me take one picture,' Lyndal admitted.

Toddlers memorise taxonomies of the adult world: the fireman with his hat, the policeman with his truncheon, the nurse with her rosy cheeks and red crosses.

'What do you want to be when you grow up?' they are asked, as soon as they have the words to answer. Squint. Remember the taxonomy. Pick the one with the nice smile, the cool outfit, or the gun.

At six, I was good at answering this question. The answer was inevitable, as though I were a beauty-pageant contestant smiling 'world peace' before I showed everyone how well I could tap dance. The right answer was precocious, and fit snugly with my parents' values. The right answer was immediately rewarded. And the question was posed again, and again, its centrality emphasised in formal education from primary through to graduate school. Not having an answer implied a lack of direction, because growing up was about selecting a role and then training to occupy it. A child's trajectory is supposed to be unfailingly towards adult success.

Getting children well situated in the school system early is a global trend among many of a certain social status. In New York City, you can hire a $300-an-hour playdate coach for your three-year-old, to iron out any social kinks that might hinder their admittance to one of the city's elite kindergartens. Harder to get into than Harvard, these preschools are said to feed children directly into a bright future. 'Many of my clients are high achievers who want the same for their offspring,' a London daycare consultant told the *Financial Times*. In their playdate training, children are taught to perform sharing acts, and not to unconsciously suggest autism through their gait or inadequate eye contact.

While most parents do not go to such extremes with their children's preparation for school, almost all agree on the importance of education. But in the twenty-first century, we have lost sight of a universal ideal for good education, and policy in this area has become a political battleground in a war over what the future will look like.

My compulsory schooling ran through the 1980s and 1990s. I graduated high school in the class of 2000, amid Y2K fears and future shock. A first-line millennial, I learned about the world during a period of great epistemological faffery, when what seemed like wild oscillations in education policy were ubiquitous across the Western world.

Though, when I thought about it, I realised: when is education not an ideological frontline? Western school systems hark back to Socratic ideas about the inseparability of education and politics, but the shape of the ideal citizen they are working to produce is subject to deliberation and change.

In 1957, when my Dad was just eight years old and the Russians launched *Sputnik 1*, Cold War America wanted to know why they had lost this first round in the Space Race. It must be the Russian schools, someone decided. They taught a hard-nosed, maths- and science-heavy curriculum and churned out engineers and fascists. This was the opposite of the so-called progressive agenda in US education, which valued airy-fairy concepts such as creativity and self-esteem. The US government think-tanked: how can we direct the energies of education, from elementary to tertiary, into the service of the military? They sent delegates over to check out Ruski High. Could American teenagers be sent to such a place? Did it align with what it meant to be an American? The United States began a series of educational reforms. Then in the 1970s, wearied by recession, they turned away from them. Education, it was decided, glumly, as the summer of love flipped over into many summers of stagflation, mattered far less than family background in influencing a person's future. Sure, educational attainment was a boon to any child, but an individual's success was influenced more by what the parents had achieved economically than by any well-meaning educational strategy. What was the point, then, in teaching foreign languages or advanced physics, or spending too long training teachers?

Test scores fell, moral panic ensued, and by the early 1980s there was backlash. Despite President Regan's emphasis on school prayer and tuition tax credit, people began to insist that if educational standards were not improved, America ran the risk of being swallowed up in a great tide of mediocrity.

During the same period in Australia, ideas about what children should learn were going in and out of style like root perms. Policy-makers seemed hard-pressed to agree on what education was for. The reports say that the late 1970s and early 1980s saw a change in educational approach from vocational and academic to egalitarian. The reports say that values about the use of knowledge changed. Imagination and creativity came into vogue, and rote learning went out. By the 1990s, there was panic about children who couldn't spell or construct a sentence. There was panic about a generation of Australian students who didn't know anything about how 'their' country was 'discovered', or what the nation's role was in the two world wars. Reports talked about a 'root and branch' approach to narrating the past, and about the importance of phonics and literacy.

What this looked like on the frontline: in the 1980s I spent a lot of time making picture books with cardboard, felt pens, and tape. No one really appeared to mind that I couldn't spell — or if they did, they didn't mention it to me — but I remember feeling ashamed of how asymmetrical my love hearts were. I played a lot of educational games in something called the 'maths task centre' (a storeroom filled with buckets of puzzles) because my tiny rural primary school had extra funding through something called the 'disadvantaged schools program', and a talented teacher who knew a thrifty and effective way to spend it. I received a partial scholarship to an Anglican-run school at ten, and for four years I was no longer subject to policy whims but engaged in a rigorous, well-funded traditional education that included maths, Latin, hockey, and fine arts. I learned what grammar I know *in curabitur aliquet ultricies* with scenarios involving some kid called Quintus, who was always hanging around in various rooms. *Quintus est in curabitur aliquet ultricies; Quintus est in culina.*

At private school I was also mildly hazed by rich boys, scolded for sitting with my legs apart ('You could drive a bus through there,' said one teacher, visibly repulsed), and sent to detention when caught eating or not wearing my blazer in public. I was judged and scrutinised continually, and I hated it.

Because of this experience, I was not surprised to read a Melbourne Institute report detailing a significant happiness drop between age fifteen and twenty-three in Australia, with the most significant year of misery being fourteen. In North America, 75 per cent of high-school students who answered a 2015 survey by the Yale Center for Emotional Intelligence responded negatively to the question 'How are you feeling?', citing stress and boredom as predominant emotions at school. In the United Kingdom in the same year, only 43 per cent of Year Eight students responded positively to their school experience in an international survey conducted by the Children's Society, and English schoolchildren were found to be among the unhappiest of fifteen countries, including Ethiopia and Algeria. If adulthood is increasingly defined by isolation, battling through entrenched hierarchies, and being judged on attainment and acculturation, many young people have an educational experience that prepares them for it perfectly.

At thirteen, I moved states geographically and psychologically — from my mother's to my father's home. I repeated Medieval but somehow skipped Australian History, though I suspect this was a good thing, as most of my peers had learned a fiction by rote. Well ahead of my classmates, I cruised through my first year back at state school, which afforded me time to get fully ensconced in the way-cool social world of an inner-city art-focused high school. In my third-last year of secondary school, when I was fifteen, it felt as though half the form transferred to the vocational high school, where you studied the 'entertainment industry' and smoked ciggies in the canteen.

I took computer studies as a science for the high-school certificate, though in 1999 a lack of computers meant that we spent most of our time looking at a picture of one in a textbook while the teacher drew an algorithm on the board. To this day I don't know where my spleen is, how to calculate velocity, or when I am splitting which infinitives, though my life does not feel depleted by this lack. The lessons that I do remember from high school were those where the disciplines collided and you found yourself learning modern history in drama class, or reading Brecht and realising that history was the world, not a fine white stream that ran alongside it.

The year I graduated, the curriculum for high-school attainment and scoring changed, and the tertiary sector was on the verge of review. Higher education was increasingly discussed in terms of a return on investment for students and the government. Reforms allowed universities to set their own student fees, in line with a government-determined cap, and increase the level of full-fee-paying students. In the early 2000s, universities competed with one another to attract fee-paying students with promises of glamorous university experiences and career outcomes.

I've outlined this potted history, which is small and local, but also common for many people my age, to illustrate how my education was marked and moulded by a market economy in which both it and I were stakes.

In 1929, British mathematician and philosopher Alfred North Whitehead wrote that the child should understand ideas and theories 'here and now in the circumstances of his actual life'. He went on, 'there is only one subject-matter for education, and that is Life in all its manifestations'. It seems to me that the way we currently understand education as a pathway to a professional identity, an investment in various futures, is formed as through a misreading of texts such as Whitehead's. We still want our education to be applied; it is our concept of life that has become impoverished. At Future Day, we chose between the teacher and the hairdresser, knowing full well that it was the same outfit every time.

'I'm just going to work in a call centre and go to parties for the rest of my life,' I told my horrified mother when she asked me to address the taxonomy in my final year of high school.

It felt good. I was done with school, with answering questions about who I was and would be. Who I would be was dreamless and free, focused only on survival and pleasure.

Unusually, my long-separated parents formed a united front to pressure me into tertiary education. Dad started going on about how all the best parties were *at* uni. It was just a thrilling social scene, an unmissable event, a total mindblower.

'Didn't you drop out?' I asked.

'Yeah, but it was the '60s. I had more interesting books to read, better things to do with my time.'

At seventeen, I'd never seen an American college, but I had seen *a lot* of teen movies. I understood the co-dependency and cachet of the sorority. I knew by heart the espresso sophistication of the New York film school, the old-money cocaine orgies in the halls of Connecticut and New England, the passions of varsity sport. I knew that college was a contentious political space that regulated class; that in America, college is where the aspirational age dawns.

But in Australia, we didn't have that same cultural narrative. And I wasn't buying Dad's line. Universities seemed tragically uncool. The uni bars were clogged with awkward-looking weirdos, and all the students I knew were miserable, juggling classes and jobs, and commuting to attend lectures on sprawling suburban campuses. They worked long hours to pay their rent and lost their minds over essay deadlines. Even more, none of the adults in my life could lay out a convincing argument as to what these students were struggling for. Discussions about higher education usually descended into platitudes such as 'education is important', 'get a head start', and 'it's important to keep your options open'. But statistics about underemployed university graduates had been making headlines for a decade. I finished high school just before the ten-year publication anniversary of Douglas Coupland's *Generation X*, the cult 1991 novel that coined the term 'McJobs'. I wasn't interested in these kinds of 'options'; I wanted independence, and whatever degree of freedom I could eke out.

The insistence that young people move straight into university or full-time work after high school is as much to do with our fear of what the young might do with their spare time as it is with our hopes for their future. Zero-tolerance policing; lockout laws in bars and nightclubs; and media furores over teen gangs, drug use, and delinquency are further evidence of this fear. Young people, with all their angst and energy, should be put to work lest chaos ensue, that's the adult fantasy. My experience with youth culture – music and art scenes run on enthusiasm and the smell of an oily rag – disposes me against this logic. What young, un- and under-employed people were doing with their time in 2001 in Sydney, a city as fiercely anti-youth then as now, seemed much more important than how it was described by grown-ups. They were creating culture. A look through the history of music and art in many cities (New York, London, Melbourne, Berlin) shows the same cultural genesis repeated many times. Our society glamourises the early twenties as a time for finding oneself – it's strange, then, how afraid we are of giving young people the time and encouragement to do so, particularly during politically and economically conservative periods.

Eventually, my parents conceded a reprieve. 'A gap year,' Mum said, desperately trying to reorder her ambition for me.

Dad bought me an old bakery van and my boyfriend built a fold-out bed-and-storage combination in the back. Annie and I packed it with tins of tomatoes, cans of mosquito repellent, and bottles of Stone's Ginger Wine. We were off to see the country we had lived in all our lives. We'd pick mangoes when we hit the Top End, and then head back down again for who knows what. Girls! On the road!

It turned out to be a six-month holiday for Annie, who decided to start tertiary study in the next school year, leaving me displaced. When I came back to Sydney, savings depleted and puppy-Cassady in tow, I was hit with how hard it was to be young in that city at the dawn of the millennium. Live music venues across the city had shut their doors. The surveillance and zero-tolerance policies that accompanied the Olympics hung around for a long afterparty, and intensified following the September 11 attacks in New York. In 2001, as the United States adjusted to the George W. Bush presidency, conservative Australian prime minister John Howard won a third term and spent much of his acceptance speech talking about family barbeques, a breeding incentive program for young families called 'the baby bonus', and being tough on drugs. He said nothing of the welfare reforms that set the agenda for my day-to-day. I felt as though politics was a force that did not and could not recognise my existence, or that of many of my friends. This sense of exclusion probably defined how I came of age, and persisted in how I saw myself right up to that moment of adult reckoning.

Living below the poverty line, I worked for unemployment benefits doing, among other menial things, maintenance in local parks. After a year of this, university looked pretty good. My mother was thrilled. She remembered her student days as a time of great inspiration and independence, of teachers jumping atop tables to recite modernist poetry, and of a psychology professor cementing the direction of her own adult life when he claimed (dubiously, it has always seemed to me) that 'psychology is a science without judgement'.

In 1972, when my parents were in their early twenties, progressive politician Gough Whitlam proclaimed that the answer to inequality and mediocrity was to 'involve the creative energies of our children and our youth in a creative, concerned community'. He made promises that won him the election, and the nation fifteen years of free higher education. 'It is our basic proposition that the people are entitled to know,' he cried. 'It is our basic belief that the people will respond to national needs once they know those needs. It is in education – the needs of our schools – that we will give prime expression to that proposition and that belief.'

These were not the ideals in 2002, when I began my undergraduate degree. There were more than two hundred students clogging the footpath on Harris Street for my first lecture. During my studies I submitted assignments for a pass/fail mark – a cunning workaround, I now realise, that eliminated marking pressure on sessional academics and tried to break recent high-school graduates of their obsession with grades. I couldn't help but notice how few whole books we read. Everything was in extract, and often delivered with only the most rudimentary context. We subsisted on a diet of fragments, designed for delivery by sessional tutors who are not paid for the hours they spend reading, while student services were cut back. Critics describe this period as the beginning of the culture of competitiveness among academics, leading to lower teaching and research standards, soft marking, and disillusionment.

Nevertheless, I took a lot from my degree. And while I don't remember the content of that first lecture, somewhere in the throng were a group who became my coterie, and with whom I navigated the next four years with enthusiasm and energy.

'We developed a critical intimacy,' my friend Alice remembered when I quizzed her about her memories of that time.

In the eleven years since we completed our first degree together, Alice has attained a PhD in cotutelle with an Ivy League college, and returned to Australia to work as a lecturer at one of the first universities established after the war to meet the needs of the baby boom.

Both Alice and I chose our university largely because of its inner-city location. It was a means to establish our independence; education was a bonus. This attitude inured us, in some sense, to the corporate culture emerging in universities and colleges: institutions now subject to economies of scale, increased enrolments, and high pressures on teaching staff.

'The university is a set of resources, and the students who get the most out of it are those who use these resources to collaborate,' Alice observed. It is as true now as when we were students, and it's a logic that she thinks will become even more entrenched as universities vie for industry support and reputation. Her guess is that within a decade the most expensive seats of learning will be those with the tightest ties to industry, from which a student emerges with a guaranteed future.

A disturbing story recently hit the national news in my country and caused ripples in policy reform that represent another change for education. In it, a door-to-door degree hawker signed an intellectually disabled woman up to diplomas in online business and management. The salesperson promised her a free laptop as an incentive, and coached her on what to say to the call-centre operator during the enrolment confirmation. The woman waited in vain for her laptop, but began to worry when she received a slew of invoices instead. As it turned out, the courses she had been enrolled in were worth $36,000.

Unfortunately, this student had just $200 a week after rent. She had never held a job, but desperately wanted one.

'I'm not good at reading,' she told the reporter.

In the newspaper, a brightly coloured diagram mapped the educational racket like a children's picture book on money laundering. A government grant trickles down to the educational provider and then to the sales reps (allowing for enticements such as the free laptop), and eventually to the student, who repays the original sum to the government, with interest.

Few would argue against the moral corruption of selling this woman a debt she had no way of repaying on the promise of a laptop and a better life. But some would say that this is a local, particularly egregious example of a trend that is happening on a much broader scale. In *The End of College*, Kevin Carey describes the sheer mass of private colleges in the United States offering 'inexpensive online courses at large profit margins', and reports on a congressional investigation that revealed similar practices in luring students into taking out loans to pay for 'largely worthless courses'.

In Australia, the current-affairs program *Four Corners* ran a story in 2015 on the use of recruitment agents to attract international students to Australian universities. The recruitment teams could help with adjusting transcripts and could offer internal language tests that were easier than the standard test. They could guarantee offers of enrolment.

The program interviewed academics who reported pressure to pass students lacking sufficient language skills. It described the case of a nursing graduate working in aged care who could not read the label on a medicine bottle. A sessional academic turned whistleblower repeated the line, 'Education is not an industry. It is not an industry.'

But she's wrong.

In Australia, education is our third largest export, behind coal and iron ore, but ahead of tourism. In 2015, the Bureau of Statistics reported the total revenue generated from international students living in Australia was $19.2 billion, up $2.2 billion in just one year. In the United Kingdom, *The Guardian* reported that in 2014 universities generated £72 billion in value on a turnover of £27.3 billion. In both countries, while universities might not commonly run for profit (as they do in the United States), their value as an industry cannot be underestimated.

In his book *Whackademia*, academic Richard Hil tracks what he describes as the rise of the enterprise university. Since the late 1980s, higher-education facilities have been forced to build their businesses by attracting students with advertising campaigns, elaborate graduation ceremonies, high-tech everything. Universities seduce what Hil calls 'student-shoppers' by promising them a flexible educational program and a top job after graduating — but there is often little focus on educational enrichment beyond the skills needed for an entry-level job.

Though Hil's nostalgic descriptions of traipsing the British halls of his 'testosterone-charged' college in '68 to the dulcet tones of 'Bob Dylan, Pink Floyd, and Van Morrison' make me want to sick up in someone's acoustic guitar, his critique of the contemporary university is incisive. Optimists such as Carey argue universities are at a threshold moment and hold forth an educational utopia for the future: the new university will be high-tech, democratic, and cheap-to-free. Students will complete courses at Oxford, Cambridge, Harvard, and Yale via responsive, personalised online learning environments. Thirteen-year-olds in Uganda will do advanced chemistry subjects at MIT and grow up to reverse drought. These are indeed exciting prospects. I worry, though, that most visions of the future of education — whether online courses that are universally accessible, regulated, and transparent, or industry-partnered specialty schools providing a near-guarantee of return on investment — are all so closely tied to economic imperatives: they smooth the transition from child to adult worker, leaving little space for personal and intellectual development. Carey's utopia cannot counter Hil's charge that universities 'take it for granted that students want to or should become embedded in a world of enterprise and productivity logic that feeds into a corporatised, capitalist world'. Educational reform over the last century — including, throughout Western democracies, standardised testing, moves to national curriculums, and competitive tertiary entry scores, seem to work on behalf of employers and parent-investors first, allowing them to efficiently read a young person's future without having to go to the trouble of listening to her. Education, from kindergarten coaching to big-ticket degrees, increasingly relies on the professionalisation of childhood and youth.

If there is an entrenched perception of degrees as essential in a competitive job market, it follows that high marks become important in order to stand out from the pack. Millennial students and those Generation Z pupils who follow them are responding to this with unhealthy levels of competitiveness. A distant cry from the class of '68, some of today's students are taking drugs, such as the narcolepsy medication Modafinil, not for recreation but to achieve and succeed. 'You take it on an empty stomach first thing in the morning and then you work really hard all day,' a British student dubbed Phoebe told *The Guardian*. 'It kills your appetite and then if you go to the gym, you do a really good workout. So you lose weight, nail your exams, and go hard at the gym all at once.' The workouts and motivation were great, but for Phoebe and the other students, the crook guts and lingering sense of fear were a definite downer. Also, the work they did was compromised, somehow. It had a narrower focus. The essays came thick and fast but they were … what's the word? Shallow.

Lest this seem another report on a baseless moral panic, it is worth noting that in the United States, the use of drugs such as Modafinil and prescription amphetamines such as Adderall has become so widespread that some colleges have issued formal statements: using performance-enhancing drugs constitutes cheating.

Such statements seem at odds with our present mode of engaging with the world, though. Do what it takes to get ahead. Make no excuses. Seize every opportunity. These are the messages of our hyper-competitive culture, and they are predominantly aimed at young people. Phoebe's description of a day on Modafinil reads like the affirmations that clog my social media newsfeeds. *Lose weight! Nail your exams! Go hard at the gym! Succeed!* I hear it with hashtags. What happens when you fulfil all these imperatives, become competent and poised for success, and yet it does not come? It's an increasingly common experience for young adults, and yet, as university-course cohorts continue to swell, we are doing very little to spare each new group from graduating into this inevitable malaise.

'I remind myself that the things that are frustrating about my job now are not the fault of my students,' Alice told me, 'or the fault of the university, but the fault of a broader cultural and economic reality. The way universities are forced to run in order to survive. The way students have to think about their economic prospects as a return on an investment in their studies. This is a global issue. The financialisation of our fucking souls.'

Alice worries that universities, in the midst of a heavy identity crisis, might end up promising the opposite of what they are set up to deliver. Which is not the same as saying that a jobless university graduate has a useless degree —

a claim that has dominated the media for the last decade, and denigrates education, subsuming it to a capitalist logic. Despite corporatisation, good teachers still teach in schools everywhere, and engaged students still make opportunities to turn their ideas out into the community. Alice sees the classroom as the last frontier of education: it is still social, relatively unregulated, and can still be radical. If a degree program is not seen exclusively as a ticket to a particular kind of adult future, universities can be spaces where young people discuss and critique what one writer describes beautifully as 'competing accounts of the good life'; that is, a place to try to nut out what a life well-lived, socially as well as economically productive, and meaningful on an individual and a cultural level, might look like.

'The strength of universities is still criticality and intellectualism,' she said. 'But if you said those words to a focus group, they'd freak out. They are terms that are so old-fashioned, and associated with elitism.'

For Alice, when teaching, the question became, 'How do I help my students value these things in a way that doesn't conflict with what the university is promising them?' She has tasked herself with helping students learn how to be critical of, and flourish within, a culture made of empty promises and continually changing social and vocational roles. It is not an easy brief.

Ultimately, I used the elective system to restructure my degree from the inside. Unlike the international students who need to return home with a bankable skill set, I dumped the more-vocational courses, and, without telling my mother she was right, picked units that looked more like what she had in mind when she pushed me through the gates. I remember one class particularly: a dozen students around a table talking about a book with a gifted teacher. The book, aptly, was Flaubert's *L'Éducation sentimentale*.

'Let's avoid indulging in moral gossip,' insisted our teacher. 'Instead, let's think for the moment about the revolution.'

I loved these books where lost and naïve young people smacked unknowingly against the political and economic forces of their time, trying to find a way to live beside them. Maybe one day I would write one, I fantasised.

Today, it is even harder than it was in Flaubert's age to have a conversation about education and adulthood without also considering debt. Degrees are more expensive than ever. In Australia, the latest proposed university fee deregulation has been scrapped, but a partial deregulation for specific courses is still on the table, as are higher student contributions and loan fees to cover the cost of our deferred payment system. Currently enrolled students study without knowing whether their courses will be impacted by these changes. In the United Kingdom, the fee cap was increased in 2014, effectively meaning that many students will emerge with £20,000 more debt than those who graduated four years earlier. North America, a leader in educational business models, has long since declared a 'student debt emergency'. More money is owed on education than on all the credit cards in the nation combined, and students have an average of more than $30,000 debt when they graduate. In 2015, *The Wall Street Journal* reported that 81 per cent of college-educated millennials in the United States have a source of long-term debt, and 34 per cent of high-income debtors and 54 per cent of all debtors over thirty worried about their ability to repay student loans.

In each of these countries, the reality was incomparable for my parents' generation. The post-war generation could graduate from higher education with comparably minimal debt, and began their lives with a degree of financial independence that a university-educated twenty-five-year-old today would be privileged to experience.

If we accept the imperative for adult lives to contain houses, cars, and children, it's easy to see one reason young people are delaying these financial commitments — they don't want to (or can't) get in even more debt. If we are looking for answers to how to build a meaningful adult life, debt has a role here, too: it's impossible to work out what gives value to your life when you are spending a great deal of your time and energy servicing and worrying about debt. Debt in this model *is* the waithood; it's what makes the kiddult and the adultescent. It is the economic responsibility for today's adult: if Rosie riveted, we borrow.

But we are borrowing a sense of forward momentum at the expense of actual security. As economic growth has slowed in most developed countries, young workers without inherited wealth need more time to save for a home, a family, and retirement, yet many also start with a large debt. If welfare and public services continue to be privatised at the rate they have been in the last twenty years, this problem will be compounded. It is not possible for one cohort to disrupt this trajectory. We sledge baby boomers, we lay our punches; the bell tolls, we do it again – but actually, we need to direct our efforts to fighting such a long-term reality. Otherwise, generations that are worse off financially than their parents will become the norm, not the outrage-inducing exception. What we will lose in all this will be a sense of the history of humanity as a progression towards a better life. Despite my petulant insistence on a commitment-free existence when I finished high school, I know now that the person who focuses only on survival is not free.

Writing in *The Huffington Post*, cultural commentator Amanda Oliver defended her peers against accusations of more millennial angst. The student debt emergency is real and unprecedented, she insisted. In the United States, tuition has risen 1,120 per cent since 1978 and, particularly for young people who were the first in their family to attend university, 'it is very likely that neither us nor our parents fully understood the lifetime burden we were foisting on ourselves when we took out these loans'. She spoke to more than two hundred people for her research on the subject, and reported that almost one-third enrolled in qualifications in addition to their first degree to increase their employability in a severe economic downturn where even experienced professionals lacked job security. This is sound in theory, but in practice it also means more debt.

The heavyweights in intergenerational sledging are not impressed by any of this. After all, aren't debtors just bad adults who can't handle money? Exploring this logic, *The Wall Street Journal* reported on a study that found only 24 per cent of millennials passed a basic financial literacy test. Unable to let an online quiz lie dormant, I surfed over to the OECD website and scored 4/5 — a win for my team! For me, though, the rising anxiety came not from working out the answers to the questions but the scenarios about invoices to pay, interest to calculate, and investments to make. Here are some maths problems I have worked on that do not make the financial literacy test: if Doyle has a $20,000 student-loan debt accumulating at low interest over a long period, and a $5,000 credit-card debt at high interest over a short term, which one should she make repayments on first? If Employer X owes Doyle $1,000 but probably won't pay the invoice for twelve weeks, how many weeks will Doyle need to buy groceries on her credit card, and at what point should she apply for a zero-interest balance transfer to equipoise her debt against her savings and give the illusion of control?

Fortunately, I had early debt training. 'You can't get blood from a stone,' I remember my dad saying as he tossed the third eviction notice in the bin and lit a cigarette. Having been a child who hid tenners in hairspray cans, major credit sounds too much like gambling to me. Maybe this is wisdom accrued from a parent's sins, or maybe it will keep me poor forever. I don't know. But these days, when I listen to my partner, Serge, on the phone to the debt collectors again, patiently trying to explain how, if they keep calling his main freelance client and bugging them, he is even less likely to get the work he needs to make payment on his debt, I'm pretty sure the stone can bleed.

Serge's debt breaks my heart. He has missed holidays because he can't afford them and I can't afford to carry him. But more than this, he feels utterly paralysed in the face of his own future. He can't talk to me about next year, let alone next decade, because right now his whole raison d'être looks like this: pay back debt.

It's a common story, if the case studies in the media are to be believed. Student debt, credit-card debt amassed when unemployed, or loans taken out against the promise of a bright future are wearing young people down. This situation is so common it raises the question: what are we not learning in school? The combination of expensive educations with aspiration as a condition of becoming, easy credit, and precarious employment is potent — it combines to make an adult life for which my generation is not adequately prepared. If the majority want millennials and those who follow to grow up and get on with it, mitigating the flow-on effects of student debt will be an important place to begin. There are lots of different ways to do this, from regulating what a university can promise a student in return for their fees, to indexing repayments to income (as is the case in Australia), and to individual debtor bailouts based on longer-term economic realities. Safeguards that prevent profiteering on educational debt by capping or eliminating interest on existing loans, and preventing the on-selling of student debt, alongside deadlines that ensure low-to-mid-income student debtors aren't making repayments in their fifties, would prevent a worsening situation.

Of course, the other option is providing free or low-cost education for all.

In 2016, I graduated from a minor university with my terminal degree. I stood in line with the other postgraduates in a balmy West Australian twilight. My peers had studied autism and slime mould, rare birds and dung beetles, in research degrees sponsored by industry partners whose logos were writ large across the program of ceremonies.

'Briohny Doyle: the postapocalyptic imagination,' read the dean, and I strode across the stage to receive my certificate. I held the handshake and smiled for the camera, for Serge and Annie and Mum and Dad, who had travelled across the country to be with me at this moment. They each knew, in their particular way, how disconnected I had been feeling as I laboured on this dissertation, mourned Cassady, and tried to strategise ways to take hold of my life. Baffled or proud, they each wanted to demonstrate that this work, my work, had value, and I was grateful to them for it. I crossed the stage and took my place on the shadowy, crowded rostrum.

During my candidacy, I lived more than 3,000 kilometres away from the university campus. I met with my supervisor through Skype, and when he came to town for a conference on nuclear ephemera or to see one of his other remote students. I made no friends in graduate school. Almost ten years after my first experience of tertiary study, the student body was being removed from the university.

At my graduation, I met the physical reality of university today. The ceremony went for four hours. At one point a biologist handed me her degree to hold while she texted her babysitter. 'We won't be home until midnight!' she said.

The undergraduates just kept coming. The audience was a sea of mortarboards that seemed to reach as far as the horizon — far more than could ever fit in the collection of buildings beyond — each one atop an individual with a piece of paper they hoped would secure their future. After the degrees were awarded, a bombastic promotional video was played, showing serious-looking young adults staring into microscopes and unfurling blueprints, a digital Earth turning on its axis, a polar bear standing perilously on a sheet of ice.

Thinking about it now reminds me of a course-outcome descriptor that Alice paraphrased: 'How will this course prepare a student to contribute to a world in crisis?'

I considered my fellow graduates, our red polyester gowns polka-dotted with mozzies. Were we prepared for this world in crisis? The video suggested that our very presence was a correction to it. But that was just a video. An advertisement for our own sense of self.

The twentieth-century philosopher Jean-François Lyotard insisted that the 'human' is something we work to produce. It sits in opposition to two forms of inhuman. The first is a system or technology produced by humans, yet bigger than us and annihilating in its power: radical free-market economics, say, or nuclear warheads. The second form is more ethereal and wondrous. 'Inhuman' in this sense designates an unknown space that the child does not enter because they are too busy learning to be human via the educational apparatus. This idea captivates me. What if there was no taxonomy of adult? No fireman, no stethoscope, no bridal veil, no gun? What if there was no Future Day, and even no future? What then?

My post-apocalyptic imagination thrummed. The Black Eyed Peas' 'I Gotta Feeling' crackled through the speakers overhead. Fireworks were let off. Beach balls were sent across the crowd. *I got my money / let's spend it up / go out and smash it / like, oh my God.* We paraded down the red carpet, past our proud (and slightly shell-shocked, due to the beach balls) families and through the sea of graduates, each with their bright future and piece of paper that made it so as the song urged them on: *Let's do it, let's do it / let's do it, and do it, and do it … and then we'll do it again.*

Maybe Lyotard's idea of the inhuman partly explains why people are fascinated by the stories of feral children raised by animals. The woman who was kidnapped, abandoned in the jungle, and subsequently taken in (up?) by monkeys, who taught her to pluck birds off branches and catch rabbits in their holes. The toddler kept alive on the streets of Chile by feral cats that fed her and kept her warm at night — a feline blanket in a dark alleyway. The Siberian four-year-old who escaped his alcoholic father to live with a pack of wild dogs for two freezing years. Feral children hiss and bark and smell their food before they eat it. Feral children are caught like animals, by leaving scraps of food out, or by throwing a blanket over their crouching bodies.

With help from his pack, the Siberian dog-boy escaped his human 'saviours' several times – an image I can't help seeing Disney-style, exaggerated and bright. Finally, social services sent him to military school to join the lower ranks of a different kind of pack. I couldn't find any information about what happened to the dogs.

But what if he had not become a soldier? What if he had gone to a regular high school – which is not so unlike a pack, or a number of packs fighting for alpha status? Would he have retained a dog's understanding of the social world? Would he have gone to university, and if so, what would he have studied? How would he parent? What insights would he have had about living and survival that we do not?

On graduation night, we former university students switched the position of our tassels and marched forth into a world we had been taught was one way, knowing that we would most likely experience it in another way entirely.

4
MY BEST FRIEND'S WEDDING DRESS

At thirty, if someone had asked me to draw my life as it felt, I would have drawn a cracking landmass. A fine-liner cartoon like those used to break up the lists of facts in elementary geography textbooks; a simple rendering of fragmenting tectonic plates, each carrying a small cargo of people – pairs, mostly, with some single bodies, some infants, dogs familiar and strange.

In this drawing, my own plate looks solid enough; it affords a pleasant view of the surrounding domestic scenes. But it has broken away from the others, and a swift tide is dragging it further out. I'm on the edge, perhaps contemplating whether to jump in and swim across to another plate. I'm reluctant, though. If I jump, I risk losing my private foothold. I'm drifting, yes, but I feel as if I can steer this plate. And if not, I can lie down and stretch out unmolested. I call out to a neighbour: 'What do you think I should do?' She shrugs, and turns to tend to her family. She's wearing a big fuck-off ring and a wedding veil, which trails across the bowl of mush she's feeding to her baby.

One of the defining characteristics of conventional adulthood seems to be a fragmenting social world, a drift from friendship and school to coupledom and work. The official cultural markers of adulthood— the careers and marriages and children and houses — all conspire to hasten this drift. Perhaps my inability to connect to adulthood derives, at least in part, from reluctance to let go of old, fierce friendships, despite the possibility they are already small oceans away.

At sixteen, Annie and I had a *Ghost World* kind of friendship. We viewed life through the same pair of second-hand shades and gained our admittance with matching fake IDs. Our personal value system was comprehensive, and complex. We had a formal line on everything from the aesthetic to the political. The finer points — vegetarianism, glitter, hottest rock stars, dumbest adults — were debated minutely on either of our balconies, set at bookends on a long street in a small inner-city Sydney suburb.

Between afternoons spent playing Iggy Pop down the phone line and evenings fuelled by illegally procured booze, we liked to make plans for the future. It was clear to both of us that once the tyranny of high school was over, we would live a life of uninhibited adventure. First we would travel, and party mightily. After a few years of that, we would probably want to settle down and have a family. Before we got too old and decrepit. Like, around twenty-three. This all sounds fairly conventional for middle-class girls, but we were not thinking of two separate families — we would start one together.

Annie, who was more interested in the experience of childbirth, would get pregnant via a sperm source still to be determined. We would raise that infant and any subsequent sprogs together. We would live together, bringing up baby in an inner-city house of our own, finally collapsing those pesky residential blocks that had kept us apart as we slept in our teenage beds. Our adult home would be large enough to allow us separate rooms, where we could entertain lovers as we saw fit. We weren't lesbians — much to the chagrin of Annie's lesbian mother, who listened to our plans with barely contained glee. No, we assured her, we would be free to embark on hetero dalliances, and could even leave the family for short trysts, bursts of travel and adventure. Isn't the inability to ensure these private adventures the reason so many marriages fail? This arrangement would spare us from the seemingly inexhaustible loneliness we identified as a defining feature of motherhood. It would also spare us the horror of divorce because, as everyone knows, you can't divorce your best friend.

'It just makes sense,' we told each other. 'Build a life with someone you love, but don't love-love.'

Love-love just complicates things. We would be savvy enough to keep that separate.

Were we serious about all this? Sometimes it felt that way. We talked about our plan so often and in so much detail. But surely we knew, even then, that this is not how our lives would go? Or did we actually think we could invent wholly new kinds of lives — and if so, when did that belief change?

While the first part of our itinerary (the travel and the parties) was easily accomplished, we soon discovered that the very tyranny we so longed to escape was part of what held us together. At school we were sisters in arms, but after graduation we were a less united front. If the plan was real, I was first to break away from it. As months turned to years, I began to realise that the space between late teens and early twenties was not so unfathomable, and my enthusiasm for having a baby at twenty-three in a non-sexual bestie union diminished. Annie, too, had other ideas. Within a year of high school, she started going on about university and employment, two social institutions in direct discordance with our already defined and inflexible code of conduct. At twenty-three, rather than being shacked up, we found ourselves at opposite ends of the country, at opposite ends of a scale of ambition, and at opposite ends of a shattered value system in a limiting adult world.

As children of the late 1980s and the 1990s, Annie and I were raised on a diet of friendship-first pop culture. In primary school, the pre-teen band of the minute was Girlfriend – also the name of the highest-selling pre-teen magazine in the country, which regularly featured the group. On television, the most-watched show was *Seinfeld*, about a bunch of thirtyish friends who spent their time together discussing their jobs, social lives, and romantic entanglements. Then it was *Friends*: same deal. The Spice Girls' 'Wannabe', a pop song about girl power and friendship forever, became the best-selling single of 1996. Too cool for serious fandom, Annie and I sang along to it ironically with our small teen girl gang.

In our final years of high school, as the 1990s inched cringingly towards the millennium, we spent every Tuesday night at Bella's house watching *Dawson's Creek*. We were just a cute, close-knit crew of teenage besties, doing bong hits and drinking green cordial, watching a show about a (slightly cuter) close-knit crew of teenage besties. Like Jen, we were angsty and sexually active. Like Joey, we had dreams of notoriety and romantic adventure, and like Pacey, we did not know what the future held but hoped we would be together for all of it.

Around the same time, the urtext for friendship — and what is now one of the most popular television shows of all time — was *Sex and the City*, chronicling a gang of thirty-something besties and their successful lives in New York City. While each half-hour was ostensibly about the women's sexual escapades with men — many of them deviants or pathetic caricatures, such as Mr Pussy and The Turtle, Mr Cocky and The Bone — the program's main arc was friendship. The show celebrated the ways these women supported one another, reducing the world to an absurd comedy that could be digested over brunch. Friendship made their glamorous and footloose lives possible. Without friendship, they were the lonely, piteous outsiders, spinsters past their prime. Samantha, the brazen slut of the group, was adamant on the priority of friendship over romance: 'We made a deal ages ago. Men, babies, it doesn't matter. We're soulmates.'

I resisted the show when I first saw it. It seemed too yuppy, too repressed. But in my mid-twenties, in the midst of a relationship breakdown, I housesat at Olivia's place in Tasmania and spent the first two weeks binge watching, freezing in her lounge room, with Cassady pulled up close. When I finally finished those 47 NYC hours, I looked out at the grey sky of Hobart, thought about how alone I was, and went right back to episode one. It's not so easy, in real life, to put friendship first.

Years later, as our twenties drew to a close, I put a season of *Girls* onto a hard drive for Annie to take with her to her new job in Fiji. I wished we could have watched it together. The show sketches a metacritique of friendship as a pop-cultural production. The characters are full of angst. Their lives are confusing. They want to lean back for at least ten seasons (plus re-runs) into friendship that is frozen, like Monica and Rachel's. But how can they, after the social bonds of high school and college have dissipated? I sympathised with the uptight and controlling Marnie when she cajoled the whole gang out to the seaside so they could 'heal' their friendship and 'prove to everyone via Instagram that we can still have fun as a group'. Marnie is awful. In that episode, she embodies some of the millennial tendencies I too possess. You can imagine her consulting internet listicles on '55 Ways to Have an Unforgettable Weekend Away with the Girls' before packing her picnic hamper and designing her floral arrangements. The pathos lies in the fact that, while any of these girls might be able to marry, get a job, or one day put a deposit on a condo, they cannot lock down something as dynamic as friendship.

Throughout our twenties, Annie and I tried, at different points, to resurrect the friendship in its adolescent intensity.

We did live together for a time, but found that 'entertaining men' in our rooms complicated the teenage utopia – men being, it turned out, subjects of their own, with all kinds of inconvenient needs and desires. It infuriated me that Dave, Annie's boyfriend, could not simply be put back in the cupboard when she was finished playing with him. He was there every night, clad in some intolerable beanie, watching hard-hitting documentaries and strumming South American folk songs on his nylon-string guitar. He was *there*, ubiquitous – on the couch, in the kitchen, beside her on a milk crate in the backyard – a barricade against my attempts to commandeer her attention. And finally, not long after we moved in together, he was there, packing up the station wagon and moving her off to some new life that did not include me. And there they are still, together on a plate in the continental drift.

As we got older, our attempts at reclaiming teen-bestie fervour became less passionate. By the time we were nearing thirty, a shared home, or even a long road trip, seemed impossible. We settled instead for a nice cup of tea wedged between more pressing commitments. We moved in different circles, had different interests and different ways of conducting our lives. Annie, a community-development worker, had always been practical, civic-minded, family-oriented, intensely social. I remained creative, reactive, at odds with almost everything, and at my best socially one on one. It's sad to look objectively at these two adults and remember that as children they thought they were the two halves of Aristophanes' primal human. Sad in that bittersweet, midday-movie way. Sad in the way *Ghost World* is sad – because the slow collision of dreams with reality can leave us all feeling like the future owns us before we have even managed to make a scratch on it.

In 2012, six months before my thirtieth birthday, I received a giddy text message from Annie's Fiji number. *Darling. Sorry to do this via text – we're on a beautiful island and can't get phone credit ... We just got engaged! It was amazing. Not a dry eye in the house.*

I sent her an appropriate burst of emoji and congratulations and then put the phone down impassively. I felt devastatingly and permanently left out. Marriage was a plan for two, designed to draw a border around two bodies. Marriage added metaphoric oceans to the literal ones between us. I also felt guilty for not feeling unreservedly happy for her; I should craft a better reply. She probably couldn't even get my emoji on her distant handset. I wandered around my quiet house, fretting. Made a cup of tea. Turned the heater up. Tried to ignore my teen memorabilia, still proudly on display: the photo-booth prints taken en route to our first music festival, the obnoxious dolphin paraphernalia we had exchanged for years. I tried to picture Annie in Fiji, over-freckled and glowing, draped in frangipani, dipped low to the sand in Dave's exclusive embrace, backdropped by a red-hot sun sinking into some distant patch of the Pacific green as envy.

I tested the feeling of 'breaking the news' to Serge when he got home.

'Annie and Dave got engaged!' I said when he walked through the door, trying for enthusiasm.

'Huh,' said Serge, unsurprised. 'And how do you feel about that?'

I squirmed. 'I dunno. Happy, I guess.'

'Great, then.'

I re-read the text message. A bulk send-out, I was sure. Annie can never resist the urge to crack a sarcastic joke, so 'darling' probably indicated a group address. Practical and funny; I both loved and hated her for it.

It wasn't a slight on me that I was among many to receive the text — of course it wasn't — but in my specific displacement from the performance of Annie's future, I realised that, even though I no longer imagined us raising a family as husbandless co-wives, I hadn't really believed in another plan since. I could see plenty of futures I didn't want. I didn't want to be stifled and contained in my relationship. I didn't want a partnership that was static, frozen in time. I didn't want to take on more than my share of the domestic or care-giving responsibilities. I didn't want to assimilate into a milieu of 'the suburban married', if such a thing still existed, and if they would even have me. I didn't want to make a declaration that aligned me with principles to which I did not subscribe. But what *did* I want? I was jealous that Annie was mapping out a future and I couldn't, or wouldn't, form my own. Annie was announcing her adult status, and I still felt like a teenager rising against the grown-up world.

'I still feel like a teenager,' I confessed to Serge later, interrupting a *Battlestar Galactica* marathon.

'Me too, darlin',' he said, his lovely voice resonating with cool melancholy.

As the details of Dave's proposal rippled out across the ocean via Facebook and rumour, I both loved and hated him as well. It was just too perfect – the element of surprise, the public display of high romance, weeping strangers, and sparkling wine. Later still, there were images of beaming individuals holding placards reading 'Congratulations' and 'Dave loves Annie' against a too-blue sky.

Their wedding was to be 'a festival of love', Dave told me upon their return. 'Obviously we don't have to get married,' he said. 'So we want it to be a celebration of us, of who we are and what we love.'

A festival of happiness where you are the headlining act: it's a seductive and very millennial idea.

When Annie got back to Melbourne, we came to the topic only after our exhaustive complaints and triumphs, recounting all the fascinating and grotesque moments that had passed since last we met. Even then, Annie spoke of her wedding only lightly, giving scant details. As months passed, I waited in vain for her to give me a job. One that made me an important part of the event. But her lips were sealed against terms like *bridesmaid* and *maid of honour*. Instead, her favourite routine was a hammed-up ignorance of tradition.

'Did you know the guy doesn't even get an engagement ring?'

'Yes,' I replied. 'Everyone knows that.'

Maybe Annie was trying to distance herself from the auspiciousness of the thing for my benefit, or perhaps she wanted to preserve her privacy. Either way, I came home sulky after our catch-ups. I re-watched *Bridesmaids*, feeling too much empathy for Kristen Wiig's character. I was just as ridiculous. Just as desperate to have my relationship with the bride acknowledged. Just as left out. I suffered the inability to move forward into the next stage of life. Mishka sat anxiously on my feet and yodelled in the scene with the puppies. Soon she would be gone, too; everything in my life was temporary. I yearned for a jubilant synchronised-dance conclusion.

When Annie finally asked me to help her, I felt like I was being proposed to. Did I want to come with her to buy a wedding dress? I do! But it was not long before the reality of the task was brought home. Annie hates shopping. A request for help to buy a dress was like a request that someone you trust be in your firing squad. What started as flicking through trashy magazines and emailing photos of 1940s Hollywood starlets quickly turned into another point on which to emphasise our difference. I was Annie's 'shopping friend'. I was the only woman she knew who was not too busy — I don't know, say, with practising human-rights law or directing theatre for the disabled — to cultivate skills in the consumerist arts. We sacrificed our paltry catch-ups to stressful marches through the arcades of Melbourne.

I asked Annie what kind of dress shape she preferred, and she traced her figure in a slick, hugging hourglass shape.

'A wiggle dress?'

'Oh, Doyle, trust you to know that.'

Everyone knows that, don't they? At least anyone who has ever attempted to buy a cut-price frock online.

At home, I anxiously mimicked Annie's hand movements for Serge. 'Let's play the what-kind-of-dress-is-this game.'

He looked at me, bemused and patient. 'A wiggle dress?'

I drew a few more, just to check. He correctly guessed A-line and baby doll before sighing, pushing his glasses back up his crumpled nose. This, I knew, was my cue to quit.

'It's common knowledge though, right? I'm not some kind of shallow clotheshorse?'

'You may not be, but I am. I'll be wearing a gold suit to my wedding.' He drew a sharp collar in the air. 'Texan cut.'

Annie didn't want to go to a bridal boutique, so we restricted ourselves to department stores and less formal dress shops. We tried on dresses that were too casual, too slutty, too cheap, too plain, too thin, too thick, too weird, too structured. We tried on blue dresses and spotted dresses and crepe dresses and dresses with impertinent bows. She looked at me suspiciously when I suggested that trying on clothes can be fun, that for some, the dress, the hair, the shoes, and the matching accessories is the main pull towards the wedding event. She shuddered.

'Why are you doing this again?' I asked.

'It will be nice to have a party.'

She pulled a giant Grecian urn of a dress over her shoulders and posed awkwardly beneath the department-store fluoros.

'Not quite right,' she said, ripping it off and attempting to hang it up again by its labyrinthine straps. 'It needs to be more …'

'Bridal?'

She gave me a look.

I proffered a silver dress, ruffled and sequined, like a swan at a disco.

'I think that's too …'

'Birdal?'

We were a week out from wedding day when I managed to drag Annie through the doors of the specialty boutique. 'At this point, we have nothing to lose,' I coaxed.

I could feel her body tensing. If we were cartoons, her toes would be excavating the concrete. There would be sparks at her heels.

In the boutique, brides and bridesmaids tittered and sparkled in floor-length gowns. These were dresses charged with making announcements. 'Look, a beautiful woman succeeding at life!' they screamed, in appropriate languages for their various contexts.

A heavily made-up woman wearing an unseasonable fascinator smiled broadly at us. 'When's the special day?'

We cowered. We'd been shamed by shop assistants all over Melbourne. In the boutique, however, they had special training for this kind of thing.

'You're like me,' replied the woman, when Annie mumbled the date. 'Keep it casual! It's all about having fun!'

She bundled Annie into the change room and began to launch dresses at her like a talented prosecutor might pose questions.

'There,' said the assistant. 'That's gorgeous, but it's also fun. Just like you.'

Beautiful seventeen-year-old girls in $500 debutante frocks paraded along the mirrored promenade between the change rooms. The store buzzed with nervous glamour, which is what glamour is: nerves pulled and prodded, insecurity and desire sewn into impractical dresses, bodies bleached and highlighted, plucked and pouted, and sent out into the world. Tottering. Unstable. Glamour is so fragile it will only hold together for a day, an hour. It's strange that we mark a lifetime's commitment with this brief magic.

Annie joined the glamour parade. She tottered. She grimaced in the mirror. She wrangled straps and boobs. She would not, could not, enjoy the spectacle she was making of herself and her life. Maybe I was cruel to ignore her discomfort. I flicked through a rack of black glomesh.

'What's the occasion?' the women asked me, in their cash-draw singsong.

'Jealousy,' I said, pulling a flashy gown over my body and staring into a mirror as if it were another world.

I know a few divorcees under thirty-five now. These are women who had weddings in their early twenties but never felt completely comfortable in their marriage. In almost every case, they got married because that's what their best friends were doing. The desire to stay together was stronger than the desire to work out what made them distinct.

In Japan, there is a rising trend for women to have solo weddings. These solo brides are reclaiming a term, '*himono onna*', which translates literally as 'dried-fish woman'. I read about them in a *Marie Claire*.

'I was brought up to believe that I could take care of myself, so marriage has never been a priority for me; getting married does not equal being happy,' thirty-seven-year-old Akiki told the magazine. She went on to describe a whole crew of thirty-something femme babes who hold the same opinions. This doesn't mean that they should miss out on the event. A wedding, the women suggested, is about more than the beginning of a marriage. It is a milestone in maturity. It announces adulthood. The *himono onna* do not want the burden of men, but they still want to make this statement.

In Japan, a solo wedding package includes the dress, professional makeup and photographs, and dinner in a glamorous restaurant, alone or with a paid escort. And a week or so later, a photo album to place strategically on the coffee table. It's something to be proud of, to mark an arrival, if not a conventional path to get there.

What else does a solo wedding prove? It's a niche product that has arisen from consumer need. Designed as a substitute for marriage, it also highlights what this institution has become: a dress, a photograph, a printed announcement. A fetishised commodity in any well-constructed adult life. But if there is commercialism here, there is feminism, too. It takes a strong will and a pragmatic mind to ignore the stigma attached to a move like this. *Dried-fish wife.* Would I be bold enough to make this statement? I could still hear, in my inner ear, the schoolyard taunt *you love yourself, go marry yourself.* It was a lonely-making taunt.

'I don't feel lonely at the moment,' said one of the solo brides. 'But I would be in trouble if my best friend was to get married.'

I left the dress on for a few extra turns.

When Annie went back into the change room, I was tempted to run. Out of the shop, across the rows of stalling traffic, the hectares of city, of offices, commerce, and bars, and on and on, in this heavy dress, straight into the blazing sun.

The change-room door opened, and Annie stood in the stall. She looked tall and gorgeous and utterly grown up. A woman in her wedding dress in a room full of kids playing dress-up.

'Is this it?' I felt my throat catch.

'I think it is,' she said.

We stood together, grinning in the room of mirrors. It was a classic lock-down shot lifted straight from a rom-com, with life continuing, uncontainable, beyond the frame. We waited, perfectly in character, for a director to yell cut.

There is a scene in the 1978 film *Girlfriends* in which the eponymous BFFs fight. Susan, depressed and disillusioned, takes the train from the city to her best friend Anne's (the name is pure coincidence) new adult abode. It's the first time we see this house. For most of the film the girls live together in a cramped apartment, writing poetry and taking photographs of each other sleeping. They tango through shabby rooms, taking their dual future for granted, until it vanishes, suddenly and irretrievably, into the adult world of marriage and careers. Initially, they try to make the best of it. At Anne's new big-girl house, she gives Susan a present she has brought back from her honeymoon: a hideous kaftan. There is a slideshow of their trip, too — photos of ruins, which the new husband (a suitably bearded academic who indeed looks like he belongs in front of a 1970s chalkboard) enjoys explaining. The visit does not end well.

'Even if we want different things, I'm still the same person,' Anne insists finally, exasperated.

'No, you're not! You're married,' yells Susan.

A married best friend is different because her needs are different. A married best friend is different because the way she accesses the world has changed. A marriage, when you strip it down and stand it in front of the mirror, is a legally recognised relationship in a way that friendships can never be. Even if friends are as important to you. Even if you are working hard, tirelessly, to keep friendship at the centre of your life.

After Cassady died, I had been angry. I felt alone in my grief, and I couldn't work out why. Dogs were not the centre of most people's lives, I knew that; but surely the people close to me would understand how vital Cassady was to me? I wanted flowers, soup, and stroked hair. Instead, I had an irreducible pit in my stomach and an aching sense of sadness.

I railed against this feeling in my psychologist's tastefully furnished office. I blamed Serge first. Why wasn't he there for me as much as I needed him?

She reminded me that although in an ideal world the people in our lives tend to our needs, in reality it is unfair to demand more from someone than they can give. Serge, who bore the brunt of my sorrow, was stressed at work; he could be more sympathetic, sure, but he had also made it clear he had enough on his plate. 'He's told you what he can provide. Now you need to decide whether that's acceptable,' she said.

'What about everyone else, though?' I demanded, shifting the conversation away from this uncomfortable reality.

'Well, do they know what you need?' she asked.

I couldn't answer. My friendships had come to seem so ethereal and fragile that I seldom dared to make demands within them. Besides, wasn't friendship supposed to be fun? On television, friendship is a place to play hooky from those other, more staid parts of life. One of our culture's favourite adult fantasies is unending friendship, goofing around without responsibility or consequence. In my past, I had been guilty of excusing myself from friendships that became too difficult, too messy and demanding. I didn't want to be a similar burden. In an adult world, a friendship that causes problems, that is not consistently enjoyable, is surely a toxic asset. Who has time for such a thing?

At home, I searched the internet for advice. In *New York* magazine, Ada Calhoun extolled the secret to friendships in your thirties. You have to 'lower the bar', she writes. 'There is no friend equivalent of the candlelit dinner and rose-strewn canopy bed. To stay friends is to make do with the social equivalent of a taco truck and bathroom quickie.'

The article, which describes once inseparable besties catching up during mutually essential trips to the pharmacy, or while walking each other to meetings, depicts a very specific kind of existence. These are adults with fancy jobs, children, and partners, trying to be everything to everyone, and feeling relieved when a friend cancels drinks. Friendship, in Calhoun's view, is an important part of successful adult life. Time with friends is like going to the gym or having a cold-pressed juice – something you should fit into a busy day because it's good for your health and wellbeing.

This didn't help me, though, not really. How could you discuss grief at the taco truck and the toilet stalls? How could you yell and scream about jealousy at the pharmacy?

Calhoun's description of adult pals is antithetical to the reputation friendship – particularly female friendship – has for being fraught and conflict-ridden. And yet is the lack of time afforded to these kinds of relationships part of the reason they are deemed volatile in the first place? Like Calhoun, I've had friendships as passionate as love affairs, but I have never fought with a friend in the entitled, unrestrained way I would with my partner.

When I eventually decided to speak to Annie about how I'd been feeling, I prepared an elaborate picnic. I made a flan. I made two types of salad and a sweet treat. I was terrified. To say 'my needs are not being met' in a friendship in your thirties felt wrong on every level – unendurably selfish. I wanted the picnic to keep things light, to maintain the element of fun that would make the difficult afternoon worthwhile. We ate two courses in the dappled sun before I worked up the guts to get serious. I tried to be articulate, but as emotions built up, I descended into a teenage vocabulary.

'I drop everything for you!' I whined. 'You don't care about me!'

'You seemed so angry that I figured it was better to leave you alone,' Annie said through tears.

A month later, she came to my house with a potted lemon tree that I have named Clementine but have no idea how to take care of. Adult friendship is hard. Ours is not volatile so much as castaway, adrift in uncharted waters.

In 2016, three years after Calhoun's article, *New York* magazine ran a very different perspective. 'When friendships are your primary relationships,' wrote Briallen Hopper, 'friendship isn't just important: it's existential.'

This has been true before. In other times, when marriage was more ubiquitous, though less emotionally central, friendship was the primary emotional relationship for many — men as well as women. While Hopper laments that her 'most important relationships are chronically underrated and legally nonexistent', at other points in history it was precisely this that sanctified them. In Ancient Greece and Rome, friendship was an ideal to which to aspire. For Erasmus and Aristotle, an ideal friendship was creative, inspiring, even transcendent. For Cicero, friendship was two bodies sharing a soul, a perfect union without the debasement of sex or the mess of children. During the Renaissance, strong friendships were akin to marriage. A friendship could be a covenant. Men were buried together. They bequeathed one another their fortunes — to the chagrin, no doubt, of many wives left in situations far less than ideal.

Women had intense friendships, too, even if their virtues were less extolled upon. Nevertheless, historians of the early modern period have mistaken ardent and pseudonymous letters written by women for the correspondence of married couples. In the seventeenth century, the poet Katherine Philips insisted that as the soul has no sex, female friendship could be of no lower order than men's. To prove this, she formed an official coterie and dubbed it the 'Society of Friendship'. To the society, friendship was about support, sharing political views and secrets, and writing poems about all of the above. In her poem 'Friendship's Mystery, to my Dearest Lucasia', she writes that friendship makes 'Both Princes, and both Subjects too' — no insignificant claim for a royalist. For Philips, friendships were a place of becoming; like writing, they were both an imperative and an active process. 'Poets and friends are born what they are,' she writes in 'A Friend'. In the Victorian era, women wore jewellery made from one another's hair. It was not unheard of for small groups of middle-class married women to move to the country together and live apart from their husbands, enjoying female company away from any force that might deem it imprudent or perverse. They were schooled and punished, of course, though mainly in literature.

Marriage, suicide, or madness was the fate of the eighteenth- and nineteenth-century fictional female, and it's a tradition we have continued into the twenty-first century. While real women have complex, challenging, and important relationships, the women of literature and popular culture are usually doomed or tamed. It is an enduring trope that friendship — particularly the exclusive, overly intimate type explored in films such as *Girlfriends* or *Frances Ha* — is something to grow out of.

Jane Austen's Elizabeth Bennet comes to her senses about marriage. Carrie and Big must have a wedding. Thelma and Louise drive off that cliff because there is no place for them in the world they come from. It's not just that we can't make space for this kind of friendship in social reality – we can't even imagine how it would work.

This tradition haunted me recently as I let everything in my life fall away to finish Elena Ferrante's Neapolitan novels. In her quartet, Ferrante eschews the marriage plots of the nineteenth century and the modern romantic comedy to present a more complex plot centred on friendship. The twinned protagonists of these novels are locked in a relationship constantly agitated by the pressures, violence, and repression that women faced in mid-century Naples. In many stages of the narrative, the reader is given to wonder what would have been possible if these two women's lives could have been lived together in a formally acknowledged partnership, like the friendship ideals of the ancients, or the marriage contracts that reify heterosexual marriage – if the pressures of patriarchal capitalism didn't conspire to keep them at opposite ends of a dyad. Writing in *n+1*, Dayna Tortorici notes how readers and critics, 'in absence of adequate vocabulary', call Lila and Lenù's bond '"female friendship" – an ambiguous catchall that's slightly evocative of a slumber party'. This phrase might be enough for shows such as *Sex and the City*, which figure friendship as a commodity, but it's insufficient in Ferrante's Neapolitan novels and in our own lives, where our connections to people mark us in indescribable ways.

This sense of an inadequate vocabulary that shadows much of Western literature also curtails my own attempt to describe my friendships without resorting to cliché or to tropes of juvenile covenants and adult loss. How do I express longing for friendship without falling into nostalgia? How do I celebrate and insist on an ideal without romanticising real relationships? Maturity, in some sense, has to be about finding ways to make complex interactions work, not transmogrifying anything difficult into a misty glade of romance.

I'm aware of the danger, in discussing friendships, of erasing queerness. Where does the undermining of same-sex friendship end and fear of homosexuality begin? Were those Victorian women in fact lesbians retreating from a culture that hated them? In one scene in the Neapolitan novels, a grown-up Lenù catches her toddler playing erotic games with Lila's. She's shocked at first, and then, feeling something else entirely, something more like recognition, she strains to remember if she and Lila had ever played such games, experienced some kind of erotic becoming, a transgressive love that was blocked as they came into competition with each other, racing to realise adult fantasies. And yet, aware of the risk, I think there is something in friendship that is seditious, a threat to heteronormativity that is distinct from non-heterosexual relationships. There is no way to know what kinds of lives would be possible or would flourish outside the social reality we in Western cultures know, but I think that 'female' friendships (it is the friendship that is female, not the friends per se), which have no institutional name or legal premise, are figured, rightly, in Ferrante's texts as acts of resistance. They are places from which we could organise different kinds of adult lives, if only we had the opportunity to do so. Unfortunately, though, despite our friendship-first popular culture, we often have less, not more, time and space for friendship than we did one hundred years ago.

Annie and I drift along side by side, occasionally braving the current between our two patches of earth. I have faith that we will keep hold of each other, and that the inevitable drifts will be temporary. But if I want my adult life to have friendship at its centre, how else might I go about this? Casual work makes it hard to forge lasting friendships at work. Renting in a seller's market means I've moved too often to befriend my neighbours, who are similarly changeable. For most, family pressures, the second shift at home after work, and council ordinances that fragment communities and subcultures in service of development all stand between us.

It is no longer unusual, in cities like mine, for people to go it alone. We are living alone. Our bank accounts have one name on them. We are raising children alone, taking holidays alone, eating alone. Alone, alone, alone. I love being alone, except when I don't — when I'm logging on to Facebook, clicking for a fix, throwing ropes between those shifting plates and thinking, *Well, it's not enough.* Perhaps we do only have time for marriage *or* friendship, and this is the price we pay for sexual relationships that are also loving and supportive, rather than mere economic and procreative pacts. Or worse, perhaps the pressure to construct recognisably 'adult' lives, with monogamous partners, houses, children, careers, and retirement plans works also to exclude those who have, or want, different kinds of primary relationships.

This thought got Mickey Rourke started in my inner ear again. To distract myself, I headed back to the long document of fragments that was becoming this book. The what-the-fuck-am-I-doing book, which was a too-long draft lacking structure and resolve.

'So what is the book about?' my psychologist asked, when I told her how I was spending my time. I dreaded this question — the manuscript was too nebulous, and so was the topic. I felt sheepish and glib when I tried to describe it to someone.

'It's about adulthood,' I said, as though that explained everything, hoping she would leave it there.

'What about adulthood?'

Once again I considered running out into the street. But if ever there's a place to get your thoughts in order, your psychologist's office must be it.

'About how these milestones we have are outmoded and actually kinda oppressive in the present moment. You know, the idea that you would have a career, kids, a house, and this is how you measure your maturity. It's about trying to think about adulthood in a different way, to become comfortable with and maybe even excited by maturity.'

To my relief, she nodded her head knowingly. 'I see people about this problem all the time. Mostly twenty-nine-year-olds coming up to their thirtieth birthday and losing it. One guy was ready to kill himself because he felt so worthless,' she said, matter-of-factly. 'His therapy was all about defining the areas of his development that were actually very advanced. He was such a caring person, for instance. He might have been, in another time, a real cornerstone of a community. But now he's just kind. He helps everyone around him, but he doesn't get any kind of validation for that. Instead, he feels inferior and depressed for want of a career or a house. That's what middle-class Australia thinks you should have to be a real person.'

'Yes, exactly!'

She drew a diagram on the back of my folder. 'I call this the Hong Kong skyline,' she said. 'Some buildings are tall, well-developed: "career", say, or "relationships", and others are smaller, like "community" or "financial freedom". But there are things to develop that we really don't talk about much, like "kindness".'

I nodded, but I only half-read the diagram because the phrase 'Hong Kong skyline' was far more evocative than the developmental schema she used it to draw. In my science-fiction novel, the roofs of the skyscrapers in future Hong Kong were so covered in water collectors and solar panels that passengers in aircraft lowered their shutters so as not to go blind.

'Another exercise I do with them comes from existential psychology. In it, you ask the patient to imagine their funeral. They are a spirit flying around the funeral home and they can see who is there, and eavesdrop on the various conversations mourners are having while they drink their tea. I ask them, who's there, and what are they saying about you?'

'What you think they are saying, or what you hope they'd say?'

'You do both – one where you die tomorrow, and one ideal funeral, at the end of a long life.'

'Sounds depressing.'

'No, it's a very good kick in the pants!' she said. 'Particularly for people who are quite materialistic, or always striving for status. Hardly anyone wants their friends to say things like "She had very nice furniture," or "She quickly ascended the corporate ladder," at their funeral. This is when something like kindness becomes an important thing to have developed.'

Conspicuously, she did not suggest that we do the funeral exercise. But on my way home I began to formulate it. I flew in through the skylight of the funeral home, where my friends and family were about to sit down to a supper including actual pieces of my body. This will be in my will. It's something I've wanted since I was a kid.

'Gross,' Annie has said, repeatedly, when I've outlined the menu for my wake. 'No one will want to do that.'

'Not like a whole steak, though – just very fine slices, perhaps lightly tossed in a salad. Then you will be digested by the people that you love, and you will actually be an energy source for them. It's a basic gesture of kindness to feed your friends.'

Annie has steadfastly been refusing to eat me for twenty years, but I know that when it comes down to it, she will.

In any case, I acknowledge that it will be a challenging meal. And there I am, the spirit person, flying around and eavesdropping while people complain about the food and joke about what a weirdo I was. A difficult person, perhaps. A person who loved dogs and the ocean, and was a pain in the arse to argue with. But also maybe they'd say I was fun, or generous, or maybe, if I'm really lucky, inspiring. I'd fly back out of the funeral home, past the staff taking a smoko and laughing about what freakish requests people who pre-pay their funerals make, and then back over the town and maybe even further — a quick round-the-world joyride — being very careful to shut my eyes tightly as I fly over the Hong Kong skyline, so I don't get blinded by all the shit that obsessed me while I was alive.

5
FORSAKING ALL OTHERS

I don't remember dreaming of white dresses and veils when I was little. I never married my dolls, but rather sent them 'to space' by flinging them out the window one night. But somewhere in my twenties, this changed. I began to think seriously about marriage. No, that's too mild; I began to obsess.

Some of the reason for this was pop culture: I always loved the film clip to Guns N' Roses 'November Rain', and Clarence and Alabama's horseshoe wedding rings in *True Romance*. Part of the reason was love: I met Serge. He had a great mouth on him, and the ability to answer any question without blushing. He had seen all my favourite films and had something insightful to say about each one. And part of the reason was more existential: my social world was fragmenting, my best friend got hitched. The final reason might be more surprising: I became a marriage celebrant.

Yep. I was a member of an industry with an annual profit in Australia estimated at more than $4.3 billion. A fundamental legal conduit for an institution that, in Australia, still actively excludes a significant proportion of the population. In retrospect, I'm not sure why I decided to do this. Caprice? The desire for another unreliable revenue stream? An enduring love of Madonna microphones? When I sent my letter of registration to the attorney-general's office, I think I just thought being a celebrant would be a lark.

It's not hard to become a marriage celebrant in Australia. I completed an online course. Upon graduation, I knew all about the mechanics of 'surprise weddings' and how to fill out a Notice of Intention to Marry form. I knew who could and who could not marry, and I could recite the legal definition of marriage in Australia — that is, the union of a man and a woman to the exclusion of all others, voluntarily entered into for life. But I did not know that this was an amended definition, written in 2004. I did not know that until then the man and woman bit, and all that exhaustive forsaking, were only assumed to be the thing. I knew about as much, I suppose, as most of the young couples who would soon be calling for my services.

For almost three years I signed forms and made speeches. I witnessed couples promise to exclude all others without my really knowing what their sexual proclivities were. Couples that were more than a little bit queer promised to be strictly heterosexual. Couples who were not particularly attached to monogamy promised to be faithful. Then everybody cheered, ate cake, got fall-down drunk.

Perhaps what I actually wanted, in this strange and awkward role, was a chance to be a significant part of other people's lives. Or maybe it was a perverse research exercise, because with each ceremony I attended, whether as a celebrant or a guest, something shifted further within me. My relationship to the institution of marriage and the spectacle of the wedding deepened. I found myself with strong opinions on subjects I had hardly considered before. I rated rituals and rites chosen by couples. I counselled against Rilke and soul music. I weighed up the political symbolism of processions and being given away. I spat smoked-salmon vol-au-vents into pink paper napkins. There will be no finger food or confetti at my wedding, I decided. There will be no acoustic balladeers or poems. These judgements were made silently, definitively. *Not at my wedding. At my wedding. My wedding.* They took concrete form: I would have a wedding. I would get married and be someone's wife.

I knew, of course, that there were plenty of reasons not to do this. Good reasons. Like the fact that in Australia you are not allowed to marry if you happen to love someone with similar reproductive organs to your own. Or that until the mid-1960s you were probably not going to be allowed to marry the person you loved if they happened to have darker skin and an older claim to the national land base than you. Or that marriage itself is an institution that operates in relation to power — that is, historically, dominant groups such as the church, the landed gentry, the colonial authorities, or the parliament allowed or disallowed marriage as a means to control the behaviour of the common folk. In Australia, marriage as a tool of social control goes back to the penal colonies, where well-behaved convicts were rewarded with the right to marry based on their willingness to kowtow to the imperatives of the authorities. When politicians argued that marriage was an institution that underpins nations, they were right, though this is not something of which to be proud.

And yet somehow none of this weakened my resolve. As my thirtieth year approached, I stopped dreaming and started planning. I learned the prices of chapels and Elvis celebrants. I hunted down the cheapest island escape packages and bulk deals on alcohol. I made a shoe wish list on Net-a-Porter, pale hoofs lined up like steps in a square dance. I loitered by jewellery-store windows, and answered all my sweetheart's questions about birthday gifts with an obvious stare.

I took it for granted that Serge would play along. He usually assented to my plans good-naturedly. I made a suggestion, and we'd flesh it out with the combined imaginative power of two only children.

I wondered, how would he propose? Would it be in public? That was embarrassing and earnest. There was something distasteful going on in the power dynamic of public proposal, but did I secretly want that? And if so, why? What do these spectacles say – what do they prove?

There is no real historical tradition behind the idea of the marriage proposal as we understand it today. Even literature can't account for the level of theatre we strive for in the twenty-first century, and that millennials in particular have popularised and made viral. Nineteenth-century literary proposals were often underwhelming, awkward, or comic: from Uriah Heep's cocky quip in *David Copperfield* – 'I've an ambition to make your Agnes my Agnes' – to Mr Collins' insulting litany of practicalities, ending with the bureaucratic declaration, 'And now nothing remains for me but to assure you in the most animated language of the violence of my affection,' in *Pride and Prejudice*.

Perhaps the first hint of the modern proposal came from the French, who were more prone to fancy – or perhaps just in thrall to the idea of the travails of love. Writer Marie-Catherine Le Jumel de Barneville, also known as Baroness d'Aulnoy (who coined the term 'fairytale' and inducted the genre), always made sure that Prince Charming had to jump through hoops to secure the hand of his beloved. Finding himself duped, over and over, across several tales, into promising to marry mean and ugly girls, Charming proved his love to the pretty and the pure by appearing as a jewellery-presenting bluebird, a shut-in meditating only on love, and an armed prince riding a winged dolphin.

Proposals from the Golden Age of Hollywood tended more towards the format of a stern yet loving word tacked on to the end of a fight, and followed by a forceful kiss. When Rhett proposes to Scarlett in *Gone with the Wind*, he first begs forgiveness for startling her with 'the impetuosity of my sentiments', and goes on to hazard that marriage might just be fun – a suggestion to which Scarlett replies, 'Marriage fun? Fiddledeedee. For men, maybe.'

But the notion of the marriage proposal as an over-the-top performance – an extravaganza of love complete with five-piece band — has reached its zenith in contemporary pop culture. Today's Hollywood films and reality-TV shows feature unsuspecting (or pseudo-unsuspecting) women being publicly serenaded, rings dropped in champagne flutes, acorns planted in the dirt where he knelt. Proposal speeches, overwhelmingly delivered by men, demonstrate exhaustive knowledge of the intended, along with a love of their petty flaws. Suitors profess the ways in which they are improved by the mere presence of the beloved. Most importantly, these speeches have an embarrassing hint of chivalry: a modern proposal does not skimp on the genuflecting. It is proof of a couple's suitability.

After my long shifts at work, Serge and I watched endless mindless rom-coms on the couch. More than once, I teared up as the proposal unfolded.

'Haha, you're moved,' he said, countless times, turning my chin around so he could look into my bleary eyes.

'Am not!' It was an embarrassing thing to be moved by.

I discovered the hashtag #proposalfail and wasted whole mornings in its company. I scrolled through proposal brag stories with terrible headings such as 'Epic Waterfall Adventure' and 'Prince Charming Goes to First Grade'. I watched Kanye West's 2014 proposal to Kim Kardashian on a loop: the couple at a sports arena, facing the fireworks and orchestra, simulcast to a nearby limousine where the Kardashian sisters look on, enthralled, Khloe repeating, *I did not know this was real life, I did not know this is real, this is a movie,* and then further out, into a wide world where the rest of us watch them watching, thinking, *no, this is not real life*. Was this the most telepresent proposal in history? Modern romance's moon landing?

'After Kanye proposed to Kim, all her friends ran into the arena and they drank champagne and danced to *Yeezus*,' I told Serge.

He laughed.

'At my wedding I will be a hologram,' he said.

We were playing a cute game, I was sure. It was all part of a shared narrative we were building. Advertising bars encroached my browser like strangler vines. My screen became busy with services that would design the perfect proposal, from romantic picnic to flash mob extravaganza. *Our twenty-per-cent-off sale*, claimed the banners, *means it's the perfect time to propose*.

Even on my thirtieth birthday, when Serge handed me an obviously book-shaped parcel, I managed to delude myself that it would be the kind of book that prison-breakers hide their picks in. A hollow with the promise of a new life buried inside. I swallowed and composed my face as I unwrapped a first edition of Kerouac's *Big Sur*. A good book. One of my favourites. A thoughtful present, on all accounts.

But I couldn't help thinking: really, though? Kerouac? The symbolism was glaring. I was thirty. The big three-oh. I saw myself in stark relief – an adult woman, no longer a youth, but not a bride. Not now, and if not now, perhaps not ever. I was hurt but also, and perhaps far worse, I was embarrassed. Why did I want this so much? What did I think it would do for me, for us? When did I become so crazy?

I decided that I was clearly brainwashed. I'd watched too many romantic comedies and read too many trashy tabloids.

I was far too concerned with what my friends were doing. Too scared of being left behind. It was time to de-program. No more rom-coms. No more #proposalfail. No more marriage celebrant. I reread *Big Sur* and loved it more than ever. This time, though, instead of noticing the ecstatic charge of the prose, I paid more attention to the protagonist, who goes mad on that coastline, drunk, high, thrashing between the desire for thought and solitude and a need to participate in his moment, in what is most intoxicating and dangerous about his own intellectual milieu, a group who were, above all, outsiders.

I smelled the pages. They smelled good.

My deprogramming worked. It worked so well that a month later, when on a road trip across the United States, Serge took a knee and offered me a ring and a profession of undying love, my first thought was, *Are you kidding?*

Of course I said yes.

I said yes and then got good and drunk. Rather, *we* got good and drunk, my fiancé and me. We got drunk and talked about our future. Because at its best that is what being a fiancé is — a shared conversation about the future, which glitters like diamonds. (Diamonds? Appalling!)

Actually, our immediate future looked colour-saturated and cliché. We would backtrack along the Sierra Nevada and then head to fabulous Las Vegas, we decided, for a quickie marriage. Elvis celebrant! Neon signs! Unfettered capitalist carnival plonked in one of the world's most pillaged deserts! But as the highway carried us closer, I began to feel less like I was living in a cool movie and more like a lame joke. Fabulous Las Vegas,

Nevada, bent across our windscreen: rows of rundown chapels, pink paint chipped and peeling. Plastic flowers yellowed and torn. Cupids aimed limp bows at our rental car. Foreclosure notices and overdue bills littered the frosted doorways of bankrupted tux-hire shops and florists. Mega casinos owned by Disney and Trump cast dark shadows on the lost end of the strip.

I had a panic attack in the lobby of Circus Circus.

I was surrounded by screaming kids and sunburnt octogenarians in fanny-packs. A bachelorette party all in pink tutus sipped insipid fluoro goo from penis-shaped yard glasses. I propped myself up against a pillar, breathing hard, the gaggle of women staring at me as if *I* was the freak. In front of us, an overweight, middle-aged couple in matching, ill-fitting cargo shorts redeemed their coupons for a 'Lucky in Love' weekend-escape package. When it was our turn, a booking agent presented us with eight package choices. There were clowns all over the booking sheet. Clowns on the bedspreads. The poker-machine ambience surrounded me like a blackout scored by Philip Glass. I couldn't breathe. I wanted to extricate myself, but I also couldn't handle the idea of walking back through the endless slot-machine disco, or the kids' playroom that now stands where the revolving bar from Hunter S. Thompson's *Fear and Loathing in Las Vegas* once stood.

'Do you wanna book one of the honeymoon suites?' Serge asked.

In the honeymoon suites there were clowns on the carpet and a slot machine in the toilet.

The booking agent watched me patiently over his faded purple boutonnière. Tiny clowns whirled in my vision like the aftermath from a crack on the skull with an Acme anvil. All my adult fantasies sunk low into the spongy carpet, bacterial and foul.

No, I thought, *I do not want to book the honeymoon suite.*

Serge, disappointed but eager to placate me, drove us to a run-down motel with an outdoor pool facing the dead end of the strip. I swam in the flickering neon, eating the reflected light and spitting it back out again. I realised that I still had no solid idea what a marriage was, beyond the ring and the paper. I didn't know what I wanted from my relationship, either. I had just wanted it sorted, recognised, notarised (though definitely not by clowns). I had wanted to lock it down, even though I knew there was no such thing. I floated in the cool blue screen. Tough young men swung their cars into the forecourt of the hotel, went in and out of rooms, taking care of business in a part of Vegas where no one was playing make-believe.

Marriage and adulthood have always been inextricable. A person is a child in the home of their parents. To marry is to become a householder, to actively form a new family unit, to be indisputably a grown woman or man.

Yet despite our legal definition of it, marriage is a historically and internationally varied practice. It's hard to pin down. The idea of love as the basis for marriage is only a few hundred years old, and the sexualisation of this love strictly a twentieth-century development. Greek and Roman philosophers concurred that too much ardour from husband to wife was obscene. For the early moderns in Europe, love was thought to be a likely result of marriage but not an occasion for it. Monogamy is also not a constant: China, Tibet, Sudan, India, and Nepal have all at some point in their histories officially eschewed two-person monogamous unions and considered the co-wife or co-husband an integral part of marriage. Anthropologists attempting to find a universal definition of marriage run into trouble as not all marriages are productive of children, or strictly heterosexual, or sexual at all, or even confined to the living. The Chinese practice of ghost marriage, for instance, saw young women seeking out the commitment of unmarried spirits to reap the benefits of familial lineage with none of the burdensome chore of marrying a live dude.

In 2011, when then prime minister Julia Gillard based her opposition to the legal recognition of gay marriage in Australia on her strident belief in the traditional definition of marriage, we could all be forgiven for not knowing exactly which tradition she meant. Was it the tradition of marriage as a contract made between parents to connect kinship groups and reinforce economic and political power? Was it the tradition of marriage as a means to extend family influence into different geographical territories? Was it marriage as a tool for class consolidation or mobility? Was it marriage as a vehicle for women to escape their status as the property of their fathers to become instead the property of their husbands? Or was she referring to the tradition of marriage as cemented relatively recently in Australian legalese, to define marriage by what it is not? That is, it is not something that happens between a brother and a sister (though it can happen between cousins, or uncle and niece), nor a decision arrived at by force (though what constitutes 'force' is not defined), and it is definitely not the result of a same-sex couple eloping to a more liberal state for a party and a bogus piece of paper. Nevertheless, we all know that every marriage is different, and none can wholly be summed up by a sentence-long definition.

So what kind of marriage was I looking for? When I closed my eyes and imagined myself married, I couldn't see anything different. It was the wedding I had been envisioning, I realised, not the marriage. In fact, when I thought of an ideal relationship, I imagined something flexible, forever changing, yet also continually inspiring and supportive. Married or not-married had little to do with it.

'What you want is the relationship from that vampire movie *Only Lovers Left Alive*,' a girlfriend said over a cup of tea.

Perhaps she was right. But what was the bigger obstacle to this goal: the fact that life is not a movie, or that Serge and I are not immortal? I'd been seduced by a vision of the future as impractical as it was irresistible.

It's a common claim of popular psychology that we get our relationship blueprints from our parents, that the first relationship we know forms the basis for all others. When we returned from our holiday unmarried, I began to look at the relationships around me and interrogate my understanding of marriage, starting with the one that produced me: the marriage I knew first and probably also the least about.

Here's what I knew already: in the 1970s my parents were hippies, sort of. Really, they were the kind of middle-class professional hippies whose utopian dream was to balance their careers and social lives with running a permaculture-aligned pick-your-own-raspberries farm. Towards this end, they bought a small, windy hill in rural Victoria. They populated it with seedlings and black-faced lambs. They bought a generator and a truck and led their two large dogs onto the land. Then they set up some marquees and got hitched. Mum got new blue jeans. Dad got inappropriately drunk. Gnarled dogs lurk at the edges of all my parents' wedding photos like the guardians of some foreign territory. It is a beautiful, Polaroid-coloured day. Or perhaps that's just the colour of the times.

After the wedding, the guests hung around for what seemed like a decade. The photo albums were littered with tall, beautiful women taking outdoor showers in mottled, scrubby light. Gradually, a pretty wooden house grew up on the spot where the marquee had been. In a few shots my mother's jeans look tight, and then she's obviously pregnant. There is an incredible image of my parents facing each other, standing on a morning street that can only be described as misty *and* golden. The infant me is strapped to my father's chest. My mother looks on with the kind of proud, maternal glow that could sell a million boxes of washing powder.

Then you turn the page and it's as if everyone simultaneously traded in their braids and blouses for high-waisted pastel pants, jumpsuits, and tortured hair. I have noticed this in many family albums of people my parents' age. Somewhere just after the birth of their millennial children, a transition occurs that reminds me of *Scarface* and *Casino*. A caption says 1986, and the mise en scène deteriorates accordingly. The leading man has a moustache now. Too much of the furniture is made from mirrors and microsuede; too much of the ardour and optimism of the previous years has sunk into the plush pile. You can just tell that someone has developed a coke habit, or at least a nasty shopping addiction.

By 1990, it's all over. My parents hung up their hoes next to their idealism and went their separate ways, my mother and I to a regional centre, my father to the city.

When pressed, my mother's most passionate complaint about marriage is people's insistence on referring to her as Mrs Doyle no matter how often she corrected them. Her second is that a wife is equally responsible for the debts of her husband. This is because my father was a poor punter, and consequently Mrs Doyle spent the best part of her own fin de siècle paying off his debts. It's easy to imagine a polyester-suited goon breathing down an old-fashioned telephone: 'Are you Mrs Doyle?'

'It's Ms Harris.'

'Same thing, lady. Cash or credit?'

When I shared my own conflict about marriage, my mother warned me to be careful to make a sound choice, as divorce was a bitch. This was a strange thing for her to say because, despite their separation of more than twenty years, my parents never got around to getting divorced.

'How would you know?' I asked her.

'Exactly,' she said.

I speculated on reasons why the divorce never eventuated, but my mother didn't care for this line of questioning. It's fair enough, I suppose, not to want to lend significance to some paperwork oversights from long ago. But to me, the irresolution seemed a sad thing, as though an official end was not needed because the marriage itself lacked potency. My parents' marriage wasn't a prison requiring a great escape, but a room one simply exited, feeling no need to return with the wrecking ball.

When you get married, you are supposed to say 'forever' and believe it. This despite statistics predicting that 33 per cent of marriages begun in the first few years of this century will end in divorce. By the time I relinquished my tiny superpower of marriage-officiating, more than half the handful of couples I married had filed for divorce. I have no real emotional reaction to this. I'm glad divorce exists, and hate the idea of bitter, loveless marriages (unless you are simultaneously allowed to move to the country house with your besties). When I spoke at weddings as a celebrant, I always stated that a wedding was a gesture of supreme optimism. It was my nod to the elephant in the pews. And optimism, I still think, is a lovely thing to celebrate. But perhaps it's not enough. Could I say forever and mean it? Did anyone really mean it, or was forever always forever-for-now?

I asked Mum if she liked being married.

'Oh, yes, I suppose,' she said, adding as an afterthought, 'We were very in love at one point.'

A question about why they married led without excuse or explanation to that old chestnut: that getting married was something hetero couples simply did.

Perhaps it was embarrassing to her to reflect back on a time when she was so idealistic, but when I looked through those old photo albums, it was all right there, open to scrutiny. Dad's only album slays me the most. He must have been thirty when he carefully curated the pictures, glued them into an old spiral notebook, and captioned them by hand: *Various views of the farm – and views from it. We don't own that much. Shack Settlement – home for last 18 months. Travelling – a place to ourselves on the Murray River.* And finally: *Kangaroo Valley – where we'd like to buy a farm if all our plans pan out.* It is hard for me to imagine my parents so easy and sanguine. What happened, I wonder whenever I reach the end of the album.

Was this part of my conflicted feelings about marriage? I was raised on romance and the utopian spirit represented in these photo albums, with fat lashings of cynicism on the side. I was raised to cut my losses.

When I emailed Dad to get another perspective on my parents' marriage, I assumed he'd share something funny and probably quite offensive. I also assumed it would be about my mother. Instead, I received a long prose poem starting with his first kiss ('like being attacked by a vacuum cleaner on heat'), leading through descriptions of his juvenile pick-up routine (which apparently always involved teaching girls to play tennis), and ending with his marriage, at nineteen, to a woman who was not my mother.

I knew some of the story of this marriage. I learned it when I was eleven and inadvertently found an unfamiliar wedding photograph. In it, my teenage father is wearing a baby-blue suit over a ruffled shirt. He stands with his new wife in front of a Sydney cathedral – it may even be the one where, just a few years earlier, he had been a choirboy. Soon, this wife would leave Dad on their European holiday to head home and explore the meaning of her crush on a female friend. Shattered, Dad walked from Paris to Gibraltar. Some time later, he returned to Australia and met my mother. Some time after that, he decided to give marriage another go, though this time with no suit, no parents, and no God in attendance. Yet the details of this later, longer, and more reproductively fruitful marriage did not make the poem.

I rang him and we talked about his eagerness to marry at nineteen, and Dad expressed a little light regret. 'If our parents had suggested that we just move in together first, it probably would have been a better idea,' he said.

Dad's first marriage was fuelled by love, he told me, but also the need to have everything of adult life, all of it, all at once, and when he was still really a kid. That's what I had wanted too, of course, though I was more than a decade older than he was when he donned his baby blue. And perhaps that was the problem: by the time Serge and I got engaged, we'd been together for six years. We had already broken each other's hearts a few times. We had already shed some ideals, and some dreams. We loved each other deeply, and we were romantic about that love, but we were not abandoned to it. We might not have been real adults, but we were thirty, after all.

The sustained perception of marriage as a transition from the juvenile to the adult was brought home in a gross and practical way for me after I got my sparkler. When wedding plans faded away, the ring became a prop. I wore it to job interviews, other people's weddings, when speaking to the neighbours about our barking dog or loud music. It was a little bit of shiny proof that I was a legit adult, a person of serious intent.

'Are you engaged?' one of my young students asked when I wore it to class. 'Lucky duck.'

Her envious smile made me nervous.

I put my ring back in the box to check the oil in the car, to do the dishes, or to have a big night out. Soon it was in the box more often than not, and eventually, I stopped taking it out entirely.

When our elopement failed to eventuate, we talked about having a big to-do, but the conversation became a stressor. Serge's mound of debt kept him up at night and off to work every morning to a job he hated. How could he save money for a wedding? There were other difficulties, too. Our families were a bunch of weirdos. Serge's relationship with his father was a string of long silences punctuated by guilt and disappointment. When he broke the news to his dad, there were no hearty congratulations or offers to help throw a party. What further disappointments would a wedding expose him to? His worry was catching — I thought about my own parents. My mum's persecution party-dress, my Dad's likely drunken speech-making or sudden disappearance. It would be like Lars von Trier's *Melancholia* on a shoestring budget, with no apocalypse to save us from our folly. As all the possibilities got fleshed out afresh, the dream wedding began to seem like a nightmare.

But really, our lack of resolve was more to do with our uncertainty. Did we actually want to get married and, if so, why? What difference would a wedding make? We loved each other – wasn't that enough?

My confusion about the significance of marriage corresponds with my times. It's trending. In Australia, while the number of weddings has increased along with the population, the Bureau of Statistics reports that the marriage rate has decreased. In the United States, the marriage rate dropped to an all-time low in 2015 – despite many states changing their legislation on same-sex marriage – and the reticence of millennial couples to marry was cited as a major part of the reason. In the United Kingdom, the ever inflammatory *Daily Mail* ran with the headline 'Marriage Will Be Extinct in 30 Years', citing statistics and expert opinions insisting that marriage is 'doomed', and in the future it will be an 'esoteric' choice, not a normative standard. In 2014, the slightly more reputable *Guardian* ran a feature on the diminishing marriage rates across Europe, interviewing couples aged between twenty-five and forty, who gave a mix of economic and political reasons for their decision to leave the knot untied. Once again, decreasing employment opportunities for college graduates, as well as the increasing age of adult children living at home, were cited.

An afternoon chat with my friend Priya reminded me that these are largely secular trends. The meaning of marriage in secular culture is diffuse, but this is not so within many religious traditions.

'I felt like being in a long-term relationship and not getting married was too much like sticking my finger up to my parents,' said Priya. 'I thought, I'll either be single forever, because that is a life choice, or I will get married.'

When Priya's Tamil parents found out she was dating a white guy, they were worried. Could this kind of man understand the importance of marriage and family? At twenty-three, it was sometimes hard to negotiate the cultural chasm, Priya admitted. Her partner had never pictured getting married – he was scarred from his parents' divorce. He wasn't even sure he was husband material.

'What's husband material?' I asked.

'Oh, you know, being together, having direction, being tied down,' Priya said with a laugh. 'It actually turned out he is much better at those things than I am.'

Before they discovered this, though, Priya wondered if she was wasting her time. 'I was happy to have met him, but then sometimes I just felt like, well, maybe I should break up with this guy and let my parents set me up. I know people who have done this. It seems like a pretty efficient way to go.'

Eventually Priya's partner came around to the idea of marriage. But given their different backgrounds, they then had a long period of negotiating what that would mean. They questioned everything: traditions old and new, secular and Hindu. 'We had questions about monogamy – do we believe in that? I had ethical issues with marriage, with how in our country it's a way to separate groups of people. Also, there was financial stuff. Our pay now goes into a shared bank account.'

I gasped. To me, a combined bank account is more of a commitment than marriage. Having your own money means independence, freedom. I had feminist arguments up the wazoo to back my position, but sitting at Priya's dining table, my first thought was, if you don't have your own money, how can you leave?

'I know, right? I've lost my independence. Feminism says this is what marriage is, and guess what, this is what marriage is!'

From the get-go, Priya's wedding planning was more community-minded than those I'd witnessed in my time as a civil celebrant. She and Jack solicited advice from older couples they admired on how to be married. And for the celebration, they decided to have two weddings: a Tamil Hindu ceremony and a secular booze-and-speeches affair, both on one weekend.

'I bawled my eyes out at my wedding,' Priya admitted. 'Twice, actually. The first time was seeing this tall white guy in Indian clothes, in his turban. As a child, I had never imagined my wedding. I'd never been there before mentally, and then I was just hit with the image. He and his family threw everything aside to be part of this.

'The other time I bawled was after the Hindu ceremony. The tradition is that you go to your parents' place and have tea and eat a sweet. When I left, I felt this great pain. I was leaving their home for my own family home. Cutting ties with my family is so immense.'

Priya experienced a threshold moment of the kind that I have no memory of. Her wedding was a decisive, culturally respected movement into adulthood.

'My parents hardly come over to our house,' she explained. 'They want to give us space. This is a family home now, and they respect that.'

I asked her if her parents would have had trouble accepting her as an adult if she had she decided to stay single forever. 'Yes! One hundred per cent. I would have had lots of responsibilities caring for them. And not have time of my own because I would still be seen as not fully developed,' she said, without hesitation. 'But I was okay with that in my thinking.'

The view that a single person is not fully developed would be deeply unfashionable to speak out loud in a secular milieu, and yet isn't this what the editorials that characterise declining marriage rates as evidence of a selfish, immature generation are suggesting? Moreover, I wondered, was there still a trace of this in my parents' perception of me? I had not moved from my family of origin to my family of (potential) procreation, and so I was lingering somehow in their list of responsibilities.

Priya insisted that getting married changed things emotionally, too. She has felt tangibly different since her weddings. 'There's nothing novel about getting married, though. You aren't special. It's so funny because the wedding industrial complex is all about being special, but actually you are doing the most ordinary thing. There is nothing special about you. It's humbling,' she added. 'It's nice.'

While there might be nothing special about marriage, there are always unique reasons for marrying, regardless of whether we acknowledge them. I presided over Poppy and Gustav's cute, brightly coloured wedding, catered by friends and hosted for free in a small local art gallery. They did not invite extended family, or blow the equivalent of a small house deposit on the party, but nonetheless I was in tears by the time their friends were throwing the confetti. The couple met in Sydney, but while Poppy was Australian, Gustav was German. They were together for three years, splitting their time between the two countries before they decided to get married and settle in Australia. This was not a so-called 'visa marriage'; however, it was a marriage in which attaining visas was one of the motivations. Without said visa, the couple couldn't remain together. When I asked Poppy, about a year after their wedding, if she would have married Gustav if there were no visa to consider, she shrugged, averted her eyes, and looked over her shoulder as if to check for immigration stooges. 'We might have waited longer,' she said.

The visa application process had a serious effect on the couple's relationship. Immigration qualification is prescriptive. In fact, nothing exemplifies the way that normative conceptions of adulthood structure our social world like opening your life to the scrutiny of government gatekeepers. Poppy decided to have a proper wedding because she knew it would be read as evidence of her relationship's legitimacy. Otherwise, she told me, she'd probably have been satisfied with one or two friends and a glass of champagne. She might have eloped. Nevertheless, she was happy with her wedding, and — perhaps equally importantly — so was the government.

The immigration department's list of other kinds of material proof of the validity of a couple's marriage includes shared assets such as houses, vehicles, boats, whitegoods, and, of course, children. Poppy and Gustav didn't own a house or a boat or a washing machine. They didn't have children. They were committed renters, and artists to boot. They had to be extra careful. Marriage, according to the standards of the immigration department, was a legal commitment made in a specific way and favouring a specific lifestyle – coincidentally, one that favoured couples with money.

I was glad, after speaking to Poppy, that I didn't have to prove my relationship's authenticity by these standards. At the time of our engagement, Serge and I lived in rental accommodation with another friend. We did not share a lease, insurance, furniture, or a car. These did not, and do not, seem like things you need in order to share a future.

In 2017, marital law in Australia and many other places means that some relationships aren't legally recognised regardless of how many possessions you co-own, or children you co-parent. Gay and lesbian marriage is simultaneously the biggest challenge to, and reaffirmation of, the institution of marriage in the twenty-first century. In the United States, the right of same-sex couples to marry was hard-won. California was the first state to issue same-sex marriage licenses in 2008, but these marriages did not turn out to be happily ever after. Proposition 8, an amendment created by opponents of same-sex marriage, was passed later that year. It found that same-sex marriage was unconstitutional. This unconstitutionality was later found to be unconstitutional in and of itself, and same-sex marriage became legal once more. It's a dance that has been repeated elsewhere. It describes the way the law can be exploited to justify and naturalise inequality.

In 2013, the ACT Marriage Act was passed in Australia, allowing same-sex couples to marry in the Australian Capital Territory. In June, the papers ran with pictures of queer couples kissing in a sea of rainbow balloons. Men stepping from limos, fingers entwined. Kids with rainbow flags painted on their cheeks. In the capital, couples lined up to marry, and then, like the Californians before them, found their marriages annulled.

We are not homophobes, insisted opponents; this is not an emotional issue, it's legal.

'It is not a question of being for or against gay marriage — it's a question of adhering to the constitution,' said then prime minister Tony Abbott, waving that same legal document that it was commonly believed classified Indigenous Australians as flora and fauna until a 1967 referendum allowed the nation to vote on it.

The next big plan for updating our legal definition of marriage in Australia was a plebiscite (we don't need a referendum because gay marriage is not actually a constitutional issue). It was a move resisted by many LGBTI groups and individuals because of its potential to stir up hate and homophobia. But the very idea of a plebiscite on same-sex marriage highlights the normative mechanisms that work to define adulthood against the status quo. What does it mean to say that the majority has a right to vote on how the minority live their personal lives, and what civil rights they should be granted or denied? Do we still think that it's important to collectively decide who is human?

In Ireland, 412 same-sex couples married the year after the country became the first to change its marriage laws via plebiscite. The vote was no small accomplishment in a place where the influence of the Catholic Church is strong, homosexuality was illegal until 1996, and abortion only permissible if the pregnancy threatens the woman's life.

'Now we can relax and get old together,' the first couple to marry told *Buzzfeed*.

It's telling that this comment conflates marriage and the ability to 'grow old'. If marriage is a milestone, the refusal to recognise same-sex marriage can also be read as the patent exclusion of LGBTI communities from mainstream adult society. Unsurprisingly, then, in the fight for marriage equality, same-sex couples are consistently represented as conservative, family-minded, nine-to-five workers, and homeowners. See? These are real, hardworking adults, just like you, insist the campaigns. The fight to be recognised has to work with, and against, recognisable models.

'Marriage is a conservative value,' Ted Olson, former lead Republican counsel and solicitor general under George W. Bush, insisted. 'It's two people who love one another and want to live together in a stable relationship, to become part of a family and part of a neighbourhood and part of our economy.'

Marriage, in other words, is about belonging. But there is something more insidious in this. What Olson was saying, as he jumped the fence to campaign for marginalised people, was that conservative groups should want gay marriage, because the alternative could only be new ways of living. This argument, I think, will be the one that wins, because economic forces engender prejudice. It is rarely the other way around.

Tahnya wants to marry her girlfriend, who is also the mother of her kids. When we spoke, she thought it was misguided to compare queer marriage to that thing that hetero couples do. She stressed that for many in the LGBTI community, marriage means something more than it means for most heterosexual couples. 'For gay couples, and particularly for trans gay couples,' she told me, 'it's not like "Janey McStraightnuts is getting married, so I better too." You appreciate it. You are committed. You are just so glad to find someone who accepts you for who you are.'

Acceptance, in her description, is defined in relation to the total rejection of non-normative identities by legal and social institutions. For Tahnya, marriage is a place of shelter from the world, not a definite role to play within it.

I realised, as I spoke to her, that this was what I wanted from a relationship, too. This was what drew me to marriage, and this is what is now pulling me away from it. Even now, sometimes I suddenly feel the need to get up and rush over to my dresser, to check that my ring is still there, dim and neglected in the gold polyester padding. I would hate if it were to get lost in a move, or swept up in the paperclips and pens that litter my desk — absent-mindedly cleared away, as though that promise were never made, whatever it meant or means. But what does it all actually signify, once you stop performing, put the ring back in the box, and get on with this business of adult life? I wondered about this as I stood in the audience last year at the wedding of an acquaintance, watching the couple exchange vows that seemed little more than emotional platitudes. Tear-jerking? Yes. Original? Hardly. Consequential? Revealing? No, not really.

Perhaps, in fact, I don't want my relationship to be recognised. Perhaps the right position politically for a heterosexual couple in 2017 is to fight to have your relationship go unrecognised; to insist it is unrepresentable, private and perverse. While I'm at it, I could try to unrecognise everything I ever heard about romance, family, emotional fulfilment, and the rest of it. Fuck the dishes. Fuck who plans your dates or holidays. Fuck pants and who wears them. Fuck your rom-com proposal. Imagine the longest lens ever made, god's macro, widening and widening, two people on a raft in a sea of other people and animals and plants and trash, until there really aren't any people at all, just shapes, bacterial and shimmering. My true wedding photograph. A glorious, incomprehensible mess, and everyone is invited.

6
APOCALYPSE, BABY

Along with a compulsion for #proposalfail, listicles, and the dubious online articles of *Psychology Today*, in my thirtieth year I became obsessed with working out the ages of characters on television.

Previously, programs for me had been divided into shows about kids (right up to the college years, and maybe a little slippage on the side), shows about adults, and shows about families. But now I found myself wondering continually, how old were the various spreads of adults? How old was Elaine on *Seinfeld*? How old were the titular Friends? How old was that New Girl? When I first watched those shows, the answer seemed 'older than me'. But was I now older than them?

Specific ages were only emphasised if they were unusual. I knew Lorelai Gilmore senior was thirty-two and junior, sixteen, at the beginning of the first season. Tony Stark graduated from MIT at age eight. Everyone else was a smeary, socially appropriate 'ish'. This on-screen obsession might have been a continuity of the habit I had as a child, of staring out the window of the school bus at the teenagers and trying to see the future. On the bus I wondered, would that be me in a few years' time? In front of the television I worried, was that supposed to be me, now?

'How old do you think they are supposed to be?' I asked my friend, as casually as possible, while we sat on the couch eating spaghetti and watching a television drama.

'Thirties?'

'Like, late thirties, right?'

'Hmm, I'd say mid-thirties.'

The distinction seemed both important and flimsy. They were whatever age you were supposed to be when you worried about children and your mortgage, or being single forever. They were everypeople, snap-frozen, with no future or past, their problems derived from an outline of our own. They lived in colour-by-numbers worlds.

We ate our spaghetti, occasionally heckling the screen. And then a scene came on that stopped us both. It was a nothing scene, graded night-time green, as though the curtains couldn't quite cover the harsh fluorescent streetlights beyond. A rich white woman (they are often rich white women on television) is sleeping. We hear the child crying before she does. She stirs, reluctance in every limb. The crying is loud and desperate. We know that she needs sleep. We know that her marriage has broken down and that she is in a toxic relationship with her boss and that she is cracking up under work pressure. But that is not important now. The child cries out again: 'Mumma!'

She opens her eyes. She pulls herself from expensive sheets as if wrenching her body up out of a swimming pool and onto wet concrete. She's dragged through the room by those tears. The camera lingers in the bedroom, shoots her heavy footsteps from behind, her agonisingly slow walk down the hall towards her crying child. There is a tiny pause in his tears, and she stops mid-step. Maybe it's over. 'Mumma!' he cries anew. Her hands cover her face in a gesture of true despair. She starts walking, slow footfalls, down the hallway again.

'Fuck,' I said to my friend, moved by the everyday brutality of the scene — a rarity in TV land.

'Fuck,' she replied.

And then I was momentarily filled with a sense of deep relief. 'I never have to do that,' I said.

My friend laughed. It was a flippant thing to say. But to say it out loud produced a feeling of certainty that I seldom have. *I never have to do that.* An incantation. An affirmation. It's a sensation I have felt at other times around children, too. *I never have to do that*, I've thought, watching parents teach their kids to share or say thank-you. *I never have to do that*, I've thought, even when watching my friends' kids play with them adoringly or listening to smart, lively children tell their parents about their day at school.

This is the one aspect of adult life that I have resolved. I know for sure that I don't want a baby. Not now. Not ever. I am one in a fluctuating number of women who are childless. Our existence is charted alarmingly in statistics. We are labelled as selfish, blamed for greying populations in covert and overt ways. We are subjected to endless questioning by friends and strangers. These questions range from the snobby ('Don't you think educated people have a responsibility to breed?') to the dynastic ('Aren't you concerned about your legacy?') to the quasi-religious ('Don't you want to pass on your beliefs?') to the batty ('But don't you just want to kiss their little baby faces — aren't babies just sooooii cuttteeee?!')

My answer, a resounding no, provokes raised eyebrows, concerned monologues, or a war call indicating the discovery of a heartless woman, a cold fish-bride/witch to be ejected from the hearth of all that is LOVELY AND WORTHWHILE.

One benefit of passing thirty is that while the questions still get asked, people accept my answers. They no longer smile knowingly and refer to my biological clock, a pea-sized time bomb set to explode somewhere in the space between gut and vagina at a preordained age (thirty, it's always thirty). It used to be inevitable that I would turn into a genetically programed baby machine, unable to shirk the imperative to replicate. Now I'm just a weirdo. A strange genetic abnormality. Or a ruined, over-educated woman who doesn't understand what it is to be human.

The biological clock is just another misogynist metaphor, but there is a cultural clock, and it is ticking loudly enough to keep me up at night. What becomes of the childless woman? Our culture insists that she is a lonely individual who will rue her choices and die unloved and unsatisfied. She is anathema to the future. Fine. I go to sleep each night ready to awake as a comic-book villainess.

News about diminishing birth rates around the developed world has flared up from time to time over the past few years. Young people aren't breeding in Italy; they aren't breeding in Japan and Greece and the well-to-do parts of North America. Or, if they are breeding, they are waiting too long to breed enough. In 2016, former Chief Rabbi of the United Kingdom and Commonwealth Lord Sacks declared that European society would 'die' because young people 'did not want the responsibilities of bringing up children'. Pope Francis delivered his edict against childless millennials in 2015: 'A society with a greedy generation,' he said, 'that doesn't want to surround itself with children, that considers them above all worrisome, a weight, a risk, is a depressed society … The choice to not have children is selfish. Life rejuvenates and acquires energy when it multiplies: it is enriched, not impoverished.'

He was right, of course. Denuding yourself of the belief that the future redeems the present and past had its existential downsides. And the Pope is old; it made sense he'd fall back on intergenerational sledging rather than consider the reasons why children have become such hefty burdens.

But when he had a go at dogs, things got personal.

'It might be better,' spake the Pope, 'more comfortable, to have a dog, two cats, and the love goes to the two cats and the dog. Then, in the end, this marriage comes to old age in solitude, with the bitterness of loneliness.'

This was too much. There was no reason to bring companion species into this kind of demagoguery. Dogs aren't to blame for women choosing not to have babies, capitalist patriarchy is.

Slowly the statistics, if not the opinions, are starting to support this. In 2014, a report on fertility by the Pew Research Center showed that older women with advanced degrees were suddenly having more children, despite the generally declining US fertility rate. Why were these women breeding when the conventional wisdom said they would not? Fertility treatments were partly responsible, but so was an increasingly equitable distribution of labour in highly educated households. Men with masters degrees (that is, greater incomes and more-flexible working hours) did more chores. Historian Stephanie Coontz argues that how much work men do around the house after the birth of their first child is the single biggest factor in determining whether a woman will want to have a second.

Generally, the mainstream media skirts around these kinds of findings. More-liberal sources emphasise cultural change as the determinant for procreation, and preserve a degree of sympathy for a generation who can't afford to own homes, couples for whom a dual income is a necessity but childcare is still too expensive, a GFC–shocked cohort who are understandably cautious about economic risks. Conservative sources are less understanding: selfish, educated women the world over are to blame for ageing populations and future economic disaster, and we know this because globally, where education levels for women go up, fertility rates go down. But as we can see from Coontz's analysis, statistics on their own can be misleading, and they can also be weaponised to bolster opinions.

In order to better understand statistics about women and babies, you need to know your terms. The commonly cited total fertility rate (TFR) is a speculative calculation. It refers to the number of children a woman will have if we sudden-age-forward through her whole life. It can be adjusted continually. If we are down by .08 this year, there is always a chance we will be up by .1 the next. The TFR cannot take into account new fertility technologies. In opinion pieces and editorials that decry the ageing population, the TFR is often linked to the replacement rate, that is, the number of babies that need to be born to make up for population loss *due to death*. Immigration is not taken into account when calculating replacement rates. In Australia, the replacement rate is approximately 2.1, according to the Australian Bureau of Statistics.

These numbers, in concert with negative attitudes towards single mothers on welfare, insist on the importance of replacing our dead with middle-class babies. But given that we currently need more than 1.2 Earths to survive at the rate we are consuming, and that middle-class kids use way more resources than kids from lower socio-economic households, it'd probably be better not to.

What we are talking about, then, when we talk about fertility, is not only babies and their bright or not-so-bright futures. We are talking about class and class consolidation. We are talking about national borders and immigration. We are talking about culture, its so-called 'character', in the way a person (let's call them a racist, for clarity) might say a new immigrant cannot replace a dead settler/coloniser. We are also talking about our fear of ageing and death and our knowledge that the way things are going, there will be no support for either in a decade or two. And finally, we are insisting women's bodies be tasked with nurturing all these things.

Recently, my doctor asked me if, given my advancing age, I was interested in freezing my eggs. 'You know, just as an insurance policy.'

She handed me a brochure for an egg bank. 'You can store them for later!'

Insurance against what? I wondered. This was, I suppose, a threshold moment. I had been identified as a person who might later have the means to avail myself of reproductive medicine and claim my inalienable right to a baby of my own. If I froze my eggs, I might be able to have my baby at fifty with a very tidy husband, or eight babies and a little light celebrity, like Octomom, putting the TFR in a spin and causing an echo of opinions across the media of the future.

But I don't want a baby. I don't want to be a mother to any of this.

It probably doesn't help my wasted fertility that I am compulsively drawn to catastrophism, disaster, and the end of things. I'm one of those people who wakes up on a forty-degree day in April and says, 'Any minute now, this whole suburb is gonna be underwater.' This is healthy or unhealthy, depending on your perspective, but my unshakable feeling that things cannot continue as they are may have impacted on my inability to make decisions about the future. I'm not building bunkers and stockpiling canned goods, but I'm not investing in oil companies and taking out massive loans, either. And so, it shocks me how little we talk about what it means to have a child in the second decade of the twenty-first century. Whenever someone proclaims that we need to think about the future of our children, I'm a little taken aback. No spoilers, but it's not looking great. Of course, no one wants to hear this kind of thing. No one gives the time of day to the dude on the freeway with the 'End Is Nigh' sign. Nor should they. But if you are that dude, even part-time, the traffic on the freeway, all those cars carrying all those people to school, to work, seems like a big fat joke.

While I think the human race will meet heat death or inertia before we stop breeding, if governments are concerned that there will not be enough young bodies to prop up economies, it might be a good idea to schedule an economic policy overhaul for some time in the next fifty years. Here's a hint: the harder it is for women in these countries to have a reasonable quality of life in addition to babies, the less likely they are to have them. Women are shrewd like that.

This shrewdness is not the same as selfishness. Neither are selfishness and childlessness mutually exclusive. I know parents whose sense of self simply incorporates their offspring at the expense of everyone else, and childless people who work tirelessly for others. The conception of childless freedom as synonymous with hard clubbing and flash holidays on islands with unadvertised colonial histories — a perception that is particularly prevalent among op-eds on the declining numbers of millennial mothers — is even more problematic. I might be an educated, childless woman, but I find the trope of the wild, unencumbered chick with money to burn on shots and shoes irksome. This isn't the life I have or want. In fact, I think the predominance of this representation is part of what is freaking me out about adulthood. The fact that childless women like me are consistently portrayed as overgrown, overfunded teenagers suggests that the only real way to be an acceptable part of adult society is to have a baby.

There are statistics that show the association between adulthood and parenthood leads some of the poorest Americans to have children young, outside of a stable relationship and therefore in a more vulnerable economic position. 'Having a baby can be a marker of adulthood,' Olga Khazan wrote in *The Atlantic* in 2014. She described an American economy where unskilled jobs are outsourced and computerised, and young adults without sufficient education are unable to secure anything beyond the 'low paying and dull'. 'Meanwhile, babies are great,' she added. 'They're like a little mini-job that you get to love. Plus, being a mother is being *someone*.'

Parenthood is a way to 'become a successful adult when all other paths are blocked', Johns Hopkins sociologist Andrew J. Cherlin confirmed.

Meanwhile, the representation of childless adults primarily as consumers masks all the ways that having children is an economic, not just a social, imperative. Australians spent $3.9 billion on baby merchandise in the 2008–09 financial year, with disposable nappies accounting for almost a quarter of this. In the United States, parents spend one trillion dollars a year on their children. As Goldman Sachs put it, enthusiastically, in their report on marketing to Millennial Mom, 'Parenthood is a catalyst for new ways of spending.'

The narratives we have about babies and what they do for the life of the parent change according to the cultural and historical moment. As critic Laura Kipnis has pointed out, the stories about 'maternal bonding', which figure the love between mother and child as borderline divine, emerged around the time of the Industrial Revolution (when women could finally leave the house for work), and strengthened again with the introduction of child-labour laws. You can't leave them at home, you can't put them to work. Someone has to look after them, and mothers need some sort of reward for their time if there's no actual pay attached.

It seems similarly conspicuous to me that the dyad of the selfish and selfless has emerged in this moment of peak capitalism, in which fast fashion, entertainment, international travel, resort holidays, and designer drugs are more readily available to the middle classes than at any point in history. It's crucial, in late capitalism, that everyone envies everyone else, and spends money accordingly. Being unfulfilled is the foundation for aspiration. It is our economic responsibility.

My own decision to remain childless has nothing to do with parties or shoes (you don't need to have a child to stop drinking in the shower). I made the decision, I think, before I even knew there was a decision to make. As a kid, when my dolls were not in space, they were less likely to be my babies than my peers. We sat together in a completely genderless, interspecies classroom where bunny, baby, transformer, and wombat puppet all spoke with one voice (it was my voice, obviously; there was no one else around to speak). Occasionally, when another little kid came over for a play date, the classroom broke up and the attendants were positioned atop one another for some interspecies fun times — smooshed together violently, as we understood the practice of copulation. When other girls wanted to take the next step and give birth to these dolls, I was totally sicked out. It was not a fun game. You just knelt there, fussing over the friend while she wailed and moaned, slowly pulling the fully clothed Cabbage Patch Kid from under her butt.

As a teenager, I liked to talk about child-rearing as an ethical project. Would you live in the city or the bush? Would you send a daughter to school or teach her at home, Rousseau-style? What was your position on amniocentesis and aborting so-called chromosomal abnormalities? At sixteen, I was fascinated by these questions. I liked my imagined family with Annie, where everything was accounted for and agreed upon in advance. When that fantasy dissolved, I tried to transfer it onto my first boyfriend.

He was five years older than my naïve seventeen. We had our own rented apartment above a Portuguese restaurant, and it seemed to me that we had it all. Then why was I spending so much time in bed eating home-brand corn chips and watching the first season of *Big Brother*? Was something missing from my life? Did I need a baby to really get into this grown-up life? We talked about babies a little less abstractly, though of course we could both see that we were probably too young, too broke, too in love. We talked alternatives — travelling or getting a dog. We even got as far as the pet store, where I cooed over a shivering miniature pincer in a baby pen. But even that was too much too soon. We compromised again, chose two fat young rats and dubbed them Joey Methyltryptamine and Afghan Kush. (He was well into weed and Aleister Crowley. I was well into The Ramones.) It didn't take long for the rats to go feral and take up residence beneath the stove. They emerged occasionally, grease-smeared and wild, to scavenge instant-noodle scraps off the peeling kitchen counter. When we broke up eighteen months later, my boyfriend set them free in a local park. A year later, I pulled Cassady from under that caravan in Humpty Doo. Just as the Pope feared, I have not felt the baby urge since.

As I progressed through my twenties, I began to really notice how hard mothers work. Again, let's not pretend that mothers work harder because they are naturally suited to childcare, and stubbornly insistent on working outside the home as well. They work harder because there is not enough infrastructure to support them. They work harder because they have been taught to. Noticing this helped me to remember, or perhaps realise for the first time, how hard my own mother worked, both domestically and in her profession. In having me, she undertook her own project of ethical parenting. She didn't home-school, but neither did she allow television, American novels, pop music, fashionable clothes or magazines, plastic toys, or snacks containing refined sugar. When I was a toddler and my parents were still together, my mother made her own fruit leathers and pasta. She took me to macrobiotic playgroup. Later, she read me ambitious old books such as *The Lion, the Witch, and the Wardrobe* and *The Waterbabies*. When I was in primary and early high school, after my parents had separated, my mother worked long hours and came home at seven each night to find her tween daughter sprawled on the floor in front of a television blaring with American accents and jingles, a trash angel amid the empty cracker packets, organic peach pits, and apple cores.

'I'll pick them all up at once!' I remember yelling at her one time, as she stood over me expectantly.

She had placed her bag on the dining-room table. Gone to the kitchen. Poured herself a scotch. Then she began chopping vegetables and boiling water for our dinner.

Looking back, I'm embarrassed and appalled.

I'm also surprised that she didn't teach me a few recipes and have me cook and wash up. A few years later, I met Annie, who, at thirteen, was the household grocery shopper and primary cook. She and her mother were a team. Surely I could have been roused to similar domestic efforts? Serge, too, had a single mother who worked long hours and shouldered all of the domestic labour. Why did they do this? I'm sure it's a pain in the arse to teach kids to cook and clean, but isn't the payoff worth it? One convincing argument was guilt. My mum did all the domestic chores *because* she worked. Because her marriage had ended and she was drowning in debt. I think for her, self-flagellation was preferable to admitting that she had not managed to pull off the ideal. I have some of this instinct in me — I try to keep it in check. Not having children helps. No one tells me that I am selfless, and it's a real load off.

There is one important way that being childless does equate with freedom and selfishness. When you don't have a child, you are free to be morose, to be depressed or angry or impulsive or joyful, without someone thinking you feel this way because of them. My parents, both so loving and supportive, were also moody people. As I child, I learned to interpret the way my mother turned her key in the lock, or the sound of my father's Zippo lighter flicking shut. I knew, by these cues, what the tenor of my immediate future would be. I quietly wished someone would call my Dad and ask him out for a beer; I longed to have heard my mother's car in time to slay the trash angel before the time of judgement. I know now that my parents' moods had nothing to do with me, but children, in their narrow cocoons, are selfish by design. They think they are the centre of everything, and very little tells them otherwise.

Even in the first-person accounts of wilful childlessness, no one wants to deemphasise the value of children. Authors feel compelled to state that they do not dislike children. In fact, they love them. They hang out with them all the time. They are wonderful aunties/uncles/godparents/mentors. Children are so important, they insist. I don't feel defensive on this account. Some children I have met are really cool. Quite a few of them are jerks. The ratio is not dissimilar from that I encounter in the adult world. The idea that all children are wonderful, joyful, caring sweetie-pies is rubbish. It is also a key fallacy on which to build a narrative of adulthood as a kind of moral decline, such as the one in *Big*.

My psychologist asked, in one of our appointments, if perhaps I don't want a child because I feel like I could fail at it. She is wrong. She forgets that I am special and I can do anything. (I should have my mother call her.) Even without a house, a reliable income, a family who could help with childcare, or a strong community network, I can imagine rising to the task of parenting. I can imagine pulling myself from bed in the middle of the night. That's why the knowledge that I don't have to is so relief-inducing. I cringe at the titles of recent books such as *I Can't Even Take Care of Myself* and *Childfree and Loving It!* Unlike the authors of these insistent titles, I don't think passing up on progeny is the fast track to a great life. Finding meaning without children is difficult. I'm still grappling with the idea that I live my life, as Harry Dean Stanton puts it, 'well-steeped in nothing', but I don't think that a lack of meaning is a good reason to have a child. I have seen too many friends have children and then sink back into that same aching nothing, still plagued by the existential questions that bother me in the small hours.

Instead of insisting that children add instant meaning to adult lives, perhaps it is time to think more about why we feel bereft of (or perhaps entitled to) meaning in the first place.

'Aren't you worried you will regret it?' is the final question in the arsenal of the disbelievers.

It's this regret that I was supposed to insure myself against by freezing my eggs. My generation is so obsessed with the spectre of regret that we have an acronym for it, FOMO, fear of missing out. But, as one childless girlfriend puts it: 'You know what, it's better to regret the baby you didn't have than the one you did.'

But could I change my mind? they want to know. I always say no, though this is not entirely true. Perhaps if I was to wake up one morning soon in a parallel universe in which I have a partner who I love as much as Serge but who, unlike Serge, cannot stand the idea of life without a child, cannot be talked around to it. And if this partner also respected – loved, even – my need for solitude, understood that writing sustains me; if they said to me, as I stood silhouetted in the bathroom doorway, crying, holding the plastic stick covered with piss and tiny blue ticks, 'Please, let's have this baby. Once it's born, you can go ahead and do what you need to do to preserve your sense of self; you are more lovable and useful to us in doing so. Pursue the ideas that enchant you. I'll take care of all the grunt work of child-rearing, as well as supporting you in every endeavour. You will always retain at least fifty per cent say in major decisions about our lives. You just need to pledge your love and play with us on the rug in the evenings after you eat the healthful dinner that I have prepared. And even if some nights you only want dinner and not to talk or play, we will still love you forever, and follow you wherever you want to go.'

If, in other words, this parallel-universe partner said, 'It's okay, you can be the Dad,' then, and only then, would I reconsider my position.

Now that many millennials are leaving their narcissistic years behind and selflessly forming families of their own, profiles of my generation as parents are beginning to show up in the media. In December 2015, *Time* ran a cover emblazoned with a typically hyperbolic headline — 'Help! My Parents are Millennials' — above a picture of a baby in one of those fancy Swedish four-wheel strollers that look like robotic insects and self-destruct in the first year. The baby's uncannily adult features (compared to millennials, babies are Renaissance-level mature again) are arranged into an expression that says 'good grief'. From the magazine's right margin, two anonymous, perhaps even genderless, but certainly parental arms aim smartphones at this little dear in the headlines like hunters at a zoo.

Smartphones, social media, and the internet feature heavily in *Time*'s characterisation of millennial parenthood, with good reason. Many of today's parents start documenting their children online from age foetus, with sonograms posted on Instagram and Facebook, followed by birth shots and important milestones, from crawl to kinder — will these parents continue to document into adolescence, or will puberty signify the beginning of the next generation's digital individuation? Time will tell. *Time* will no doubt tell us too. Meanwhile, here's a statement for the times: my Facebook page is covered in babies. There are babies sucking, crawling, cuddling, clapping, and co-opting my social network.

For a while, Facebook was dominated by the 'motherhood challenge', in which women posted five photos that made them 'happy to be mothers' and then tagged five other great mothers in their network, inviting them to do the same. These photos became indistinguishable from one another in my feed and also, poignantly, from a news item that dominated Australian media outlets the very same morning. My city's major daily ran with a front page featuring a similar photo collage: images of smiling and gurgling refugee babies, slated for deportation to offshore processing centres. The headline was 'Babies Bound for Hell'. There was no mention of their mothers.

While I quietly judged the women of the Facebook motherhood challenge, noting their inelegant timing, there were others who took to trolling, and even posting a 'childfree challenge', featuring photos of themselves napping with bottles of plonk, stacks of cash, international air-travel tickets, and molecular degustations, all of which were far more gratuitous and distasteful than the onslaught of babies.

The internet impacts everything we do now, and arguably for millennials more than any generation before. It is a place to perform the self, to make connections and seek information. I cannot tell you how many times, while trying to write this book, I have slipped into a digital trance, snapping back into focus just as I hit search on terms as asinine as 'how to write a book in less than three months' or 'should I eat carbohydrates before I write a book'. I can only imagine what you would find yourself searching when you haven't slept in days and your baby hasn't stopped screaming for just as long. One friend says she was sucked into a rabbit hole of forums and dubious articles after searching 'how do I tell if my baby is a jerk?'

'I got a bad case of mummy finger,' she laughed, using the new hospital slang for repetitive strain injury of the thumb. 'Sometimes I wonder what he thinks our phones are. To him, it's just this box of light that all the adults are totally transfixed by, that has the power to make them go completely still and silent.'

While the internet also helps connect parents who might otherwise be isolated, social media jealousy and guilt reaches its apex when the lives being compared are not our own but our children's. Millennial parents are anxious about their children's development compared to the other sprogs in their feed. They are wracked with envy or derision over shots of homemade organic baby food, elaborate cakes, smiling children participating in craft activities. It's a 'mompetition'.

Intensive-parenting trends, such as attachment parenting, extended breastfeeding, and other conceptual approaches centring on children's wellbeing have paved a moral terrain. 'Parental determinism', the concept that parenting is the key determinant in the future lives of their children, has made getting through the day like cutting across a minefield for many parents. (And this is despite the fact that where a child is born, to whom, and what school they go to are the single biggest predictors of adult prosperity. Today, statistics carve up school districts into prophetic zones for the future wealthy: the statistical line that divides Sydney almost exactly in half, predicting the future income, health, and even life expectancy of babies born to the east or west, and the colour-mottled map of London showing a deep purple 'knowledge class' at the centre of the city, fading out to the pinks and blues of 'service' and 'working' classes on the outskirts of the megalopolis. In some ways, a child's personal adult taxonomy is designed before they are out of nappies, let alone able to tap dance for Instagram.)

Such grave responsibility also has a significant impact on adult identities. 'As the "work" of parenting (emotional and physical) expands to engulf more and more of parents' lives, clearly the time and energy available for everything else will be drained,' argued Charlotte Faircloth, founding member of the Centre for Parenting Culture Studies at the University of Kent. 'This fits into a wider conversation around risk consciousness and the demise of confidence about how to approach the future. Put simply, our paranoia about parenting is a symptom of a society that feels less and less certain about what matters in life, and why.'

This statement resonated with me. It helped me to connect my feelings about performed parenting, babies as a central determinant of identity, and my sense of adult life as unformed and disconnected. Children are objectively important, and require care, attention, stimulation, education. In lives that lack centres, it makes sense that these concrete tasks could fill the void: if we cannot name the moral terrain of our lives, we can make parenting our crucial moral task. And if this results in giving too much space to our children, it is only because we do not know what that space might otherwise contain. It's time, then, to have an adult conversation about it. Such a move is necessary if we are to create an engaged, connected, and intelligent adult culture.

I hit peak child-bearing age at a time in which adult culture was distinctly undervalued. The Australian government paid new parents five grand per baby, and the media maligned mothers for spending it selfishly, on big-screen plasmas and clothes. Meanwhile, our first female prime minister was attacked for her childlessness, for her too-clean kitchen and empty fruit bowl. In 2007, Liberal senator Bill Heffernan said, 'I mean, anyone who chooses to remain deliberately barren … they've got no idea what life's about.'

In the United States, female reproductive freedom was also under attack by conservative politicians. In 2012, US Representative for Missouri's 2nd congressional district Todd Akin told a local news program that women who had been victims of 'legitimate rape' would not need abortions as they were unlikely to become pregnant. 'The female body has ways to try to shut that whole thing down,' he said. 'But let's assume that maybe that didn't work or something. I think there should be some punishment, but the punishment ought to be on the rapist and not attacking the child.' The punishment, in every case, seemed to come down sharply across the backs of women, and it's a preference that is increasing in 2017, with President Donald Trump making a global gag rule – which prevents US-funded NGOs from providing, cancelling, or issuing referrals for abortions – one of his first actions in office.

Now, as then, the deadlocking of the female body to the sacred task of maternity sicks me out. As does the suggestion that a woman without a child can never understand the life of a woman with one, women's intellects and imaginations being limited to the things they have experienced firsthand, naturally.

Unfortunately, these sentiments were echoed by well-meaning female friends, hopped up on post-birth hormones.

'You've never experienced love like this,' gushed one new mother when I visited her.

'It's amazing to think that I will never be alone again,' said another.

I concentrated on controlling my facial expressions.

Meanwhile, in the tabloids, we were having a mommy moment. Celebrities by the dozen were taking to glossy magazines and lifestyle television shows to claim that they were just 'regular moms'. I picked up a gossip magazine in a waiting room and became incensed by Gwyneth Paltrow's claim that she was of this ilk, 'just a regular mom wiping butts and warming bottles'. *Sure,* I thought, *and stacking your millions.* (Some years later, Paltrow would be vilified for allegedly not allowing her children to eat carbohydrates.) A few pages on, the actress Minnie Driver claimed her regular-mommy status too. Women's magazines featured parent-and-toddler fashion spreads. *Find out what Brooklyn Beckham or Pax Jolie-Pitt wore to the Yo Gabba Gabba! live show.*

I read Jennifer Egan's *A Visit from the Goon Squad* and found it chillingly prophetic. In Egan's future world, adults text one another in a vowel-stripped baby babble rather than talk because subtext has become exhausting, tone an unnecessary way to complicate meaning. Texting is, one character says, 'pure — no philosophy, no metaphors, no judgments'. Meanwhile, toddlers, nicknamed 'pointers', monopolise culture through their natural aptitude with smartphones. Manhattan — the capital of grown-up culture, where the women of *Sex and the City* brunched, and so many of the art and music movements

I adore emerged – has become, in Egan's dystopia, the place 'where the density of children is highest in the nation'. Babies fill Times Square, and the sepulchral streets surrounding Ground Zero – 'An army of children: the incarnation of faith in those who weren't aware of having any left.'

if thr r childrn, thr mst b a fUtr, rt? one adult texts another.

It would be two more years before I read Lee Edelman's *No Future*, a polemic against the power of exactly this insistence, which he calls 'reproductive futurism'.

'What,' writes Edelman, 'would it signify *not* to be "fighting for the children"? How could one take the *other* "side", when taking any side at all necessarily constrains one to take the side *of*, by virtue of taking a side *within*, a political order that returns to the Child as the image of the future it intends?'

While I was often called to defend my choice not to have children, I realised, as I waded through the swamps of pro-baby popular culture, that no one had ever articulated to me why they wanted a child. It was supposed to remain sacredly obvious, I gathered. Far from being a topic around which adult positions could comingle and mutate through impassioned debate, most of those I knew dodged accounting for their choice to procreate. Many, in fact, claimed that their baby was an accident. These accidents, I observed, usually occurred after the couple had quietly established that they wanted kids at some point and then promptly stopped using any form of birth control. This, I thought, pushed the boundaries of the term. It was the sort of accident I might have if I decided I did not want to go to work today and then turned off my alarm and went back to sleep.

Why did everyone want to tell me about their child's nap schedule, or sweet temperament, or let me in on the intricacies of their bowel movements, yet no one could tell me how it felt to want a child? I decided I needed to talk to someone who had been open about their desire for a baby. I called Stacy, a friend of Annie's with two children, whose existence she had spoken about long before it was manifest. Did she always know she wanted kids? I asked in an online chat thread after a few pleasantries.

'Oh, I always knew! Yes.'

Stacy promptly invited me over for lunch at her home, one hour west of Melbourne in a small, deindustrialised country town with a growing population of urbanites pushed out of the city by high rents and low prospects. Tree-changers, they have been dubbed in the media, though there were not so many trees around Stacy's huge, rented home in the centre of the town.

As soon as I walked through the gate, I saw the trends outlined in descriptions of Millennial Mom. Though Stacy was born in the late 1970s, missing the cap for some definitions of Generation Y, she fit the profile from *Time*; she was the very woman whose habits Goldman Sachs evaluated for spending implications. Her three-year-old daughter was reading a library book on the lawn when I arrived, munching on a homemade sausage roll covered in what looked suspiciously like chia seeds. The little girl was a delight: soft-spoken, thoughtful, and cautious. Stacy ushered me into her bright kitchen and the girl asked politely if she could watch something before her nap. Stacy handed her an iPad, and the child shuffled off down a hallway lined with organised boxes of toys.

Stacy's broad kitchen table was spread with an array of fermented vegetables in jars — her award-winning sauerkraut, as judged by the local agricultural show. A brightly coloured craft project was laid out in the adjacent room, felt and pegs and baskets of this and that. Useful boxes, as they called them on *Play School* when I was little. The whole thing was pastoral, neat, idyllic, and, in a way, enviable.

'Millennial parents put self-expression first,' said the marketing profiles. 'Millennial parents are more idealistic.'

'So what did you want to talk about?' Stacy asked.

'No one ever tells me why they want kids,' I explained.

'Right. Because it's just something you do.'

'Exactly.'

Stacy told me about her childhood. She was the eldest girl in a family of four and was often tasked with looking after the younger kids, feeding them and putting them to bed. It was not the first time I'd heard a story like this. Anecdotally, it seemed to me that people who played carer roles from an early age were more comfortable with assuming them later on, a fact that makes perfect sense and is probably obvious to people who grew up with siblings. One new dad I interviewed in my search to find someone to talk about their desire for children spent his teen years caring for his developmentally disabled brother, and attributed the comparative ease of transitioning into fatherhood and then single fatherhood to that experience. 'It's just what you do,' he told me when I goaded him to complain or rant or protest.

I'm not sure it's what I would do, I had thought then, and I thought it again now in Stacy's kitchen, sampling her pickles and picking apart her life.

'I was eight years old, making two-minute noodles for dinner and helping with homework,' Stacy said. 'I knew then that I would never feed my own kids shit food.'

I nodded, helping myself to another quinoa burger.

At age eleven, Stacy started planning for a family of her own. 'I even have a list somewhere I wrote back then of exactly the man I wanted to marry.'

'Oh, yeah?'

'Yeah!' she said. 'No beards!'

We both laughed. Chris, her husband, is thoroughly bearded.

Stacy had a glory box, too, still at her parents', filled with 'cheap crap' that never made it to her married life, though in some sense her entire twenties were a glory box. Right up until the age-thirty deadline, which was very real for her, Stacy collected crockery, beautiful old toys and puzzles, and experiences.

'I didn't want to have kids until I was thirty,' she said. 'Now we can show them pictures of us in Paris. They can see we had a life before them.'

The phrase 'a life before them' resonates with loss on paper, but listening to Stacy, I got the sense that it was waiting to have children that was more difficult. She did it not because she wanted that life she had without children, but because she wanted to present it to them, like a human glory box, filled with experience rather than with napkins. She probably also did it because of the contempt that our culture reserves for mothers who are too young. There is a window, between too young and too old, and it is about the same amount of time as a graduate degree.

I looked at Stacy's fridge, tacked with drawings and photographs. 'So you basically got everything you dreamed of.'

'We don't own the house.'

'No, but it's a very nice rental.'

'That's truuuuue,' she said, cracking her appealing, fox-like smile. 'Then why are we so fucking unhappy?'

I smiled. *Because happiness is not indexed to achievements*, I thought. Instead of saying this out loud, I paraphrased Tom Waits: 'There's nothing wrong with you a hundred thousand dollars wouldn't fix.'

Stacy broke into laughter. 'That's true, too. Then we could take a holiday and put a deposit on a house. Then we could afford some daycare.'

Stacy insisted that she does not feel pressured by her peers on Facebook. Her ethical parenting style and DIY aesthetic (not dissimilar from my own mother's early *Whole Earth Catalogue* aspirations) was all her, and she stuck to her guns even if it meant explaining what a sweatshop was to her kids when they demanded some cheap imported toy at the supermarket (*I never have to do that,* I thought). Her insistence and her reasoning simultaneously problematise the kind of research that takes place in order to identify trends. Millennial Mom might have a strong profile that is open to exploitation, but the millions of women who make her up have come to these conclusions for many different reasons. One thing we know for sure about millennials is that they are more abundantly and carefully marketed to than any previous generation. Are good intentions cheapened when they are used in marketing strategies? Probably. But cynicism isn't an antidote.

If Stacy is locked in a mompetition with anyone, it is her own mother. She hated seeing the waste her parents generated, the impractical way they spent their money. 'I wanted to see if I could do a better job,' she said, laughing. 'I wanted to make better humans.'

If you put aside the vengeful glee in this, it's an undeniably civic-minded sentiment. Stacy is a bake-sale and PTA kind of mother, but an updated, cooler version. She is active in her community, always available to help out with some worthwhile cause. It's a good adult life, if a hard one, in the way that living idealistically is often hard – and because her oldest child is only six, she is only at the start of it.

Stacy handed me a jar of similarly award-winning pickle on my way out the door. I'm glad for the future that she has children. I'm still equally glad that I don't have to.

On the drive home, I thought more about community and friendship. I had wrongly assumed it was the childless who were excluded from communities, comprising happy, self-contained families. Selfishly, I hadn't thought of this lonely drift from the other side.

When researching marriage, I'd had the opportunity to visit the home of a non-monogamous triad. A family with two women, a man, and a small kid, all sharing the load together and working without models towards a different kind of adult life. Love was the main factor in this decision, Gillian, one of the women, told me, but it also turned out to be intensely pragmatic. 'None of my friends with kids have time to themselves – it doesn't matter how much support they have. I've watched the women I know have kids and then kind of flounder. The jobs they get afterwards are nowhere near as good as those they were getting before. Plus there's the boredom. Parenting is relentlessly boring,' she said, with such candour I felt ready to move in with them myself. 'We work it out between us, and everyone has time to do the things that make them feel whole.'

Feeling whole, for Gillian, came not only from family life but also from creative endeavour, paid work, and opportunities for travel. For her, parenting was isolating, but parenting in a monogamous marriage would have been impossible. How could you maintain a life beyond your family when there were only two of you to care for the child?

'I can't even finish my thoughts sometimes. I hate it,' Stacy had said, when I asked her about how she finds time for herself or for friendships. 'One friend called three times last night, and every time was still bedtime. Bedtime goes for three hours here. If your friends work nine to five, it hardly leaves time for a chat. It's so hard to maintain that contact, and you really yearn for it.'

How, I wondered, could we bridge this gap? I vowed privately to be more engaged, to be more patient when catching up with girlfriends while their children play between us; but I also knew that this effort would only help a little bit, and could only be committed to short-term. The organisation of work, the domestic space, the city, all conspire to make it difficult for parents and nonparents to form close-knit communities. This distance is also a hangover from a long and concerted effort to keep women out of the public sphere, out of the streets and cafés, out of democracy. Labelling women selfish because they choose not to have children when doing so still means undertaking more than half the domestic labour, in addition to working for a wage, is a last-ditch attempt to consolidate this effort and, as usual, wherever there is a new paradigm or a so-called choice, there is a set of consumer patterns to solidify it.

The statistics on childlessness suggest distance is not just emotional but also geographical. In 2013, *Newsweek* declared a 'postfamilial America'. Harry Siegel wrote that

> the strong correlation between childlessness and high-density city living has created essentially two Americas: child-oriented and affordable areas, and urban centers that have become increasingly expensive and child-free over the last 30 years — not coincidentally the same span over which middle-class incomes have stagnated.

Seattle, apparently, now has more dogs than children, a fact that would appal the Pope but I find appealing.

Why then, when I got back to my city, did I find myself standing beside the local primary school for a long time, too long, hanging off the fence like the kind of creep your mother warned you not to talk to, watching the children play? Why then did I find myself asking the same question women who don't want the things they're told to want have been asking themselves for centuries — that is, *what the hell is wrong with me?*

Behind the fence, the children were unperturbed by my scrutiny. There were patterns in their play. Hierarchies, negotiations, expulsions, and allegiances formed and dismantled. *I can't be a parent*, I thought, *because I don't want to teach anyone the rules to the game, and I don't have the heart to tell them not to play.*

When the bell rang, these disciplined bodies turned, rigid and quick, as though they'd received a shock of electricity to the temple. Small tornadoes spun out across the field, gathering folders and bags and lunchboxes, leaving chip packets and forgotten jumpers in their wake. For a moment, the cacophony of laughter and shouting rose to crescendo. Then it disbursed, like a flock of birds squawking before a storm. The field was suddenly quiet, still, as though no one had been there in months. It was just the kind of empty space on which an apocalyptic imagination indulgently superimposes a new world.

A ball of cling wrap skipped over the basketball court like a tumbleweed.

'Everyone is having babies!' I wailed at Serge in a bar. 'What are we going to do instead?'

'I dunno, darlin'.'

Serge was still reluctant to talk about the future. He was forever stressed. Forever sorting through his own private adult angst and leaving me to mine. If I thought about it too much, I would cry until my ears popped, until the pressure split straight through my skull.

Early on, Serge and I had constructed a very romantic adult fantasy. Strictly Hollywood, it involved eloping, making music and art together, living all over the world, being a totally self-sufficient community of two. As the years passed, not only did this fantasy fail to materialise, but it also began to seem totally impractical. Where would the money come from? Also, humans like to be around other humans. A community of two, romantic though it may be, was hard to sustain. By the time we figured this out, many of the people we knew were solving the problem by making more people. The cult of romance feeds seamlessly into the adult fantasy of the nuclear family. Before the age-thirty deadline, I had never looked past the romance, glutting myself on it — all those rom-coms and road movies, first-person pop music — until it oozed out my pores and formed a haze across my eyeballs, across the reality of my assumed social and cultural imperative.

But I don't want to have a baby.

While the Australian Bureau of Statistics predicts that couples without kids will account for 43 per cent of families by 2031, they do not provide their names or addresses, or the places they like to hang out. My life might one day provide an example of a different kind of adult existence for my friends' kids, but for now, my future is like that playground after the bell rings.

Serge stared at his phone, sighing at something in his newsfeed or inbox. Distractedly, I took out my own device and scrolled, sipping my wine, hardly noticing as my fingers tapped in the search: 'What do adults do?'

A storm of screech rose up from the palm of my hand.

MAKE THEIR BED. My life felt contingent; I often said to people that I could not make a solid plan – keep my current foster dog, for instance. OWN TWO SETS OF SHEETS A PET OR CHILD because I did not yet know WHICH BREED OF DOG ARE YOU? the shape of my adult life HOW TO DESIGN YOUR PERFECT LIFE. Would I stay in one place or move around? THESE TINY HOUSES WILL MAKE YOU WANT TO THROW OUT EVERYTHING YOU OWN Would I get a permanent full-time job? 7 UNCONVENTIONAL WAYS TO GET YOUR DREAM JOB WHY GEN Y ARE SMARTER THAN WE THINK HOW TECH CAN MAKE YOUR CAREER BY 30 Would I buy a home? TOP 20 WAYS TO SAVE FOR A HOME DEPOSIT, FAST! Would I MARRY (WHY THESE CELEBS WON'T TIE THE KNOT) Serge? The answer to every question 20 THINGS YOU SHOULD ASK YOUR PARTNER/BEST FRIEND/EMPLOYER led to the next, and so forth, until 100 WAYS YOU CAN GIVE BACK I felt like I was a little kid spinning around in circles INCREASE

YOUR CIRCLES OF INFLUENCE with the deliberate aim of becoming dizzy to the point of passing out. BEDROOM WORKOUTS THAT WILL BURN YOUR BUTT GET YOUR DREAM BODY SWEAT IT OUT Of course, the best part of this game TAKE THIS QUIZ TO FIND OUT WHICH SIMPSONS CHARACTER YOU ARE was always when, lying on the grass, GARDENING FOR A SUSTAINABLE FUTURE you suddenly realised that the sky had stopped spinning and your body seemed solid once more. That was the point you could get up and try it all again.

7
BUSY WORK

What do adults really do? Mostly, they work. Work is adult business. Work is hard to get and hard to keep. Work always means more than what work is: the jobs in which we spend an average 90,000 hours a lifetime. The conference calls. The cash registers. The projects. The products. MYOB and Powerpoint and power tools and boots and clearing tables. The bosses. The office or worksite gossip. The absorbing or unabsorbing tasks that are endless. Work. The thing we say when, as adults, we are asked once more what we do. We work. We make our contribution. We know that work is code for our economic capital. We think that work should be interesting, worth talking about, fulfilling, but often it's just work.

My first 'real job' was after my undergraduate degree, as an online content producer in talkback radio. Three days a week I listened to notorious local haters rail against the inconvenience of sharing the road with cyclists, the deviousness of single mothers, the idiocy of environmentalists, and the vapidity and entitlement of people under thirty. I snipped the most inflammatory audio from each polemic and uploaded it to the web alongside some incendiary statements of my own composition. Something like, 'Youth unemployment levels at an all-time high — should lazy youngsters be forced into military service?' I located a stock image of some dreadlocked reprobate stuffed into sloppy fatigues and uploaded the whole package. Periodically, I also moderated the responses of listeners, carefully dividing popular hatred from defamation, and taking down the essayistic single-issue posts of someone named NevilleTheGreat.

The job, equal parts depressing and thrilling, was at least interesting. Fun, even. It was a lark to generate more of this bad noise, this 'content'. On good days, I imagined myself as a writer of flash fiction somewhere between dada and negative-zen. I thought that I could neutralise the sledging machine from within by rendering it absurd. But the wall between satire and sincerity crumbled, and on bad days I felt like a scoundrel. I started coming to work hung-over. I sat sentinel in the empty office on weekends, head thumping, catching each spit-flecked monologue by its tendril. I began to sing along to the various theme songs of presenters: 'El Presidente', 'Less of Me', and 'My Way'. I began to laugh out loud, to talk back to the talkback — a kind of madness, chortling and tsk-tsking along with the long-time-listener-first-time-callers. The bad days soon outnumbered the good. To stave off the building sense of isolation, I smuggled Cassady in, and, at moments when I felt as if my brain would break, I threw a pen across the empty office. Cassady's brown body would spring up from beneath my desk, lithe and zealous, unconcerned with human acrimony and employment.

On paper I'd made it, and I wasn't even twenty-five. This was one of the jobs listed in the course handbook for my degree under 'outcomes'. This was The Media, though it bore little resemblance to the newsrooms my father had taken me to as a child. I knew very few of my colleagues beyond our office interaction. We had no long lunches, big leads to follow, or important stories to tell. We communicated with one another via sarcastic instant messages, thick with ASCII emoji. The radio stations we worked alongside viewed us with suspicion. Radio, they insisted, did not need the internet and its totalising, obliterating future. Everyone I worked with was hostile or confused. I was both. Was this the beginning of my career, my adult life? Was I a journalist or a writer? I felt like neither.

One morning I sent a pen skittering across the office floor and leaned back into the aural embrace of a broadcaster they called the Golden Tonsils.

'Look,' he said. 'I understand that Chinese drivers are probably the worst drivers on the face of the Earth.'

I clipped the audio, and typed a caption: 'Can Asians drive? Lawsy says no.'

Then I put my head on my desk and pictured returning to the sea.

Unable to afford inner-city rent, I commuted an hour and a half to work and slept in the back of my panel van, or at a friend's. Three months into my contract, I jumped at the chance to move stations, south to the colder and more affordable Melbourne, and its ever-so-slightly-more-moderate talkback culture.

At that time, moving to Melbourne was a popular thing to do. All my friends were making the transition. It felt like another new start to my adult life.

Within six months of moving, the radio network was bought by one of Australia's two big broadcasting corporations. I was retrenched and on welfare again. I put my false start behind me and fell back into the underemployment I had dwelled in when I first left home. It felt good to be doing something I understood. Drawing unemployment benefits without seeing your life become submerged in bureaucracy, in unpaid labour or spurious skills-training courses, requires particular aptitude. You need to be patient, and impervious to humiliation. You need to keep your cool, speak impeccable English, make your arguments succinctly using deductive logic, be digitally literate, be firm but not pushy, be sober (or sober-passing), and know how to present yourself across multiple contexts. This, perhaps, was the true outcome of my humanities degree, the very thing I had been training for all along.

After a few months on welfare, the state allocated me a personal arse-whipper, a kind of professional nagging mum to badger me into a job, any job. In order to bank my $20 or so a day and prove my worth to the nation, every Tuesday I sat in Anja's tiny, pilling cubicle. Anja was a small Eastern European ex-goth with a sharp black bob and heavy eyeliner. As far as arse-whippers went, I liked her.

'I think it is time you got a job, no?' she said, one afternoon after a few easy months.

I cringed under her gaze. She drew me out with her Slavic silence. 'I'm writing.'

'Be practical,' she said. 'The time is up. You need to get a job. Think of something that you want to do, or I will choose for you.'

Up until now she had been patient with me, but I could see the threat burning in her heavily kohled eyes. I was one wrong move away from getting put on one of those jobseeker buses to the local shopping centre, forced by pain of cancellation to march from store to store canvassing for employment, chest bestickered: 'Hi, I'm Briohny and I want to WORK!'

I needed to think fast.

'I'd like to work with animals,' I said.

Anja sighed. She turned to her computer and scrolled through the columns of bold type. The mouse ball groaned beneath her black lacquered fingernails. Above her desk, a laser-printed smiley face was captioned with 'GET JOBACTIVE!' Another flyer showed a pleased-looking bald man with a plate of cupcakes he'd presumably baked, a thirty-something woman smiling patiently with a broom, and the owner of the job network herself, hair a plume of feathered lowlights, earrings not dangling but rather stabbing at the air. Framed from below, she looked like a promo still for a sequel to *Attack of the 50 Foot Woman*, in which the giant tames menopause and moves to the Gold Coast.

Anja's expression began to lift, taking on ironic pleasure

laced with cruelty. 'You are in luck,' she said. 'You want to work with animals, you can work with animals.'

I was suspicious. 'What kind of animals?'

'Cats.'

I looked down at the puce carpet. She had me.

'I'm really more of a dog person.'

'It's in your suburb,' Anja said.

'I'm allergic to cats.'

'Take a pill.'

She dialled the number. The time for talent was over. The time for dreams had run out. It was time to empty the kitty litter.

The cattery was not the first so-called unskilled job I worked, and it would not be the last. Actually, scratches, allergies, and faeces notwithstanding, I liked the work. But as I pulled on the long rubber gloves and wrangled hissing felines from their cages, I found the occasion to meditate on the relationship between adult identity and work. The cattery was not a 'real job' in the eyes of my parents and many of my peers. My mother sighed when I told her about it. My father cracked a joke. I fought with a friend on a career track when I said that I didn't believe having a job doing what you love was possible, or at least not for me. But working in the media had been depressing and shallow, and I'd been retrenched before the year was out. The only benefits had been the pay and the sense of satisfaction on the faces of older relatives.

For most of my twenties, when Dad and I talked about jobs and money, I felt as though we were from different planets. His success at carving out a career was, to him, proof positive that I could achieve the same. He found my patchy working life of cobbled-together jobs baffling. He wondered, perhaps, if I did not want to have a career and make some money.

'Just call up *The Age*,' he said, referring to the biggest newspaper in my city as though it were a heavily leisured relative, happy to do favours. 'Tell them you will do a column for them at twenty-five cents a word. Something sassy. You know, a bit *Sex and the City* with Doc Martens on.'

He heard my embarrassed laughter as recalcitrance. A failure of imagination.

My dad's career path looked like this: copy boy, conscripted soldier (non-combatant), court reporter, news reporter, TV reporter, editor, brief tree change and disastrous experiment with the restaurant business, magazine writer, editor, subeditor. It was, I think, a pretty typical middle-class baby boomer one-track path, with a little deviation for adventure/midlife crisis. Other than as a parent, Dad had never worked for free.

Perhaps because of this, his career advice over the years was infelicitous. Before the column, he had advised me to do a photography diploma focused on working with 35mm film.

'It's a skill that's always in demand!' he said.

He insisted that moonlighting in advertising was a fun, undemanding way to earn some pocket money. 'Peter Carey wrote his first two books while working part-time in advertising,' he explained.

He would not countenance discussion of the competitive degree programs and long unpaid internships in advertising.

He watched, bemused, as I took on more study, moved from the cattery to a produce market, and worked my career track to be a greengrocer with a PhD.

If social change was the storm that swept my parents to new horizons, economic change is the version for the millennial generation. The neo-liberal agenda of casualisation and deregulation that began in the 1970s in Western democracies across the world has changed the workforce. Where once you advanced in a job by staying there long term, now you will earn more if you change jobs regularly. Where once employers trained their staff, and sought to keep them as a return on their investment, now workers typically pay to learn their skills through an institution and are expected to apply for jobs close to work-ready. People my age and younger will, on average, come to full-time work later, with higher expectations and, in many cases, lower prospects than our parents did. If we can afford to, we will complete internships, volunteer programs, industry-specific short courses, or launch our own projects related to our industry in order to get jobs, or we will work hard in casual, unskilled positions, while other people read this as evidence that we are immature and lacking in drive.

In 2015, amid the smeary neon of New York's Times Square — where a suddenly thirty Tom Hanks stumbled, where posters of Rosie the Riveter once were pasted — a billboard depicted a kiddult à la mode: a young man, pallid, slack-jawed, lazy belly protruding beneath threadbare t-shirt, backwards baseball cap, one headphone lifted as if to hear the sweet news. 'What, I get $30,000 a year with no experience or skills?' ran the caption.

The retort: 'Who needs an education or hard work when Gov. Cuomo is raising the minimum wage to $15 an hour?'

Higher wages for the slack, overprivileged workers drawn to the fast-food industry is, according to the billboard, an attack on American Values. (No surprise: it was paid for by a group financially supported by the restaurant industry.) High wages – though it should be noted that $30,000 is only a smidge over the minimum living expenses for the greater New York area, as calculated by MIT – are a sign of intelligence, a better work ethic, and a generally higher-quality individual. Stable, well-remunerated employment and financial assets are the markers of successful adulthood. In America, any baby can become president if they work hard enough. ANY BABY. If you squint, though, or don the magic sunglasses from John Carpenter's *They Live*, you can see the real message of this billboard in bold black type: suck it up, loser.

Yet if decreasing opportunity for younger workers is occurring on a global scale, how can it be the fault of an individual, or even a cohort? In the United Kingdom, young-adult incomes are 20 per cent below the national average. Europe is currently experiencing what some commentators have called a 'youth unemployment tragedy'. This is a time in which 'young people are stuck with lower-paid, temporary contracts and get fired first in crisis times', said Mario Draghi, the president of the European Central Bank, in 2016. 'The crucial question is whether a person can participate fully in the economy over his or her lifetime – get a good education, find a job, buy a home for the family. What makes me worry is that increasing inequality might prevent people from doing that.'

In America, census data analysed by the Georgetown University Center on Education and the Workforce in 2014 showed that my millennial cohort comprise 40 per cent of the country's unemployed, with a surge in the number of people from this demographic working for less than $25,000 a year. Many young people today grow up into the precariat regardless of their education or many other traditional measures of class. A big part of this is the increase in deregulated or casual employment. In Australia, 'casual worker' is a term that applies to employment agreements, which provide no access to benefits such as sick or holiday pay, no job security, and little chance for advancement. Casual work is typically low-income and often found in the so-called unskilled occupations such as labouring, sales, and hospitality, but increasingly also in education and health. In 2015, according to the Australian parliament, this workforce comprised 39.3 per cent under the age of twenty-five and 20 per cent twenty-five to thirty-four-year-olds. Despite this, in 2017 the government supported a proposed reduction in penalty rates for these workers, a move that privileges business owners over what is becoming a class of working poor who are also largely young and/or female. Think, then, how it must be to experience other kinds of disadvantage — discrimination due to race, gender, disability, mental health, or commitments such as caring for children, the ill, and the elderly.

By the time I reached thirty, I had worked in the media, hospitality, call centres, retail, and education. I was in a privileged position to have had so many jobs, but I'd never held a contract for longer than a year. I'd been made redundant, mostly without any severance pay, from more than 50 per cent of my jobs. I had less than $5,000 to my name, and far less than zero if you subtracted my deferred student debt. But at the greengrocer, penalty rates meant that I could work double shifts or pre-dawn opens for better money. I wasn't killing myself for a career track that might not exist in a few years, as some of my friends were. I was working quietly on projects of my own, and in an unskilled job that kept me social, active, and engaged with different kinds of people. When the weather was right, I felt as though I had made the smartest choice. Was I missing something? Had I, as my friend suggested when we fought, sold myself short and been too cynical about the opportunities that exist for someone of my skills? When I began writing about these questions, I found I still did not have answers. I'd been working for more than a decade, but I still didn't understand why my working life was so patchy and insecure. I decided to ask an expert.

Rod the careers coach is my dad's age, but cut from a different cloth — a rich, starched cotton. His office, when he let me in, was minimally but tastefully furnished. A window with minor city views covered one whole wall. Both his shoes and his hair glimmered. When I told him my level of education and my job, he looked utterly unsurprised. *Good,* I thought, *a realist*. I remembered my high-school careers counsellors, their focus on aptitude and bright, Venn-diagrammed futures. It wasn't that I didn't understand how careers worked in an ideal world. It was the real that troubled me.

Rod's appointment before me had been a thirty-two-year-old administrative officer in possession of two undergraduate qualifications and a masters degree. 'Nothing that was going to lead to a job, really,' Rod said. 'When we are talking about the group called millennials, there are a lot of people with degrees, or multiple degrees, who want to use their skills and qualifications but end up in survival jobs.'

A survival job, Rod explained, is like the one I had at the produce market. It pays the bills, sort of. There's no inbuilt security and few prospects for promotion, but it will do for now. The trouble is, 'for now' is a stretchy concept.

'When I first started working, the question was "which job should I take?" not "will I get a job?" It's been a buyer's market for labour for twenty-plus years. People coming into the job market now, that's all they've ever known.'

Rod's facts were relentless and cool; his hustle, mercenary. He was expert in breaking people down into saleable parts. For jobs that have only existed for a few years, he recommended reverse-engineering LinkedIn profiles. He could also spin-doctor a résumé and play the numbers — not with the gay abandon of a gambler, but with the precision of a statistician. I wanted desperately to drag him out of his office, pack him up, and take him to talk to my dad, to serve it out cold. Rod's pragmatic vision of a world in transition was antithetical to the insistence that life adheres to unwavering principles that an individual must learn and exploit.

'People do various sorts of qualifications, but no one gives them a sense of how to access the job market. You go to secondary school, the deal is to get into the best possible tertiary qualification. Sometimes you have a sense of what that will be; other times, you are driven on marks. So high achievers are pushed down the law or medicine path. Then of course there are various arts and business degrees. But you don't know what that means. You engage in a process of three to four years, and the goal is to get the qualification. It's very easy to see that as an endpoint. But it's not. It's a transition point. All you really have is the capacity to go into a graduate or entry-level position, and those are highly contested.'

I told him about a voicemail message I woke up to one day when I was twenty-three. It was my supervisor from the call centre where I worked, inappropriately jolly for a Monday morning, explaining how the whole operation was moving offshore and 'what that means for you is that you won't need to come in for your Wednesday shift … Or any shift … here … again … ever. Anyway, sorry for the long message … I'm actually pretty drunk.'

Rod nodded without laughing. 'I saw a shift in the late 1980s, early 1990s, when it became okay to use retrenchment as a mechanism to manage your business,' he said. 'It meant that you didn't have to invest in people anymore; you could hire them or fire them as you needed. At the same time, we saw the casualisation of the workforce. This working environment is totally new, less than thirty years old. Naturally, it's radical and unusual.'

The working world Rod first encountered was also new, though the implications of the change were different. 'I was born in 1949. That's the only reason I'm not a butcher like my father and grandfather,' he said.

My paternal grandfather was a soldier and a building superintendent. My paternal grandmother was a cleaner and, from all reports, a social climber. In 1967, my eighteen-year-old father felt exceptional, as though he could do anything. After he dropped out of teachers' college to be a journalist, he was on the career track by twenty, the first person in his family to own a car, and not just to buy a television but to work in television. It makes me wonder, if his was the first generation that didn't have to become their parents, is mine the generation that couldn't if we tried?

There are so many more of us. We are more educated. Life is more competitive. The new opportunities that open up barely replace the old ones we have been training for. It would have been unheard of in Dad's youth for an educated young person to have been made redundant three times before the age of twenty-five.

When Serge and I met, he was trying to swing himself up out of survival jobs and into a career. He put himself out there, way out past the breakers. He did expensive private courses and unpaid internships and eventually landed a fancy job in a competitive industry. On paper, he had sorted the whole career thing and was on his way to adult success. It was a joy to introduce him to my parents. His job was a kind of spell, its fizzy powers reaching across my life too. While I had never thought of my parents as traditionalists in the realm of gender roles, I felt their relief. They seemed to believe that Serge could look after me while I pursued my whims and worked part-time. His job was evidence that we were on the right track. That I was finally growing up. They didn't need to worry anymore.

'I suppose with your job, you can take off and work in the States or in the UK?' Dad said.

'Yep, that's the plan.' Serge smiled, squeezing my hand.

'Good, good,' said Dad, raising his eyebrows, impressed and relieved. He stubbed his cigarette out decisively as if to say 'that's that then'.

Meanwhile, little clues made me suspect this career of Serge's was unsustainable. Once, when we were very fresh in love, I asked him to come home with me, and he refused because he had to mentally prepare for work.

'Being with you is magical,' he said. 'And work is so, so grey. The contrast is too much of a shock.' It was an utterance both lovely and heartbreaking. It was a sign of things to come.

By the time we moved in together, Serge commonly worked thirteen-hour days, back to back. His job was technical and screen-based, and if he messed up, he expected retribution: snide remarks and cold-shouldering at best, bullying at worst. I lost track of how many times he claimed he'd been 'black flagged on the last lap' and 'stitched up a treat' and therefore would not be home until the wee small hours. Sometimes I held him tight on a Sunday night while he shook with anxiety about Monday morning. His health suffered, his heart suffered, our life together suffered. He would not quit, though. Quitting was akin to leaping into an abyss. Besides, what else would he do? Would he go back to selling DVDs at a shopping centre? He looked at reskilling as an electrician, a sound engineer. How would he support himself while he studied? How would he deal with more debt? Each question seemed like another stress-bomb. Often, conversations about these options ended with a fight, with Serge's body tense, his face grim, his hands moving compulsively to smooth the space between his eyebrows. 'I can't talk about this right now,' he'd say, and I'd know we had hit the wall.

I didn't want to become another source of stress in his life, another person asking 'what are you going to do?' when every answer seemed untenable.

On good days at work, Serge seemed to forget all of this. He was eager to forgive his boss and redeem his workplace. This was just as frustrating. He would come home and excuse everyone I was supposed to hate last week. He was trying hard — too hard, I sometimes thought, though his family disagreed.

Then suddenly he was retrenched. A small-business concession meant that he did not receive any severance. Instead, he worked out the year at the place that was letting him go, under bosses who thought that sudden unemployment was just the way of the world, not anyone's fault or responsibility. Work stress was replaced by straight-up depression. During this time, he dreaded contact with his parents and relatives. It is hard to grit your teeth and admit you are not okay, knowing that the response, though loving, will be an accusation.

'What will you do differently next time?' asked one uncle, capitalising on what he saw as a teachable moment.

Unlike my own parents, who taught the imperative to follow your dreams, Serge's insisted that to be a man, you needed to have a job, and that job was a conduit for your self-respect. For Serge, whose mother had marched him down to the local computer shop to take on a $5-an-hour retail apprenticeship as a teenager, job loss was shattering. For a year after his retrenchment, I watched him struggle to reprogram his thinking. He took a survival job. He wrote songs and spent more time playing in his band. He tried to find value in his life of which no one could strip him. It wasn't easy, and it wasn't short-term labour, but it might be the most important job he will ever have.

If Serge's work history is a familiar sob story, his half-brother Chris embodied exactly the kind of go-getter spirit that conservative politicians in my country think young adults should have. Side by side, they are a version of *Rich Dad Poor Dad*, a good brother, bad brother for the millennial sledging machine.

Chris is a great taker of advice. When he finished high school, he listened to his parents and, instead of bumming around, going to parties, and faffing at an impractical arts degree, as was his aptitude, he packed up his station wagon and went to work as a trainee farmer.

It was beautiful out there on the remote saltwater flats. He liked the work and the adventure. He liked the solitude. But his boss was abusive. He'd bully Chris daily. And the pay was untenable — less than $5 an hour, a trainee rate that favoured employers and opened young workers up to exploitation in the same way that work-for-welfare schemes tend to. Chris spent two years living in a caravan and learning to farm, while his parents insisted that this was the hard-knocks approach to growing up and becoming a man. It didn't make sense to him. At twenty-two, when his traineeship ended and he was due a proper wage, the manager started trying to look for ways to get rid of him. The bullying amped up. 'We'd be repairing a fence, and he'd stand there and stare at me down his riflescope. I mean, we were only thirty minutes from town, but it was a big property and we were alone. I kept thinking there would be so many ways for him to get out of it. So many holes he could dig.' Chris laughed grimly.

Chris wanted out. He wanted to become a pilot. He tried to enrol in an aviation degree, but it wasn't covered by government funding and, despite two years of full-time work and almost no living expenses, he didn't have enough for a deposit. His parents were staunchly opposed to hand-outs. They were also opposed to unoccupied young people. You need to make money straightaway, his father advised. You need security. Finally, Chris dealt with unemployment the way one recent prime minister thought all young Australians should be forced to: he showed his initiative and went to work in the mines.

'I had to give away my dog,' he said.

I gasped.

'I know! That was the hardest thing. I'll never get over it. I went out there with a week's worth of clothes and a thousand bucks. I spent the money on a course in basic haul-truck operations. Pretty much just driving a little dump truck in a limestone quarry until I got the hang of it. Luckily the people who ran the course liked me and gave me a place to stay, because pretty soon I couldn't even afford to eat.'

He worked in a timber mill and a factory before he finally got a job as a trainee dump-truck operator for a big mining corporation. 'It was a full-on thing to do at twenty-two. Everyone on the plane had a beard. When we got to the site I was like, oh man, this place is so tough. I couldn't believe what I was doing.'

Chris talked me through ten years of work in the mines. How it was difficult, even at such a young age, to get used to the drinking culture. How you could get fired for cutting your nails wrong. How the brain starts malfunctioning on rosters of seven days on, seven nights on, and then seven days off. It wore away at him. He lost his partner and sometimes, he felt, his mind.

'I became a pretty angry man,' he said. 'I was angry for years and took it out on everyone.'

Chris told work horror stories with a playful tone, making it sound like a lark, making me laugh at stories about being run over by a dump truck, of snapping his vertebrae changing a tyre, of attempts to 'humiliate me into quitting' when he returned to work after injury.

'I grew up really loving the whole cowboy take on masculinity,' he said. This narrative was the only way he could integrate his work into his sense of self, like a kid playing role-play while the other parts of him detached, collected the funny anecdotes. I understood this implicitly; it's a defensive position I have practised for years.

At thirty, Chris got married and mortgaged and had a baby. But since the price of iron ore is due for another fall, he's been feeling more precarious than ever. At the time I spoke to him, he didn't have a contract and wasn't sure what would happen next. He suspected a firing squad. 'Last time they set up a little portable redundancy office and people lined up,' he said. 'There was a plane waiting for them on the tarmac to take them back to Perth. It was pretty dramatic.'

'Are you stressed?'

'I don't care,' he said with a laugh. 'I spent ten years moving back and forth across the country and working insane hours and being treated like shit. I still don't know if it was worth it.'

'Do you feel like you grew up out there?'

'No way!' He laughed again.

What made Chris feel grown up, finally, was installing an oven. 'Instead of smashing up the bench like I would have a few years ago, I stopped and worked out another way to do it,' he told me proudly.

I understood what Chris meant by invoking the oven as a symbol of adulthood. He needed autonomy, time, and space, to figure out how best to do something, but he had never had that luxury. His job, and with it his twenties, had been about forcing something into a space that it didn't belong. He had never really wanted to work in the mines. He persevered in anger, at great cost to his body and his mental health. He did it for money. He did it because it was expected of him. He spent all his money on toys; he fought with his girlfriend and friends, stayed out all night, imagined he was a cowboy. He was bored and confused and acting out. Then he realised that he wasn't the problem, and found the confidence and resolve to take his time, to do things in a way that made sense to him.

'I think that's evidence of maturity,' he said, putting on a mock-serious voice.

I agreed, though I suspected that surviving trauma, and finding a new, more rewarding social role as husband and father, could as easily be catalysts for this revelation as the oven. Or maybe it was because he'd finally saved the money to train for his pilot's licence: 'When I'm flying alone, that's the most grown-up feeling,' he said. 'It's like, I can't believe someone is actually letting me pilot the plane.'

When I got off the phone, I started thinking about Mishka, my foster dog. I still felt sad about the dog Chris had to give up, but living with Mishka had taught me a lot about the nature of work. She was a frantic and confused animal: a kelpie who had never seen a farm but wanted to round up the traffic, and leapt onto every high surface to get a broader view of her domesticated terrain. She jumped on the table, the kitchen counter, the hoods of strangers' cars. She strained at her lead when walking, constantly looking around and taking in everything, getting a read on every moving object. When she was excited, she could run huge circles at motorbike speed or shriek like a death-metal vocalist. She was happiest when she had herded everyone into the corner of the room and was sitting on their feet. These are annoying behaviours. She was what some might call a 'bad dog' and, in her previous homes, she had taken some mighty wallops for it. The first time

I picked up a stick to throw for her, she cowered in the grass. Some humans had tried to beat her instincts out of her.

About six months into our time together, I took her to a herding camp for dispossessed working dogs. The gnarled and gentle farmer who ran it had eyes that twinkled like sapphires. He fed me and the other attendees tea and Iced VoVos and patiently explained what a dog is. 'They have different drives and desires. Humans love dogs because they have high pack drive. They want to be with us. But they also have prey drive, and we need to understand that, too.'

The farmer did a healthy business with city dogs in trouble on account of their prey drive. These dogs tore up the couch, ripped the washing from the clothesline, and wouldn't let little Billie out of her playpen. They hid in the hedges, waiting for the fast car in order to race it down the suburban street, and one day soon there was going to be an accident and someone might get killed.

'They're bored and confused,' said the farmer. 'Their lives lack purpose.'

Working dogs, like people, need jobs that make sense to them, and thrive when that work is rewarded.

We humans lined up by the paddock, each with a straining, yowling dog on a string, watching as three bedraggled and much-put-upon sheep were led in, bleating protests. *Here it comes again*, they must have been thinking. *That arsehole is sending in the rookies*.

One at a time, the dogs entered the pen, the farmer murmuring incomprehensibly at them. And one by one these delinquent city dogs began to listen. Mishka barked and whined and spun around in the dirt until it was her turn to get to work.

'Make her sit,' said the farmer.

He unleashed her and began his call: 'Eeeeeeergiddee-giddee.'

Mishka flattened her ears against her skull.

'Eeeeeeergiddeegiddee.' The farmer began to move, holding his hands out in front of him, palms up.

Soon the kelpie moved, too. She mirrored the farmer's movements; she ran left, and then, when he gave her the cue, she ran right. She ran circles around those sheep, nipping the air at their heels. When she had them packed in the corner, the farmer said 'come', and she ran up and sat on his foot, her eyes never leaving the bleating sheep.

The winter sun beamed across the paddock. City dogs yipped and strained on their leashes, and Mishka, maybe for the first time, walked a straight line, with purpose.

'It's beautiful to watch her work,' said the farmer. 'She's so natural.'

I held onto her lead and cried with joy.

If you have work that moves you, you will nip the air with glee. If you work only to survive, or have little opportunity for undertaking fulfilling work, you will howl and destroy the furniture.

As I thought about and researched workplace trends for young people, I became increasingly aware of the limits of my methodology. I was asking around, and therefore not expanding my worldview much beyond the network of people (and dogs) I knew. This was a problem in my conception of what constituted adulthood, too — I didn't know how young people related to work in Iceland or Peru. I read an article that asserted in France, it's déclassé to talk about work over lunch. You are expected to have other, more important interests. I read, too, that some companies in Sweden began transitioning to a six-hour work day in 2016, to allow employees to give priority to their families. I also knew that even in middle-class Australia, there were young professionals who loved their jobs, who had established careers, and had firm visions of their futures. I racked my brains and rattled my network to find one.

'I think that satisfying careers are still possible in lots of industries,' Chloe, a thirty-two-year-old marketing professional told me, delivering exactly the dose of flat optimism I was craving.

Chloe was pretty much on track, adult-wise. In her twenties she travelled, lived overseas, studied in a decidedly non-vocational discipline that she loved, and then had an aha moment when she took a marketing unit and realised that this was something she could do for money and actually enjoy. She completed her masters and took some unpaid work experience. Less than five years later, she was a bona fide career woman.

'I'm an assistant marketing manager — the next step is marketing manager. I'm certainly in a role that corresponds to roles in other places, and there are steps up the ladder that everyone can see,' she said.

I asked her if she felt as if she has job security and, even though she is on a rolling one-year contract, she said she thinks so. 'If you are good at your job, they keep you, right?'

I stayed quiet. I'd read too many statistics on workplace discrimination, and particularly after Serge's redundancy, sentiments like this felt like betrayal.

Chloe had impressively adult work problems, such as training a new assistant. We talked a little about the expectations of young people in her field (she does not consider herself young), and she explained that many of the fresh-out-of-uni people in her workplace seemed to expect their careers to move fast and would job-hop to make it so, while workers with a few more years of experience, like her, stuck around.

'Do you think that is entitlement?'

'Yes and no.' Chloe knew the statistics that suggest moving workplaces is the best way to progress in terms of salary and seniority. 'It's a shame, though. Organisations don't value staff retention,' she said. 'But every time we lose a staff member, we lose an incredible amount of institutional knowledge. And then there's the digital disruption. The number-one job in marketing now didn't exist five years ago. People who took jobs in social media and digital marketing five years ago have it made.'

'For now,' I said with a laugh, but Chloe's view was brighter – so much so that I began to wonder why. We went to different kinds of schools and had different families, but otherwise we have had similar privileges. And we had similar interests, as well as friends and some politics in common.

Why, then, did we feel so differently on the subject of work?

'I used to start each birthday with a personal business plan. I'd try to identify where I was going and what I was doing,' Chloe confided. She had other disciplinary measures, too. Applying for five jobs a day, for instance, even if she didn't want any of them, just to stay limber. This sounded pathological to me, but then I remembered the time I heard Chloe say 'I will not accept failure,' over a plate of lacklustre gingerbread and decided it was probably just determination. The same kind of determination, perhaps, that kept me in my bedroom writing while my friends took holidays and started families. The difference, then, between Chloe and me was not so much one of character or drive. It was about economic validation.

'It's an interesting question,' Chloe mused. 'Would I do this work if I wasn't getting paid?'

'Well, would you?'

'No! Or yes, I would, but less of it. I work bloody hard, and there are people who work even harder than me. The cost of living is relentless. I'd love to buy an apartment, even though I know that is such a traditional and impossible goal. But also, I'm anxious that in having a career and working so much, I am missing out on travelling, and doing the stuff that I think of as constituting my identity.' Suddenly, she got wistful. 'That really is an interesting thought … that people need to be generating wealth to have worth. It's definitely true for me. That's where I struggle, as well, with maternity leave — I don't know if being a mother would be *enough*. Not that I wouldn't love my children, but …' I waited for her to continue, but she didn't.

In her musings, Chloe illustrated some of the arguments for and against the Universal Basic Income, a welfare replacement plan once favoured by both Martin Luther King Jr and Milton Friedman. The UBI has come back into vogue over the last few years as unemployment and poverty striate the populations of rich countries. The concept is a guaranteed payment just above the poverty line for every person. I would get a UBI, and so would someone living on the street, and so would a mining company CEO. The payment would be equal: we would not be means- or activity-tested for it; we would not have to prove our commitment to it or show proof of how we spend it. It's an expensive but, some argue, necessary salve to the prevalence of unpaid, lowly paid, and casual work; workplace deregulation; and technological and environmental disruption to the labour market. It would be a safety net for everyone who can't drive ride-share in a world of self-driving cars, can't frack a depleted landmass or leave their small coastal town every low season to find other work. It would give people time and autonomy to start their own endeavours, give parents support to care for their children, and help young people to establish themselves, study, and volunteer.

In 2016, Switzerland held a referendum on the notion of a UBI. In 2017, a two-year government-testing program began in Utrecht, Netherlands. The trial seeks to discover whether a UBI will lead to better health outcomes, longer-term job satisfaction, and more wealth creation, as it did in trials in the developing world, or if the Dutch recipients will just sit around on their divans all day doing bucket bongs.

A UBI sounds like a radical plan, but it's actually kinda conservative. It's a way to save capitalism, rather than to overhaul or undermine it. To make the UBI work, there would be no tax concessions, but middle- and higher-income people would be able to invest their payments and become richer, as is their wont. Poor folk could just live. There would still be plenty of people to do the casual work that's around because living on the poverty line isn't much fun. However, if a job is so stultifying, so body- and soul-destroying, that people do not want to do it, the employer would need to entice workers with good conditions, rather than simply relying on a punished underclass.

The most compelling thing about the UBI to me, though, is the potential cultural shift that it would engender. The very premise of a UBI is the insistence that everyone has value independent of their labour. What would that have meant to Serge, or to Chris? How would it have impacted my own feelings of self-worth as I worked to solidify my place in the world? I can't know for sure, but I think it would have stopped the Mickey Rourke monologue. I think it would have allowed me to locate myself within and beside, instead of continuously, and adolescently, against the world.

Rod the careers coach thinks that unpaid internships and volunteering positions at corporations is akin to slavery. Nevertheless, it is an important part of many young people's working lives. It certainly was for Chloe, and for Serge. So I decided to follow their lead, and my father's advice, and put myself out there. I began browsing the extensive unpaid-job ads in my city. Australia is a long way from introducing a UBI, and so my lack of time put me at a disadvantage. I couldn't spend three to five days per week working unpaid in an advertising agency or for an online magazine, earn enough to pay my bills, and have the time to finish this book. Also, being a thirty-something intern is a joke. Vince Vaughn already made a comedy about it. I imagined a staff of twenty-five-year-olds reading my application out loud and giggling, forwarding it around the office. Subject: *Nice PhD, loser*.

For weeks, my inbox was peppered with proforma rejection. I was about to give up when I received a sunny pink email. 'Congratulations! You have been accepted as a volunteer at Business Chicks.' I would be one in a team of volunteers running an event, the email informed me. It would be inspiring. I would learn new skills. I would have the opportunity to 'network with the chicks'.

I dressed for the occasion: a vintage pencil skirt, low court shoes, and a white button-up shirt, the same one I wore in high-school stage band, the same one I have worn for every corporate job interview since. I felt very undercover reporter as I crossed the floor at the casino. It was oddly calm and cool at two in the afternoon on a Monday – sedate, like an airport that no one takes off from. When I got to the River Room, I realised my mistake. Off-duty and aspiring business chicks did not dress like secretaries in *Mad Men*. Their uniform was activewear, black Nikes, and heavy makeup. The volunteers were mostly university students, and a few women in their fifties.

Also, we were not, as it turned out, going to learn anything about business. Instead, we would be working as an assembly line, stuffing gift bags for guests at a corporate breakfast.

The gift bags were pink and poorly made, with 'Business Chicks' scrawled on one side and 'Well-behaved women rarely make history' on the other. They were to be stuffed with 'product', singular, as if the abstract noun would disguise the utter shittiness of these objects. Product was little packets of boob tape and bright green facemasks and dehydrated blueberry powder (for super smoothies!). It was gluten-free crackers and bottles of flavoured oil and plastic salad bowls with fork and spoon moulded into them; bags of sweet-potato chips and sugar-free vodka cruisers and strawberry chia pudding and organic goat soap and discount codes on credit-card rectangles (a subsection of product referred to as 'collateral') and vouchers for cupcakes and coffee and organic cotton tampons in patterned wrappers and water infused with ancient Australian flower essence. Product was unilaterally choked in plastic and utterly pointless. Even the Business Chicks administrators knew this. 'By the time you pull it all together, we could have given out, like, a five-thousand-dollar scholarship or something,' one observed, fanning herself with a stack of collateral.

We worked for six hours without a break. It was hard work, but I tried to chat with the women around me. There were students of economics and business, mostly in their early twenties, ambitious and conservative. I felt self-conscious. I wondered if I passed for a student in my twenties. Two women interned full-time at PricewaterhouseCoopers. One regretted not being able to take more time off work to come back tomorrow. None seemed to have a definite answer to my question about what they wanted to do after uni.

'Something in business,' said one.

Among the non-student volunteers, there was an office manager who re-did everyone else's work, and a former homemaker who spent much of her time volunteering at a food bank but seemed glad she didn't actually have to meet any poor people. One woman announced proudly that she had her own business and was just about to launch her first product. We cheered. 'A true business chick!' said one of the paid workers.

'Why are you here?' I asked a nutritionist who had also recently started her own business.

She thought it would be interesting and, 'just, you know, for the business environment'.

Great piles of trash bordered the River Room: cardboard and bubble wrap and plastic of all kinds. In the Palladium, pinked and streamered for the occasion, we placed goodie bags on seats and decorated the tables with an array of product — pens, nut milk, packets of muesli, and powdered coconut water. The goal was to overwhelm the diners. Each table was crowned with an affirmation: 'The world is your goddamn oyster' or 'Be a goal digger'. Everything was pink, pink, pink here. Positive thinking. Fat- and sugar-free. FAME. PORSCHE. MILLION DOLLARS. HOT YOUNG WIFE.

I peered into the gift bags dubiously. The next morning at dawn, 1,200 women who worked for banks and accounting firms, for real-estate developers and fitness franchises, would turn this room into a tornado of trash and exclamation. The syllables of *beau-ti-ful* would bounce back and forth beneath the chandeliers like tennis balls, punctuated by the faint sound of alarm clocks in the hotel above us. The room would become a human sculpture of the internal mechanisms of a poker machine, replete with spinning cherries and dancing kittens. A winning melody, electronic and upbeat; women cheering for the new Business Chicks CEO. Cheering for the word 'entrepreneur', a word that designates the genius progenitors of product. Cheering monumentally for the guest speaker — a famous domestic goddess. But the most important thing was that, amid the hoopla, they signed up to become premium members of Business Chicks.

'It costs one-ninety-nine but they will receive more than three hundred dollars of beau-ti-ful product, so it's a no-brainer,' I was told.

The most important job of volunteers, then — more important even than wrangling the product — was to get those sign-up sheets. It made me feel like Avon calling. It made me feel as if I rang the number on one of those photocopied telephone posters from the 1990s: 'Make a thousand dollars a week from home, I show you how.' A Ponzi scheme that unfolds like this: you make money selling the idea of making money to someone else, who onsells the idea, and so forth.

After six hours with no break — snacking on oily crisps soaked in synthetic-tasting herb, and pink pudding orbs with the texture and smell of Gak — I needed to get the fuck out of there. I could hear the casino hotting up. Whoops and sighs. Fake waterfalls of money. I slipped out of the River Room and made my way through the punters, past the stores selling handbags and the bars selling too-pink cocktails, and soon I was out on the street. The world expanded to its natural size once more, and my brain loosened.

A few weeks later, I read this in a book by Laurie Penny:

> The 'career woman' is the new aspirational ideal for young girls everywhere: she is a walking CV, her clothing, make-up and cosmetic-surgery choices merely means of upgrading her 'erotic capital' to generate more income for herself and her boss. She is always beautiful, invariably white, and almost entirely fictional. Nonetheless, it is her freedom that is prioritised, as states across the world cut services and provisions for poor women while championing the cause of 'women in boardrooms'.

It's too long to fit on a gift bag for Business Chicks, and it is not *beau-ti-ful*, but it is so, so true.

In the last months of my thirtieth year (I can't write that phrase without thinking of the Ingeborg Bachmann short story that bears that title, describes a morose, disconnected life, and ends with the biblical line 'Rise up and walk! None of your bones is broken'), I had a windfall. I sold the idea for this book to a publisher, and in so doing I became, for the first time, a validated writer, rather than a hobbyist and aspirant quickly ageing out of the opportunities for emerging writers. I got paid an advance of a bit more than nine weeks' pay at minimum wage, and I even had an editor, a woman my age, experiencing similar dilemmas, who was paid to talk to me about them, and about my work, as part of her job. She sent me emails at midnight denaturing my shitty drafts. She clearly had a job she believed in, or at least could not put down.

Suddenly I too was in possession of the magic spell. I did not have to defend myself or my choices. It was wonderful, and fraught. I thought about Chloe's observation. Did I need other people to validate the very real work I had been doing? Clearly, the answer was yes. I found something else out, too: nothing makes you feel grown-up quite like having people to listen to what you have to say.

During the period in which I planned, researched, and wrote this book, several other things happened that impacted on my thinking about work. I finished my PhD and began teaching at universities. The job was fiercely casual and only available half the year. I ran from class to class, ate standing up next to the vending machine, deflected student questions about where they could find me, and wondered, more than once, after reading this or that report on the erosion of our tertiary sector, if I was the modern equivalent of a scab worker. Despite this, the job was undeniably *fancy*. People gave me a different kind of look when I answered the 'what do you do?' question. They looked at me with surprise. They looked at me like I was an adult.

Better yet, I found that I loved teaching. For the first time in my life, I actually looked forward to going to work. It was a revelation. Some days I tilted my nose to sniff the air and smelled cut grass right there in the classroom. At those moments, a student's enthusiasm could rattle in my inner ear like a command, a low, guttural sound: 'Eeeeergiddeegiddeee-giddee.'

At the same time, there were massive and well-reported changes in the two big media corporations in Australia. Fairfax and Murdoch, I read, would no longer preserve the local newsroom model in which journalists write copy and then march it down the hall for subeditors like Dad to fix all the grammatical errors and send back snarky memos about split infinitives and missing conjunctions. Rather, all subediting would now be done in a centralised office, with journalists and subs uploading and downloading copy from a remote database. The news broke, and almost immediately, Dad took a redundancy. He was stoic, but switched from wine to vodka. The money in his severance package was great, but being suddenly unemployed in a remote area at sixty is sad, increasingly common, and puts to mind the fate of Buster, the hard-working horse in *Animal Farm* who is turned into glue and pet food by the pig rulers he worked so hard to instate.

I worried about my younger friends in the media, too. Alice had cracked up laughing when she noted that most of our university peers became journalists. 'They must be the last crop of journalists,' she'd observed. I thought of Priya, whose career in journalism began just as my Dad's was wrapping up.

'It's really bad because management always said we won't be letting any journos go, and yet here we are,' she told me.

'Are you worried about your job?'

'My contract is almost up. Anyway, I'm too worried for my colleagues right now. Some of them have much more to lose. And you know, even though they're letting so many people go, they are still trying to work out a way to keep people like me because I'm young and digitally literate. It's so ageist, actually. I'm under no illusion that I will be the hot young thing for long.'

Priya's comments reminded me of Rod's observation that seniority is not what it used to be, that the modern workplace is geared to the new and cutting-edge. I told her how Dad's redundancy was tantamount to a loss of identity.

'It's sad,' she agreed. 'The industry has totally changed. But you know, if it was like it used to be then, I wouldn't be working there, because I'm a woman and I'm brown. So sometimes I think, what are we actually mourning when we eulogise the good old days?'

Dad thought he would work in newspapers until he died, without taking cuts in grade or salary. In his head, that was how the work hierarchy functioned, and I felt awful watching his sudden and ugly realisation. But I was also worried for Serge, and Chris, and Priya, and me. Were Serge and I hot young things who had missed our chance? Was youth fetishism in the workplace the new narrative of decline? Was it all downhill from thirty? How far down does a hill go before it's a valley, or the ocean floor? And what about all the people who never had a shot at a career-track job?

After the redundancy, Dad valiantly took his own advice and put himself out there. He flew to Melbourne and Sydney to talk to editors at the major papers.

'Listen,' he told them. 'I've been in this game for forty-five years. I can write you a weekly, syndicatable eight-hundred-word column on life in the Top End. "Diary of a Geriatric Crocodile Dundee", or something to that effect.'

The young editors listened patiently. They smiled and nodded while Dad made inappropriate comments about their sex appeal and rattled off the names of long-dead legends. Then they informed him that he was more than welcome to send articles to the relevant editor to be assessed for publication.

'They want me to do the work before I get paid!' Dad said, outraged, chain-smoking and drinking Canadian whiskey on my front stoop. 'This is a brave new world, Junior. I don't envy you.'

At this point, Dad was still three years from retirement age. For a little while he took a job as an online content producer, that same patronisingly titled position I held in talkback radio when I first got out of university.

'I'm a super-user,' he proclaimed with mock pride, referring to his new social media status. His eyes were glazed, though, his shoulders slumped. He was far too thin. 'It's not journalism. I don't know what the fuck it is, but it's not that.'

'Content production?'

'Content. Yeah, right. More Newspeak. It's data entry.'

To commiserate, I told him about the people I knew who manage the social-media profiles of brands, emerging or established. I'd told my psychologist the same story and she shook her head in sympathy, admitting that the first thing she asks a depressed young person is what they do because nine times out of ten it is something vacuous, lonely, and remote.

'They tweet as coffee and socks,' I told Dad. 'They Facebook as minor celebrities.'

He shook his head and took a drink. 'When did Facebook become a verb?'

'Remember Jen from school? Companies send her products and she puts them on top of her boobs and takes photographs.'

'Whatever.'

He'd taken on the vernacular of a 1990s slacker, and seemed to be worse every time I saw him. At dinner, he ate nothing and told the same stories over and over. His hands shook as he lit fresh cigarettes, while others smouldered in the ashtray. Still, he was always ready to glove up for a sledging match. In fact, the matches were deadly, his fighting style kamikaze. Short-term memory shot, he would repeat the same sequence and frustrate me out of the ring. We fought about my life, about his life. I felt as if he wasn't listening. He felt like I was an overgrown brat. After one particularly intense visit, I went home sore, and for a little while, we didn't want to speak to each other.

Dad worked in web-content production for two more years before he received his final redundancy. His career was over, had been over, he realised, for a while. Watching Serge and Dad lose their jobs, and with them, their sense of themselves in the world, was hard. It reminded me not to let myself fall face-first into my work, like falling into a deep pool on a hot day, water filling my ears, eyes squinched shut to the world around me. It also heightened my conception of myself as contingent. Because I am not just a bad adult, but a reaction to this new, radical, and unusual labour environment. I own nothing I couldn't throw in a pile tomorrow. I'm educated and middle class without the security or the economic resources that those words imply. I'm not yet radicalised – I'm still nostalgic, missing things I never had – but I'm poised, paused, ready.

Around the time of Dad's first redundancy, we had our last-ever sledging match. I was visiting over mid-semester break, clutching a draft of my dissertation covered in red pen marks. I knew better than to ask Dad to sub it: academic language galled him, and when we squabbled about the definition of words, it was like fighting in two different martial-arts disciplines, me spinning around in some wild capoeira sequence while Dad just jabbed me repeatedly in the snout. It was better to provoke him in other ways. I left out an article about how late my generation starts working, and the flow-on effects this has in terms of housing, starting families, and our projected retirement savings.

Dad read it, narrowing his eyes under pharmacy bifocals.

'I think it's wrong,' I offered, sparring lightly, bouncing, warming up. 'People still work early, just not in jobs that become their careers. The so-called unskilled jobs are poorly paid and casual, so you are working, but you can't actually save for anything.'

'Young people don't work as early as they used to,' he said.

I gloved up and took a swing. 'I worked at fourteen!'

'Where? The art-supply store?'

'The hairdresser.'

He snorted. 'That's weekend, pocket-money stuff.'

'Yes, because during the week I was at school.'

'You're still at school!' he said with another snort.

I took the hit and got back up.

He sighed. 'Well, if you'd work full-time, you'd have —'

'I'd have what? Money? A house?'

'Probably not.' He grimaced. 'I was going to say you'd have had your confidence shot.'

My arms dropped like lead at my side. The ring dissolved. Maybe it was never really there to begin with. We were together now, bruised, side by side in a hostile terrain that Dad had not been able to see before. *This is what happens*, I thought, *when you attach people's value to their job*. Labour markets fluctuate, but people's needs are fairly stable. We need enough money to live. We need to feel useful. We need to be connected to one another. We need to be accepted and validated in our small place in the world. I didn't know what to say. Finally, we could see each other more clearly, but instead of relief, I felt as if my heart was breaking.

Dad took off his glasses.

'Whatever,' he said, and went back inside the house.

8
FOREVER HOME

Once, as we walked hand in hand across the park, Serge observed that dogs liked my voice. I blushed – it was an excellent compliment. I found myself coming back to it often, and the more I thought about it, the more I understood that if dogs liked my voice, it was because a dog taught me to speak, at nineteen, when I was pliable and eager to please. It was an enjoyable idea, like a real-world version of the t-shirt that claims 'All I know about life I learned from my dog'.

The idea that dogs are faithful and devoted is anthropomorphic and romantic. In fact, dogs are a successful companion species (they are thriving; conservative estimates place 525 million domestic dogs on Earth right now) because they are skilled at getting their needs met. Anyone who has trained a dog has also in turn been trained by a dog. Some of this is common sense. You learn to predict their behaviours, and adjust your own accordingly. Some of this is more profound. A dog teaches you how to love, not in a romantic or emotional sense, but in a practical way. Love as a verb: to love.

Mishka the wayward kelpie cross was with me for over a year before she found what rescue organisations have, adorably, come to call a forever home. I felt awful letting her go. In many ways, she had become my dog. Living with Serge and I had restored her confidence and trust. She learned to chase a stick without worrying that it would become a weapon. She learned to focus a little better, to stop scanning the horizon for threats. She also helped me with my grief. I might never get over Cassady's death, but Mishka showed me that I could love an animal again, and that dog companionship, as praxis, was not lost.

On the day she left, her eyes were white, wide and frightened, staring out of the back of her new person's station wagon. Betrayal! Abandonment! I wanted to grab her, throw my body over her, tell the kind old man who already loved her, no deal! But I bit my lip and walked away because I knew something Mishka did not. Her forever home was a fifty-acre olive farm at the base of a mountain range. The twilight was purple there, and the dawn golden. She'd sleep nights on the end of the bed, and in the morning, she'd survey her fiefdom. *What's that, Mishka? Could it be? By the olive grove: sheep.*

My second foster dog, Boyfriend, arrived six months later. Serge and I had been reticent to take on another hound. Our new lease did not permit pets (though I have never had one that does), and we were enjoying some of the benefits of radical doglessness: the impromptu weekends away, the guiltless late nights, and the freedom to leave butter out on the bench.

Nevertheless, when Boyfriend trotted down our hallway and sat his gangly mass between us on the couch, we were goners.

Boyfriend was just my type. Butch but pretty, with striking eyeliner, and brown markings that formed a dapper suit jacket over his broad white chest and pink stomach. He could jump up and put a paw on each of my shoulders. He was bossy and aggressive in his affections. After a month, I fell in deep love with him. It was as intense as any human crush. We lay on the couch looking into each other's eyes. We ran on the beach, swam together in gentle waves. We took long drives in my recently acquired '93 VW convertible, Boyfriend's giant ears flapping in the warm summer breeze.

If Cassady taught me how to care for others, and Mishka taught me the importance of working with your instincts, Boyfriend taught me how to win friends and influence people. I have never seen such a good illustration of the BDSM concept of 'topping from the bottom' than Boyfriend playing with other dogs at the park. He could make himself as spry as an Italian greyhound, as low to the ground as a dachshund, as gentle and floppy as a puppy, as careful and slow as an aged labrador. Whatever the dog, he would find their level and play to it — or rather, play just below it so that they felt themselves in charge, despite his 40 kilograms of rippling musculature.

'He has such a good nature,' people said, enchanted, watching him play so gently with their toy spoodle, cavoodle, or doodle.

They were half right. Boyfriend was a nice guy, for sure. But he was a politician, too. He was in the practice of getting what he wanted. He wanted to be the centre of attention. He did not want to hear the word 'no' or its guttural, growly doggy equivalent.

Boyfriend was nine months old. This is the most common age for abandoned dogs. Their puppyhood is spent and, if they have not learned a thing or two about living with people, they become unruly or even downright unmanageable. They need help, as all of us do, to grow up. Despite this, when I first brought Boyfriend home, I was amazed at how well behaved he was. It was a ruse. He had me pegged. I realised how foolishly I'd anthropomorphised him when the rescue organisation sent around the behaviourist to assess him.

'The thing is, you are meeting his needs before he even articulates them,' said the behaviourist.

She stood in my lounge room, arms folded, talking only to me. Boyfriend skidded and cavorted between us. He took a flying leap off the couch into the space between us. The behaviourist ignored him.

This drove Boyfriend crazy.

Desperate to get her to look at him, he worked through every trick in the new-dog book. He rolled around at her feet, showing her his belly. He yelped as though he'd been shot. He ran around in circles, sheep-dogging. Spun on the spot chasing his tail. He picked up a magazine from the coffee table and shredded it, looking up adorably. Then he peed on it. He jumped up and barked and cajoled and tried everything again until, exhausted, he did the only thing left and sat placidly at her feet. Only then did she look down and give him that validating scratch behind the ear.

'He wants to set the terms of engagement. You need to set them first,' she said sagely.

It was a daunting charge, and contained another lesson. Part of growing up, I thought, is learning to articulate your needs. This can feel near impossible for humans in a time when one of the key economic activities is generating needs and meeting them before a person even has a chance to formulate them.

I, shopped out and cultured up, had very little idea what I needed, but Boyfriend seemingly needed everything he could get. It was undeniably fun to let him set the terms of engagement, to watch him thrive, his personality developing faster than his caboose. This is the master–slave dialectic, I thought as Boyfriend pulled me down the street in his no-pull harness. Dog training: a perpetual struggle to the death between human and nonhuman, in which neither can die.

Because of Boyfriend's advanced social skills, I too met new people. The dog park near our house became my first proximity-based community since I left the city I grew up in. I looked forward to daily chats with fellow dog owners. I came to rely on them: sometimes chatting to the people at the park would be my only social interaction in a day. Other times I'd go there after a long shift at the produce market, and someone would hand me a cold beer and we'd shoot the shit for an hour or so while the dogs played. Finally, I had friends from other generations, friends who worked and lived in entirely different ways from me. I had stumbled into a 'bumping zone', said my friend Kelly, who worked in community development. It was a spot in which different people collided with one another, broadening their worldviews. Bumping zones, she assured me, were crucial to both community consolidation and social change. But they are also endangered zones. The curated online worlds and real-life social cliques we mostly inhabit these days tend not to bump but to snowball, as similar people all together add false bulk to their own narrow worldviews.

I was pleased. It was a golden period.

It wouldn't last.

When Boyfriend got an excellent adoption application, I cried for a week. Serge and I stayed up late, glumly talking over our options. Could we keep Boyfriend? We desperately wanted to. But to keep him would mean fixing our lives hastily. We would always need to have some outdoor space, which meant, as rent increased, we would need to think about moving rural. I thought about Stacy's house in the country. Would I be involved in the local community, like her, or isolated, as my mother had been? How would we deal with the commute, my six o'clock starts on Sunday morning in the city? I would have to find another survival job, or I could try to get work at a regional university or online. Serge's job would always be in the city, though. We would need to be very organised about work. Boyfriend did not like to be alone for long, so we would have to make arrangements. We checked the prices of doggy daycare. We wondered if we could, eventually, get another dog for company. An attractive, yet radically other, hypothetical life blazed in front of us.

'This is what people do when they decide to have kids,' Serge observed.

He was right. We were even displaying the characteristics of Millennial Mom: we were cautious, anxious to be the perfect parents, and ready to lay down our cash to do so.

'It's kind of worse, because there is much more infrastructure in the city for kids than for giant dogs,' I said, scrolling through an outlandish price list for dog-walking services.

We could do it, though. It would be hard work to organise, but it would be worth it to have Boyfriend in our lives forever. Maybe it was just what we needed. Like the Pope said, it's easier to give your love to the dog.

Wracked with anxiety, we drove out to meet Boyfriend's potential adoptive family.

'Maybe they'll be jerks,' I said hopefully.

I drove with my fingers crossed on the wheel. *Let them have a fence made of puppy skulls*, I thought. *Let them have trucks with offensive bumper stickers.*

Instead, they were a large family who loved one another, and lived on acreage beside the sea. Two other well-cared-for dogs ran to meet us at the gate. Boyfriend immediately struck up a rapport and got playing. The humans showed us their various outdoor living spaces, sharing anecdotes about all the great quality time they spent together enjoying their property and their totally intact and functional adult fantasy. They were wistful, full of love, and charmed by Boyfriend, already imagining him as one of them.

Serge and I cried on the drive home. Boyfriend, sandy and satisfied, slept on the back seat.

'The thing is,' I said, in one of the many painful conversations we had to reassure ourselves that we were doing the right thing, 'if that's Boyfriend's forever home, then he will never have to move. He will always have friends. He will never be left alone when his owners go to work. He will hardly ever be bored. We don't know what our futures will be like, but Boyfriend has the chance to lock it down.'

'It's the right thing to do,' Serge agreed. 'But it makes my heart hurt so bad.'

I made an appointment with my psychologist.

'The dog-lover in me wants to say keep him,' she said. 'But I think you're right to be cautious. You don't know what the next few years hold. There's a lot of uncertainty in your life, and who knows when that will change. You might have to move interstate or overseas to find a job. You might find you move and you still don't have financial or emotional security. You'd give that dog a good life, but you might do it at the expense of your own.'

I snuffled.

'Whatever decision you make, you will be okay. And so will he. So I say hold off. Let him go. You can keep fostering, keep doing this good work that you have started.'

The snuffle became a heave.

'But listen,' she said, pushing the tissues towards me. 'Here's something you have learned: you are a woman who needs a dog. So spend a few years finding out more about the world. Take all the opportunities that present themselves, find a place for yourself, and then get one.'

I closed my eyes and, through the fog, conjured up a small block, a sea breeze and, galumphing through the trees, a canine with the heft and sociability of Boyfriend, the determination and intelligence of Cassady, and the full heart of Mishka. I opened my eyes before it could turn, panting, to face me.

Forever home. I snuffled into the tissue.

It was a dream-board moment. A secular prayer to the gods of love and real estate.

In Hong Kong, the city with the most expensive real estate in the world, a think tank found that it would take a couple under thirty-five years old 14.5 years to save enough for a deposit on a small apartment. The government, the think tank advised, should get out in front of the crisis and build 'hostels' for young people to live in while they save. It's an evocative real-estate dystopia: rows of young people prostrate in bunks, exhausted, saving every cent of their income for their own tiny box in which to teeter on the edge of one of the most densely populated islands on Earth.

At its most basic level, real estate is code for the amount of private space you can draw around your body. Culturally, though, owning a home can seem like the most important adult accoutrement, no matter the cost. In late capitalism, the American Dream – which involves throwing words such as 'liberty' and 'freedom' around, and is an insistence that a person who works hard can achieve anything – coalesces in the home as a site in which to exercise those freedoms. In the country I live in, we have a more recent and explicit version. Our Great Australian Dream ditches the appeal to higher values and insists that hard work *and* real estate are essential for a good life.

Like many people my age, I have never been a homeowner. Recently, after being evicted from two rental homes in two years (no fault of my own — the market was booming, and the owners wanted to sell), I wrote an op-ed about the plight of the renter. In it, I expressed my feeling that renters pay top dollar but are usually treated poorly. On Facebook and Twitter, I received a lot of support. My article resonated with the experience of many of my peers who rent in family groups or with friends. Online comments were another matter. Here, people seemed legitimately flummoxed by my complaints. After all, if I wanted to, I could have simply bought a house and avoided all this unpleasantness. Apparently, it was inconceivable to some that there were thirty-somethings walking around without home-deposit-size bank balances, and, if this truth had to be conceded, the fault must surely rest with the individual.

'Owning a property is not a right,' ran one comment. 'If you have made decisions in your life (having kids for example) that now preclude you from owning, then bad luck. Be thankful you have a roof over your head at all.'

Of course I was thankful, in the same way I was thankful to have money for food and access to clean water.

Generational sledging is ugliest when the subject is real estate.

Every Australian of my parents' generation seems to have a story about a terrace home with water glimpses that they almost bought for twenty grand and a hand job. These stories — monotonous, formally identical with those of lottery tickets lost or found — bubble up with the warm beer at intergenerational social events. They sour the coleslaw and cause sausage chunks to stick in the throat.

'Did I tell you about the three-bedroom terrace on the harbour that your mother and I . . .' says Dad, again.

I plug my ears with indignation.

Some people his age bought those houses and now they are wealthy. In Australia, real-estate investment is class consolidation. Being locked out of the housing market is, for middle-class young people, like having the privileges your status implies suspended indefinitely. Stamped with some official line: 'The middle class is currently under review. Check back later.'

In 2014, Australia's federal treasurer, Joe Hockey, stated, like a dullard commenter on an online op-ed, that 'if housing was unaffordable, no one would be buying it,' and advised entitled young people that the first step to buying a house is 'getting a good job that pays good money'.

Right. Yep. Got it. I'll make a list of great advice I've been given regarding home ownership and put this pearl right up there next to 'move somewhere cheaper' and 'don't eat out'.

As always, though, the sledging goes both ways. A memorable article in *The Sydney Morning Herald* deployed generational warfare, accusing older people of Bogarting all the freestanding houses. *Won't you think of the children!* the article cried out, insisting on the deprivation of those forced to grow up in apartments, bonsaied and gnarled (presumably like those in developing nations?). Clickbaiting, the comments section began with the prompt 'should older homeowners be forced to downsize?' It was the kind of copy I used to bang out at the radio station. Another real-estate dystopia flashed before my eyes: retirees marched out of their lifelong homes by armed guards as hordes of children descended on well-tended Victorians, trampling the daffodils, swinging from the cracking boughs of the crab-apple tree, as their hip, young parents looked on.

In Australia, as in many parts of the world, population growth has led to housing shortages, and high purchase and rental costs. Two of our capital cities are in the top-ten most expensive housing markets in the world; Sydney is number two. Unsustainable sprawl creeps from their perimeters into the scrub and farmland beyond. We suffer from a lack of housing diversity: four-bedroom 'McMansions' are out of reach for lower-income families, while tiny apartments in toaster buildings are suitable only for students, singles, and trippers. Inner-city real estate is unaffordable, outer-suburban life isolated – unless you happen to be one in a growing number of families sharing apartments on the outskirts of the city, in which case your troubles have a different timbre.

Unsurprisingly, homelessness is on the rise in cities globally, and yet the view that the fault for this lies with the individual still holds prominence. In Melbourne in January 2017, while the mayor reportedly began talks about the forced removal of the homeless, the Victoria Police Chief Commissioner insisted that the people who are sleeping rough are not homeless at all but 'choosing to camp' because 'there's more people to shake down for money' in the summer, when the Australian Open is on. In winter, though, the *Herald Sun* insisted that homeless freeloaders were flocking to Melbourne for 'free food, clothes, showers and dental treatment'. A more sympathetic article in *The Age* ran with a photograph captioned 'a mother and child pass the homeless people camp on Flinders Street', contrasting the procreative image of adult success with the abject failure of being homeless. When I saw this picture, I remembered how Serge's boss had turned up his nose at this rising visibility of homelessness. 'You don't want your kids to have to see that,' he had said, over his morning latte.

Housing unaffordability is not limited to capital cities. Australia also achieves a global ranking of 'severely unaffordable' in areas outside the cities: Wingecarribee and Tweed Heads in New South Wales, and the Gold Coast and the Sunshine Coast in Queensland, are all brightly decorated. In 2015, the median price for a house in the Bendigo suburb of Ascot rose by 31 per cent. And there are other problems in the regional centres, too. Kelly recently came back to the city from a desert town where she had been living for more than seven years. She wanted to reconnect with city life, needed the infrastructure that was there, but also, at thirty-five, she wanted to settle in her desert home if only fracking was not affecting the groundwater. 'I just can't afford to buy a house in a town that will have no drinking water in five years,' she said. She wasn't referring to her bank account, but rather to the increasing political divide in which rural areas are seen as resource hubs to support the cities, at any cost to the people who live there.

Sometimes buying a piece of the land brings a whole new insecurity. Officially declared 'affordable' places such as

Karratha, Port Hedland, and Kalgoorlie in Western Australia, and Gladstone in Queensland, quake in the aftershock of the mining boom. What kinds of investments were these places before and then after their minerals were extracted? What kinds of homes do they make now?

Decreasing home ownership for young adults is a global trend. In the United States in 2014, home-ownership rates for people under thirty-five dropped to the lowest ever recorded and then, in 2015, soaring rental costs saw a slight nudge in this trend, as young people tried to work out whether to pitch their tent on the rock or in the hard place. In the last quarter of 2016, these rates were only slightly (.08%) lower, but the eighteen-to-thirty-five demographic took the smallest share of home ownership, with the lowest recorded ownership rates since 1965. And rent is steadily increasing in most cities. A Harvard University–run study predicted that by 2025, fifteen million North American households will spend more than half their income on rent.

In my state, recent changes to tax laws for first home buyers will give middle-income earners looking to buy their first home a leg up into the market. My mum sent me through the news item marked with a row of exclamation points in the subject line. I read it through twice. *This will help me,* I thought joylessly. I couldn't shake the cringing feeling that this help came at a higher cost than the figures on the page. Giving middle-class young people placating tax breaks to maintain the illusion of a stable economic reality is a short-sighted approach to a problem that is exacerbating the gap between comfortable and homeless in this country. An equitable solution would limit tax concessions on investment properties in order to halt the eternally increasing cost of houses, or better yet, make renting affordable and secure for tenants. House prices, even with concessions, are still too high for the majority.

Apart from the expense, my own experience as a renter is of begging and hustling for small repairs, being treated as an enemy by the people to whom I pay a third of my income, and finally, inevitably, being booted out unceremoniously when the market looks tasty. As a renter, particularly in the inner city, you are to take what you are given and be thankful. A friend recently relayed how a property manager, after rejecting her application for a bedsit, had asked why she didn't just get a boyfriend she could move in with. When I got the keys to my first rental in Melbourne, there was a shrivelled roast chicken in the oven that was certainly not on the condition report. Nevertheless, the renter must treat the real-estate agent like a high-ranking government official. I wear high-heels when house-hunting; I carry a smart black folio full of documentation. I lick arse and smile thank you.

Unsurprisingly, then, the appeal of the Dream endures. To have your own space. To be free of the rental grind. To put nails in the wall and plant a garden. To live with an animal — without the fear of the neighbour dobbing you in to the property manager. To make friends with your neighbours. These are seductive adult fantasies many of us have been training for since we were children playing house.

Despite my own lack of a stable income, I have been obsessively monitoring real-estate websites for years, typing in search words like wishing on stars.

'We could afford to move to [insert far off pseudo-city here],' I would quip to Serge, enlarging interactive sales maps.

He would smile dubiously. There's no point talking to me when I have floated away in the real-estate bubble. My brain no longer functions logically. It becomes clogged with bathroom fixtures, off-street car parks, and rooftop entertainment spaces. I become convinced that only home ownership will make me feel, finally, like a real adult. Even though I know that what most people own isn't a home but a mortgage product, I still scroll through floor plans, heart aching, trying to imagine a more habitable future.

I was surprised one morning when I discovered that my bank was more than happy to preapprove me for a home loan – my lack of stable income and the infamy of the recent subprime mortgage crisis notwithstanding. My jaw dropped in disbelief when the hold music cut out and the kind young man on the other end of the phone line said, 'Good news, Miss Doyle – we can preapprove a loan of $330,000. You can go and start bidding today!'

It was a Saturday. I was hung-over. Melancholic. Looking for distraction from the adult fantasies of others in my Facebook feed. I had been despondently browsing real-estate sites and had called the bank on a whim. I flushed with a strange pride when the operator evaluated and praised my 'good financial conduct'. He was not concerned with my casual employment.

He could see my savings history down to the school banking program, to those dollar-coin deposits. Back then, I used a bank-supplied plastic moneybox. It was a space alien, squat, not grey but orange, descended from a far-flung intergalactic civilisation to recruit six-year-old terrestrial banking customers.

The man in the call centre could follow my financial life story all the way to the overcautious adult I had become. He could see, at a glance, the $10 bottles of red, the vast sums spent on rent, and my tricky method of never letting my credit-card debt exceed my savings, carefully balancing the two so that I have both the illusion of thrift and of largesse. He could see enough to surmise that I'm the kind of gal who could service a fat loan. Does that sound dirty? I mean it that way: *service my fat loan.*

Besides, what's the worst that could happen? I take a third job to meet my repayments and avoid homelessness? I'm forced to sell early and the bank takes the property, along with my repayments, while I fall into penury and debt? They don't have debtor's prison anymore — or at least, not right now.

Full of adrenaline and aspiration, I dragged Serge to an auction.

'Welcome to Edgewater Towers,' declared a framed 1960s print advertisement. 'Fabulous Manhattan living comes to Melbourne.' The print hung strategically in the lobby of what I later learned was the first privately developed high-rise apartment block in inner Melbourne. I had just finished watching the final season of *Mad Men*, so to me, it was a pop-cultural omen. The apartment for sale — three conservatively valued rooms with views of a rollercoaster – had shag carpet on the wall. In my mind, I was already rubbing up against it, singing 'Zou Bisou Bisou'.

A small crowd squeezed into the lounge-room-cum-kitchen.

'I think you should buy it,' Serge whispered in my ear, his passion for shopping transferred effortlessly to big-ticket items.

'I don't even know how to bid.'

'Do you want me to do the bidding?'

Was he serious? I could smell last night's bourbon on his breath.

We did not discuss the pile of unpaid bills on top of the fridge or the fact that Serge already carries an unmanageable debt. Neither of us mentioned how the last home-ownership conversation we had involved building a semi-permanent tent out of plexiglass on a semi-remote piece of coastline known for its wind and sand flies. All at once, we were ready for a new life. We were ready to make our own Great Australian Dream come true. We felt good. We felt grown up.

The auctioneer opened the bidding at $250,000.

Serge squeezed my hand. 'Should I?' he said.

Earlier, he had dragged me away from a woman who was telling me how the body corporate fees were astronomical. 'She's trying to psych you out,' he explained.

'Do I hear two hundred and eighty thousand?' said the auctioneer.

Serge looked at me expectantly.

'Four hundred and fifty thousand,' said a voice from the back.

Annnd, we're out.

Our hands slackened. We giggled foolishly as the roller-coaster rattled and crashed like nothing you would find in Manhattan. I suddenly remembered that in 1979 it came right off those brittle wooden rails and crashed into playground lore forever. Perhaps someone stood in this very apartment and watched it splinter and fall, listening to the screams, unable to finish their apéritif. That person probably bought the joint for twenty grand and a hand job.

'Five hundred thousand.'

A gasp went up. This was double the real estate agent's estimated price.

I looked around at the auction contenders. A woman with a flash handbag and a severe hairstyle, gripping a black folder, refusing to smile at her eager twentyish daughter. A fifty-something couple in his 'n' hers boat shoes. A middle-aged woman who, when the auctioneer goaded her by suggesting that another bid might secure a beach lifestyle in time for summer, admitted she 'already owns one in this building'.

'Even better — buy this for a higher price and your own goes up in value,' said the auctioneer. 'Ladies and gentlemen, this is one smart investor.'

Rollercoasters splintered and fell in my mind's eye.

Finally, a couple in their late thirties secured the place. She looked pregnant. He looked shaken. They may just have gone $200,000 over budget, but you have to follow the dream.

Some millennials are taking ingenious routes in order to secure their piece of the dream. Serge's best friend Nora, her two sisters, and their parents, partners, and children all went in on the mortgage on a huge stucco palace in a rapidly gentrifying inner-western suburb of Sydney. The home, with its columns, fancy brickwork, and outdoor pizza oven, was probably built by a successful Italian family some time during the disco era. Nora's family split the house into multiple apartments. They all live together, sharing babysitting duties and gardening in a way that is sometimes utopian and sometimes smothering.

'There are downsides,' Nora said. 'Like, I look out my window and there's my whole family standing there. I don't really get the option to not engage. It can be hard to establish boundaries. But the pros outweigh the cons, for sure. When I moved in, I was pregnant. I was also alone. It was kind of a case of having a plan versus having no plan, you know?'

I did know.

'I couldn't afford to buy, or even rent anything on my own — at least, not anywhere I would want to live. I probably would have brought up my kid in a share house rather than move out to the middle of nowhere.' She paused. 'That probably sounds really boojie.'

I understood her cringing feeling. There is something icky about middle-class people in Australia, a country with a deplorable colonial history of violent displacement, whining about housing, insisting on living in the suburbs we like to socialise and work in. There is something gross, too, about newspaper articles insisting that Australian children need backyards and that apartment living is totally unsuitable for families. But the idea of Nora and her child in an apartment, hours from her friends and family, her work and community, made me feel anxious anyway.

'I was just thinking the other day how lucky all our kids are. They get their own space, but there are always other kids around to play with. Plus, my sisters and I help each other with the domestic stuff, and we all chip in for a cleaner,' said Nora, reminding me of Gillian and her polyamorous triad.

Multiple generations in one house is an increasingly popular way to deal with the cost of housing in the United Kingdom, too. In 2012, *The Independent* reported that there were more than 500,000 households containing three or more generations, predicting that another 50,000 will be added by 2019.

And anyway, arrangements such as Nora's are not innovative, but hark back to other places and times. In traditional Chinese culture, multiple generations often live in one household. It's not unusual for Spanish and Italian households to contain parents, adult children, and grandchildren. The nuclear family is, tellingly, a Western term that came to prominence during the post-war prosperity in which my parents grew up. It is an exceptional moment in history, not a long-term standard that we should expect to last forever.

The current conversation about real estate is mainly about the loss of what have been seen as middle-class entitlements. While inner-urban millennials with the resources and skills to turn a shed into a tiny house can be celebrated for their ingenuity and ethics, and siblings who pull together to buy together are adapting to a cutthroat market, people living in public housing, squats, or on the street are still treated with disdain.

There is disdain left over, of course, for kiddults who live with their parents for too long. In Japan, they are dubbed the *parasaito shinguru*, 'parasite singles', and scapegoated for social problems ranging from the ageing population to the economic recession. In the United States and Australia, they are 'boomerang children', because when you throw them out they come right back to you. In Italy, a cabinet minister described adults who live with their parents as 'bamboccioni', translated variously as 'big babies' or 'big dummy boys'.

At thirty-three, Alex is a bamboccioni of the Melbourne suburbs. He lives in the backyard of his parents' brick home in a cul-de-sac reminiscent of Ramsay Street from *Neighbours*, along with his two younger brothers, and, at various other times, his older sisters and their partners. 'I did move out for a little while,' he told me. 'The rent was huge, and the house was cramped and kind of a dump. At some point I had to come home for health reasons, and then I just stayed. I mean, it's really nice out here.'

Alex showed me his bungalow at the edge of an extensive and neatly trimmed lawn. His bed looked too short for him. It was flanked by an old lamp and a La-Z-Boy recliner. His books were piled in neat stacks, and he'd tacked a couple of newspaper prints to the wall above an old upright piano. It could be the room of a teenager, albeit a very studious one.

'I don't know if I'm, you know, infantilised, because my mum is just over there,' he said, laughing, pointing to the big house. 'I suppose it took me a long time to find myself. I was in my late twenties before I started to understand who I was and what I wanted – or what I didn't want, which is sometimes an easier place to start.'

Alex doesn't want a lot of the same things that I don't want. He doesn't want to work full-time in a job he hates. He doesn't want kids. He doesn't want to pay rent. He embodies almost every reason the media totes for labelling my generation as irresponsible kiddults. I asked Alex what he thinks about that, and he laughed. 'I think fuck off! I have been responsible for myself since I was seventeen. I just happen to live at home because that way I can save. And because I like it here. My brothers are here too. We all get along. We look after each other.'

We went inside to meet his family. His mother hugged me. There was a cheese platter. There was champagne with strawberries in the bottom of the glass. It was a warm and gorgeous night. Dinner was served as to a television family. A window above the dining table looked onto a reserve where neighbourhood dogs chased sticks and rolled jubilantly in the cut grass. A soccer ball bounced against a fence.

'I told my neighbours you were coming around, and they said to send you over to them,' said Kathy, the matriarch. 'No one can get rid of their kids 'round here.'

A heavily pregnant daughter and her partner picked at a plate of crudités. One by one, Kathy's sons emerged: healthy, suntanned men who worked together as electricians and parked their new vans in a row on the lawn.

'Do you think you will ever move out?' I asked the youngest.

'I think Mum might be giving me a nudge,' he said, smiling broadly and cutting another piece of smoked Gouda.

Kathy's face contracted into a happy wince. 'You should get a sense of it,' she said, and I got the feeling that in this family, moving out is an important experience, like travelling or sports. Something you can always come home from.

We plated up four kinds of barbeque and switched from champagne to shiraz. I made a gag about wanting to move in too, and Kathy laughed, pleased. Then her face settled into a look of utter seriousness. 'You are always welcome,' she said.

Perhaps she wanted an extra daughter, I thought, or perhaps she was looking to palm off a son.

We sat down to dine amid sepia-toned scenes: Kathy's parents, sheep farmers from the country. Her grandmother and great aunt walking their horses into the schoolyard. A dapper-looking gent in what looked like the 1940s, crouching by a swell motorcycle. Alex's Dad, Mick, in his heyday, with a splendid handlebar moustache.

There were also baby photos, of course. All five children and their friends at various stages of 1980s and 1990s shame.

The difference between the photos of Kathy's family of origin and those of her own kids was as distinct as their lives. She was shipped off to boarding school from the farm and never went back. After high school, she trained as a nurse, living in dormitories guarded by nuns, until she and some friends could afford to rent their own house. 'It was all so much fun!' she said. 'But these are different times.'

Kathy and Mick didn't seem worried about their bamboccioni.

The dinner was characterised by a distinct lack of judgement: no mean quips, very little sarcasm. The boys cleared the table.

'Do you have to leave?' said Kathy, when, at eleven, I said my goodbyes.

I wished I didn't. If this was my family, I might have got myself another wine, another bowl of ice-cream, and taken a nap on the couch in front of the tennis.

Then again, I might not. I was out of home at seventeen, aching for life to start. At that age, adulthood meant independence; it's only now that I see it also means connection. How do you find this sense of permanence and community when the nuts and bolts of your life – your home and your neighbourhood – is leased to you on a twelve-month basis?

Seeking my own alternatives, I took off early from the produce market one Sunday and drove east to the oldest intentional community in Victoria. It was a drab summer afternoon: overcast, with the promise of swelter. I'd been working since dawn – stacking carrots, giving advice on which grain to choose for which purpose, listening to the desperate rubrics of people who think that organic food will cure their cancers and make them immortal. It did strike me that I might not be in the right mood to go and hang out with real hippies, but the commune only opened its doors once a month for a work day and tour, the first point of contact for those searching for another way to live.

On the website, the community manifesto resonated with my experience, even though it was written in the late 1970s. It spoke of the isolation of the suburban nuclear family.

It discussed pollution, crowding, unaffordable rent, lack of public infrastructure, and loss of community. An accompanying photograph of the residents showed a happy group of adults and children, assembled together in a rotunda. Some clutched tinnies of local beer or glasses of plonk, some held the hands of children ready to scamper out of the picture. It looked like a pin-up family Christmas, with not even a fuzz of dreadlock or a swirl of tie-dye to suggest anything countercultural.

My spirits lifted as the city diminished in my rear-view. The highway, a by-product of sprawl and unsustainable industry, is my happy place. I love driving fast over long, straight flats. When the sprawl finally gave way to the more picturesque valley beyond, I felt light and free. I passed through the golden wine country and climbed a mountain, singing Loretta Lynn loud, singing it right to the end of the album, at which point I realised I was lost.

'Turn left,' insisted the schoolma'am voice of the GPS, gesturing into a plunging wisp of track snaking through the thick bush.

I ignored her, going offline and further up the mountain. Somewhere near the crest, I almost T-barred a slick black BMW paused dangerously, mid three-point-turn across the narrow road. The harried driver regarded me with wide, desperate eyes. 'I'm trying to find an intentional community that's around here,' she said.

'Me, too!'

Frankie, a thirty-year-old from the affluent bayside suburbs of Melbourne, was commune shopping. She was also a dream interview: a millennial malcontent, anxious about adulthood, looking for alternatives in all the hidden places. She'd spent the last six months learning permaculture principles at a place in Queensland, and was now looking for somewhere to settle in Victoria. She wanted to split her time fifty-fifty between the southern bush and the northern rainforest, and avoid the blasting heat of Australian summers. Frankie had known 'since high school' that she wanted a different kind of living arrangement, she told me. She was single, polyamorous, optimistic, and scathing of nuclear families and suburban life. Or perhaps scathing was too strong a word — all her opinions were carefully tempered with university-taught defensiveness. She prefaced every statement with disclaimers like 'I hear what you are saying, and I totally respect that, but …'

After we located the commune, we wandered around the grounds until we found John, a sixty-something hippy dressed like a sports photographer, with a Gandalf beard. In an old Victorian house that acted as a community-centre-cum-clubhouse and smelled like Play-Doh and toast, he delivered a portentous monologue about the 245-hectare site, which used to be a country hotel. His co-residents, the younger Ethan and Emma, arrived to balance out his measured perspective and call bullshit at every opportunity.

'I'm one of the newer members of the community,' said Ethan, a handsome man in his mid-forties. 'Well, actually, John is the newest.'

John blushed red under his beard. 'I was a member in the 1970s for a few years,' he said. 'I've been away for a long time.'

Sledging! Frankie looked uncomfortable, but I felt right at home.

The community, while founded around shared values and as an alternative to what everyone I met there referred to as 'mainstream society', still had some fairly mainstream social characteristics.

'Oh, yeah,' said Emma, smirking at the display of competiveness between the two men. 'Everything you've got out there is concentrated here.'

We snaked out across the ridgeline. Clusters of houses, organised by personality and lifestyle, dotted the clearings in the bush. One cluster belonged to young families with kids, another to single people in their midlife, still another to retirees. It was the whole lifecycle arranged perfectly in the scrub.

'This is the best cluster,' declared Ethan, in his British accent, waving his hand across a small glen like a lord. 'For this is where Emma and I live.'

He showed us the mudbrick and strawbale homes favoured by the community members. They reminded me of the hippy houses in the town where I was born, an architecture of mid-century optimism. The separate dwellings ostensibly shared a garden, but no commune members toiled there, as in the paintings of socialist realism. Frankie looked disappointed. 'Do you have much time all together?' she asked.

Ethan and Emma exchanged a searching look.

'I think we had a thing last Christmas?' said Ethan.

Frankie looked destroyed.

'At the beginning, all we did was build,' John explained. 'We kept saying to one another, won't it be great when the building is done so we can get down to community building? What we didn't realise was that working hard together like that was the community.'

It was a cliff note to the history of all utopian movements: once you build your utopia, you have to live in it.

We three women hung back as the tour continued. We bashed our way through the scrub and, with the skilled precision possessed by most female outsiders, casually got to the core of one another's lives. Frankie, so earnest she seared my corneas, reminded me of Julianne Moore's character in the movie *Safe*, with her sensitivity to city toxins and her yearning to be sucked into a pristine bubble. Emma was more pragmatic, tempering her New Age affirmations ('You have to be the change you want to see in the world') with some refreshing frankness. 'I'm not one of these vagina worshippers,' she told me, confidentially. 'A lot of that menstrual moon-goddess stuff goes on up here, but you can leave me right out of it, that's for sure.'

I laughed, rolling my eyes in agreement. If I lived here, we would be BFFs in no time.

As Emma showed us her tiny house site, I locked eyes on a tall young man with scruffy hair and rippling, work-wrought muscles. Suddenly, I was transported into a possible future: me and the hotty in a mudbrick, working on collaborative welding projects, tending the garden, and practising some hardcore naked Reiki.

I smiled coquettishly.

In fact, this kind of future was the only possibility at the commune. Its heteronormativity and failure to cater for other models of living was the thing that initially made Emma reticent to commit. 'It can be pretty isolating for a childfree woman. Mostly it's families, and all anyone wants to talk about is their kids, their friends' kids, teaching the kids, what the kids think, wear, do. It's so boring. I used to have a single girlfriend up here, but she moved away. It just got too hard for her.'

The vast space, the great slope of the mountain, suddenly felt as sad as a cocktail lounge at closing time.

'What's your story?' Frankie asked me, breaking the morose silence.

My cheeks flushed with guilt. *I'm a writer!* I wanted to say. *A parasite! Don't talk candidly with me, you wonderful, earnest people.*

But actually, we three had a lot in common. I was drawn to this kind of arrangement for similar reasons to Frankie and Emma — I wanted to feel part of a community, I didn't want to work three jobs to service a city mortgage, I didn't want kids of my own but I liked the idea of having them around (especially the teenagers, whom Emma was proud to be a confidant to in difficult times). I wanted long evenings talking politics, literature, and floor plans while the possums scurried through the scrub and the dogs barked in the valley below. And I'm an uncomfortable mass of contradictions, as they all were. I'm territorial but desperate for connection, like John; pragmatic yet idealistic, like Emma; competitive and irreverent, like Ethan; thirty and searching for a satisfying life, like Frankie.

Oh, please love me, shelter me, have me at your collective table!

'I want to find out more about the alternatives,' I said instead.

Frankie nodded enthusiastically. She had some of the same fervour I saw in the eyes of the Business Chicks, despite her opposite worldview.

A car pulled up, the boomer occupants smiling sharkishly. 'Are any of you interested in the Deans' place?' the driver asked.

'We'll talk about that later,' John muttered.

We all felt suddenly undressed. Ethan tried to cover by making a joke about hawkers, but it fell flat. The beast of real estate had run his sharp claw through the scrim of ideals. A tiny tractor moved a flock of sheep through a green square below us. Rows of olive trees stood to bitter attention.

'So there are vacant houses for sale here?'

'Yes,' said Mark. 'We have one that has been empty for almost five years. There was one family who were interested, but the cluster has to vote unanimously in favour of them. The last buyers didn't get the vote.'

'How much is it?'

Mark stalled. He talked about shares and full membership petitioning and how moving onto the commune is a process. He talked about the future and the past, and about the philosophy of the place.

Finally, he gave me a number.

Annnnnd, I'm out.

Safely ensconced in the unintentionality of the city, I wondered what my generation's model for intentional living would be. Are we too jaded and locked out for utopian aspirations?

Al doesn't think so. I read about the twenty-year-old 'entrepreneur and change-maker' in an article on a real-estate website. (It's not lost on me, the transmutation of the old cry 'I'm only reading this for the articles' from the porno to the real-estate classifieds.) In the article, Al talked about the power of our generation. He insisted we were at a better moment in history than we thought. He focused his change-making drive on the way that millennials arrange their lives. Base, his newest business endeavour, sought to 'create and invest in spaces and experiences to cultivate communities, culture, and personal growth'. Al, it seemed, had found a way to capitalise on both the imperative for young people to share space in an increasingly expensive rental market, and their need to feel as though their lives are making an impact, in a time when activism and getting involved in the community is a matter of clicking 'share' or 'like'. Base would be a 'curated sharehouse' for 'nomadic changemakers'. Something like a cross between *Big Brother* and a hippy commune in an inner-city warehouse. But all the locks on the doors would open with an iPhone app. That was an important feature. When I interviewed him on the phone, Al repeated it twice.

The idea for Base came to him when he was doing the festival circuit, introducing crowds at Rainbow Serpent and Burning Man to his vision for 'living onely' – that is, 'coming together, alive'.

'What if we could work together to create the abundance, the sustainability, and the love that we truly are?' he asked an audience of fourteen-year-olds in his TEDxYouth talk. 'We are a rainforest, the sun can be a shared vision ... My mission is to become the mycorrhizal fungi that the trees use to communicate.'

In my experience, share houses usually communicated via passive-aggressive notes and suggestively placed cleaning products, but that was the past, according to Al. The future is Base: abundant, onely, and fungal.

An ardent young man, Al possessed a tick-like propensity for dropping nonsensical motivational platitudes. 'You only see the wind when it causes a disturbance,' he said. 'That's a quote I like to use.' He was fervent about the power of the internet. And sharing. And diagrams and permaculture. He took the idea for Base to an incubator, one that 'incubates people rather than ideas'. He toured similar ventures in the United States and then came back to Australia, looked for a corporate sponsor, and began curating the Base applicants.

'They had to be hungry and driven,' he told me. 'With a clear idea of where they are going. Being driven towards something. Or away from something. We asked them, "If you had the wealth of Bill Gates, would you drive it in a particular direction?" We asked them their favourite colour, why they are wearing the shoes they are wearing. All these choices are important. You drive the car you drive for a reason.'

I swallowed.

Al saw his generation as driven towards connection. 'It's hard to find people without a social conscience now,' he said, sounding not unlike the Goldman Sachs report on marketing to millennials. 'People are so connected; they have networks all over the world. But when we want to look someone in the eye, give them a hug, all this anxiety comes up. Today, all these autoimmune diseases come from stress. The stress we put on ourselves. We are so reactive. We want to control everything. We are not breathing properly. But also, we are not outletting.'

For Al, all words were well-placed to become verbs. As he spoke, his speakerphone picked up the yogic gush of city streets across the car windscreen.

'Base is a way to approach that. It's a hybrid space. A hostel doesn't have a sense of groundedness, but in a typical share house you don't have that influx of ideas. We are asking, how do we bring the tribal living philosophy into the modern world?'

I did not ask him which particular tribal living philosophy he was referring to. Probably not one with a gift economy.

'We want to use the space as an incubator. Some of the profits will be to develop the space. But a portion will go into a hedge fund to invest in the ideas that come out of the space. The ideas that come out of Base will be a lot more heart-centred,' he said. 'We want to create exponential impact … And residual impact.'

So far, all impact is theoretical. But after a spate of press coverage (the article went minor-viral in a look-at-this-douchebag kind of way), Al began making connections that were less about social change and more about real estate. If Al can play his cards right, he could become a new kind of ideologically packaged pseudo-landlord, a real-estate curator.

'We want to create a culture,' he insisted, earnestly, as though he were actually born and raised in an incubator and emerged just yesterday, sticky, feathered, and tweeting. 'The culture can be seen as the wind — we want to create the wind. That's just a little analogy I use.'

'Cool,' I replied. Because what else can you say?

It's easy to rag on Al. He is everything people hate about millennials. And he is his very own real-estate dystopia: the one where young people are so desperate to control their space and make money from it to boot that they are willing to draw up minor cosmologies and enlist everything from ancient ritual to actuarial principles to make it seem meaningful. But like all canny investors, he also has some insights into what is trending — in this case, the way that younger people live now, and will in the future. Al insisted that living arrangements need to make space for the fact that his generation (it's my generation too, though I feel curmudgeonly beyond belief) are more nomadic and connected. Base will have 'nomad rooms' for short stays because the occupants might have 'collaborators' across the world who they haven't met IRL. Its occupancy will fluctuate — a continual flow of new ideas and perspectives filtering through the space, incubating everything, fungal and otherwise.

I was fairly sure that Al had never read William Gibson's *Neuromancer*, with its evocation of youth in storage, renting their bodies and minds while they save money and energy through induced hibernation. When I asked about the future of Base, I realised that Al's future was posthumanist, not in the Gibsonian sense but in the way anticipated by Ray Kurzweil, who insists that soon we will reach the singularity, a point where technology hits the exponential curve, nanobots self-replicate, and we can saturate the universe with intelligence.

'Living is life,' said Al, explaining his position. 'It's not just where we actually sleep. Living is exactly that, life.'

Another dystopia emerged, this from his pen: scribbled diagrams of the concept of onely unfurled across the sky, blocking the sun, the stars, and every private thought you ever had. The whole universe as just more real estate for our asinine self-contemplations.

A feeling of desperation rose in my gullet. I could taste metal, as if I'd been sucking on a brass coin. Al reminded me of the rupture that snakes through my cohort. There are those of us who believe that our eco-branded property development, or corporate breakfast Ponzi scheme, or tech start-up, or social enterprise, or diet will change the world, and there are those of us who stand on highways holding doomsday signs up to each other and trading wisecracks as another Prius drives by. Is this just the timeless division between the earnest and the cynical, or is it something particularly of-the-now? As a highway-sign holder, it feels as if the entrepreneur pin-ups can see the danger, but cannot think outside the vocabulary of acquisition and innovation they were raised on. In late capitalism, social change is a commodity.

I needed to get out of the house and into the anonymous streets. I wanted to interact with the world *as it was*. I wanted to experience the kind of connection I often found in being just one more human trying to get along in an imperfect but pleasant day-to-day. I rode my bike through the back streets of my gentrifying neighbourhood. In Melbourne, people are out and about all the time, even midday. Young mothers in activewear pushed strollers along café strips. Men with beards overtook me on sleek, minimal bicycles. Groups of friends occupied tables at outdoor cafes and bars.

This, I thought, is what would pass for German sociologist Jürgen Habermas' 'bourgeois public sphere' today. The place where democracy exists. A bumping zone. A place where people come together to discuss civic life. Though actually, here, they were more likely to be discussing real estate.

I passed a development site every couple of blocks. Lately, it seemed as though advertisements for these off-the-plan apartments were aimed particularly at me. Billboards showed happy bearded men on bicycles and happy groups at cafes, reflecting the neighbourhood back at itself, insisting that you, yes you, belong here. Buy in now.

A few years ago, a study of water usage revealed how many new apartments were empty, owned by offshore investors who would rather wait out the term of appreciation than trouble with renters. 'Ghost Tower Warning', ran the headline.

I rode past an old warehouse site with banners out the front. It looked like a display suite, and I was drawn in, despite myself, yanked through the doors by my real-estate obsession.

The warehouse was actually filled with a local university's interior architecture graduate exhibition. I wandered around, looking at the models and plans, struck by the depressingly urgent contexts they took on. Projects cited increasing urban homelessness, the need for public space in the face of diminishing residential space per capita, the imperative for meaningful intersections between architecture, the body, and everyday life: architecture as a way to endure increasingly volatile environmental conditions and scarcity of resources.

The images and models, however, all looked oddly similar — greyscale figures in their twenties and thirties, some alone, some in couples, a few children. Shadow-puppet lives in hyper-functional spaces. The labels read 'Toilet Pavilion', 'Bathing Pavilion', 'Meditation Alcove'. It was the design equivalent of a 'Keep Calm and Carry On' sticker. One project showed the skeletal substructure of a building, revealed post-catastrophe as a usable space. In the drawing, a young couple gazed, unthinkably, at an artwork (flood- and fire-resistant, I assumed) hanging on a steel beam. In other images, people stared at the exposed brick as though this, in view of events, had become an anchor for calm reflection. Through all of these stark, designed worlds, lone youthful figures tramped, wearing headphones, suggesting rich inner worlds, despite life in a bunker or the ruins of the city. I sniffed the air: the sweet odour of apocalypse.

Looking around the actual space of the exhibition confirmed that we were already living in this context. We were all staring at beams and exposed brick, listening to something privately through headphones. Contemplating shelter and the problems that arise beyond it. We were all anticipating, aestheticising, buying and selling our crisis.

The idea of an intentional community, of having the means to make a decision about where and how to live, is a dream for many people. Policy that substantially restricts property investments and tax breaks might change this somewhat. So might rent-capping and long leases. But for all my dystopian imagination, I can not see an Australian government making these kinds of moves in a way that will genuinely allow lower-income people to afford housing. Especially not the kind that advises young home-seekers to 'get a good job that pays good money', or awards tax breaks as a palliative measure for middle-class expectations instead of addressing the broader economic reality in which we come of age.

Serge and I would not be moving into a commune or any of our parents' backyards. We couldn't share 40 metres of converted shed, even if a team of designers came around every Sunday to beat us over the head with *The Life-Changing Magic of Tidying Up*. We didn't take out a mortgage on an ultra-modern shoebox, despite the bonus that the bank would be able to hose it down and flip it for a profit after we slay each other in it.

Finally, and more pressingly, we did not keep Boyfriend.

Boyfriend left. He trotted down the hall as casually as when he arrived. He did not look back. We were torn right up to the last week, when we received a letter, like a missive from our mean reality. Our landlord was selling; we needed to vacate in twelve weeks.

'I guess we did the right thing,' I whimpered at the dog park the last time, as I said goodbye to my friends.

I had lived in this neighbourhood, within walking distance of this dog park, for the longest I'd lived anywhere. I had been expecting this moment for some time, anxiously watching our letterbox for the tell-tale agent's stamp as the two-bedder up the street sold for $1.2 million.

Looking through the rental listings, Serge and I considered our options and suddenly found ourselves articulating very different needs, both in terms of housing and what we wanted from our lives. It was a shock, even though we had been squabbling. We were still unable to have conversations about the future without dredging up the silt of the past. We were exhausted, desperate, and confused.

When Boyfriend left, it highlighted, once more, how we did not know the shape of our adult lives, either singularly or together. We had been a couple for seven years and engaged for two, but after our eviction, instead of reigniting the wedding discussion, we took two separate leases and prepared, intentionally and with love, to live apart.

9
POST-ADULT

'How is your new living situation?' my psychologist asked when I saw her after the big move.

'Actually, it's kind of amazing.'

She raised an eyebrow. I had moved north, far north of the city and my former list of desirable suburbs to live. It had been a difficult thing to explain to people. Mostly, it went something like, 'Yes, we are moving out … No, we're not breaking up … Yes, we are still engaged,' though this last status had lost its particularity and assumed a foggy, private meaning.

Some people got it.

'I think what you two are doing is really loving and generous,' Olivia said to me, sitting in the large garden of my new, adult share house in the suburbs. 'And I know it's hard. The whole game is set up for couples. But if you guys had just moved into some tiny flat together because the alternatives are too logistically and emotionally fraught, I'd be so sad for you both.'

Some people kind of got it.

'So Serge will live with musicians and you will live with feminists,' Dad said, emptying his glass. 'Do you think that will actually *help*?'

My mother grimaced. 'What I'm hearing is that you need to take some time to re-evaluate,' she active-listened, pushing a piece of fennel around a plate.

Serge and I persevered. 'We are doing the right thing,' we reminded ourselves, a mantra we'd been repeating ever since Boyfriend trotted out of our lives. But there were moments when even we didn't get it. On the first night in my new room, I was suddenly stricken with anxiety. I called Serge, in tears. 'What have we done?' I lamented. 'I've turned into a thirty-something shed-dwelling weirdo.'

One of my first boyfriends had been just this kind of weirdo, thirty and living out the back of a share house full of younger people, smoking bongs and listening to Sonic Youth all day. I loved him, for sure, and I respected his rebellious choices, but at nineteen had never thought for a minute that I would become him.

My new house was large and lovely, though, and my detached room was more of a bungalow than a shed. Crucially, it afforded privacy and space to write. And my housemates – two women on the cusp of thirty who called themselves 'the singletons' and baulked at the idea of sharing a bedroom with anyone – were wonderful. After a month in these new digs, I felt light and energised.

'I've got all this time,' I told my psychologist. 'There are three of us doing the housework, so the place is basically always clean.

Plus, sometimes they cook me a meal. We hang out, but it's no problem to get up and go to your room. I write at strange times now. The other day I was writing at nine at night, which used to be the time for watching TV, cleaning the kitchen after cooking – you know, couple time.'

My psychologist looked impressed. She was thinking, no doubt, about her husband and twenty-nine-year-old daughter, who lived at home. About her house and the noisy neighbours who had been renovating for far too long. 'It's an incredible concept, isn't it,' she said, wistfully. 'Just grown-up women working and living together in a space.'

We went on to talk about emotional labour: the work associated with being female. We agreed that it was most often the women who listened, and cleaned, and took care of the administrative work. Women badgered about eating well and going to the doctor and getting exercise. They problem-solved and tried to brighten the lives of the people they were close to. I had been doing this for years, long before Serge and I even met. Where had I learned this? When had I accepted it was my role?

In the last few years of cohabitation, Serge and I were either tripping over each other or rippling through the other's life like sudden breeze. So much of the time we spent together was exhausted, stressed, and needy. Most evenings we were unable to do anything but slump into each other. At other times, domestic obstacles blocked the flow of love through our house. A pile of dishes in the sink. A door slamming accidentally as someone crept into or out of the house at dawn. Wet washing removed from the machine and placed back in the basket or, worst of all, a handwritten note on the refrigerator door. It doesn't matter how many *x*s or hearts you append to such texts, their meaning is unequivocal: no one is getting what they want, and there is no time to talk about it.

This is a horribly adult problem.

Living apart heralded a new honeymoon period. We went on dates. We were kinder to one another. We began, once more, to brighten each other's lives. Our time together was scanter, yes, but more substantial. We noticed how often we could not spend an evening together because we were too tired, and realised that living apart meant that any choice to share our time was conscious. The move felt, to me at least, like the first truly mature decision we had made together in a long time. We were far from Vegas now, and it was wonderful. For a while I felt as if we had been handed a cheat that allowed us to move through a really hard level of the game of life.

Then Dad's partner, Kate, called out of the blue.

'He's not doing well,' she said. 'I want him to go to the hospital, but he's so stubborn.'

'The hospital?' I had no idea what she was talking about. It took me a while to get it straight. Dad had been drinking. No, not like he always had. This was different, and it had been going on for a while. Kate admitted she'd taken him to hospital once already that year, and had warned him that the next time she'd pick up the phone and call me.

I got her to put him on. 'Dad?'

He sighed. A resigned, almost musical sound.

'I'm dying, Briohny,' he said.

For a moment, I couldn't speak. When I finally did, my voice was tiny, like a child's. 'Why do you think that, Dad?'

He sighed again. 'I can't do it, I really can't.'

His voice was light with booze and sorrow. A wispy thing that slid across the phone line. A memory emerged, of being ten, heading home from the pub with Dad as he sang and I skipped ahead to pat the neighbourhood cats. 'Oh, Barry was going to cook tonight, but he's not now,' he sung in that balmy Sydney twilight. 'He was going to, but he's not now, but he's not now.'

It was a strangely sad song.

'Please let Kate take you to the hospital,' I said.

When he hung up the phone, I booked a flight.

Psychologists say that the children of addicts, who take on emotional tasks well before they are developmentally ready for them, grow up to feel like imposters in their adult lives, constantly sure that someone will find them out for what they are — just kids, silly, unsure, and afraid. Perhaps if I had read that before I began writing this book, I would have ditched the project, chalked my interest in adult fantasies up to a glitch in early development and spent some extra time and cash with my own psychologist. It would have been easier, less painful. But if this is a resonant description of my position in the world, it might also be true for my dad, and probably his dad, and so on, back down the lineage to that ancient village distillery where the Doyles first eased their restless souls. If so, Dad worked up one hell of a performance in his lifetime. He delivered his lines, his edicts, his declarations of how things are and will be, all the while pushing those imposter feelings down, deep down. Those uncomfortable questions and thoughts that demand an audience: *What do I know about the world? Who the hell am I to say? I hope no one finds out about me.*

He took the shot and refilled. He delivered his lines.

Maybe he thought that the most important thing was to be believed. Maybe the booze made him drunk with belief. Then, finally, it didn't work anymore.

And maybe, too, he always suspected that this was where his path would lead. 'There goes another old subeditor,' he had often said, with real compassion, when we saw an old man living rough.

When I was eight, Dad had a restaurant, and I lived with him during school holidays. He let me bring appetisers to tables, and collect a share of the tips at the end of the night. I saved those tips up for years in a catering-size mustard jar, adding to it every time I visited. When the restaurant closed, he brought it with him to Sydney, throwing his own change in at the end of each day. Finally, it was full to the brim. A fortune. Dad walked me through the shopping centre to the bank so that I could change my nest egg for notes, but on the way there we passed a Salvation Army collector and, without hesitation, Dad handed over the loot. He met the old man's look of stunned gratitude with deference, palm forward as he walked away quickly, dragging his outraged child behind him. 'They take care of us when no one else will,' he said, and handed me a fresh fifty from his wallet.

The discussion was over. Did he have a flash that twenty-five years later, he would move into one of their residential programs, with a stack of detective novels and a carton of smokes?

Dad looked like hell when I got to him, but he wasn't dying. He was strong enough to check out of the hospital, against the doctor's advice, and take his place in the chair on the front deck. He was wracked with DTs. Shockingly frail. Just bones, birdlike when I tried to hug him. I bit my lip to keep from crying. He tried to talk, but only the cadence of his voice was intact. The words were abstract and disconnected, a surreal semantics. He'd lost his hold on language.

Kate was worn down. She'd been protecting his privacy and fretting over his health for more than a year, alone. Their relationship had become caustic, sour, like spilled whiskey. She loved him, sure, but he needed to get clean. And he needed to do it somewhere else.

'If this had happened six months ago, he could have come down to stay with me and Serge. But I can't put him on the couch in my share house,' I said, and the realisation sent me into a spiral, a new kind of real-estate panic. Living in a share house forever wasn't a cheat! It was a temporary fix at best. Where the hell would my dad go? What happened if my mother's health suffered? And if I had to rent forever, where would I go when I was old? Later, Serge and I joked that this was the only way we'd become landlords — presiding over a sublet shantytown of backyard bungalows tenanted by our single parents, whose fierce independence outlasted the infrastructure it was built on.

As soon as Kate left for work, Dad requested whiskey, and I spent an hour on the phone to the drug and alcohol people, who explained the mechanics of withdrawals. We had been withholding the booze, soap-opera style. But Dad couldn't stop drinking all at once outside the hospital environment, they told me, or he'd more than likely have a fit and die. It takes time to change the needs of a body. We habituate to our lives.

I found it incredible that I'd loved an alcoholic for so long, yet knew nothing about what alcoholism actually was.

Dad had always been an alcoholic. I realised that when, on more than one occasion, an estranged friend of his had enquired after his health with knowing, regretful tones. The first time this happened, it was a shock. The friend had not seen Dad since he was my age. Back then, he was a respected journalist and hobby farmer who read me *The Magic Pudding*, doing all the voices. I remembered him in other times and places: in his early forties, for example, waiting at the front gate as we pulled into the drive, a sheepish look on his face that made my mother's hands turn white around the steering wheel. He had a halcyon of sorts when he moved away from us, to a seaside town. At the restaurant, he danced me around on his feet while a jazz trio sung 'Don't Get Around Much Anymore', but it was only a few years later that he was sleeping on a mattress on the floor of a Glebe bedsit, washing shirts in the kitchen sink, tying his border collie to the Hills Hoist when he left for work. I remembered him squabbling with reporters at a pub in Surry Hills. I remembered young women slamming the door on him, theatrics I did not realise were unusual. Later, we lived together for five years, while I finished high school. It must have been a tough adjustment for him, but perhaps it was also another halcyon. Another chance at something meaningful. By that time, I knew he had struggled with alcohol, but it didn't ever seem to matter. He got along fine, and so did I. When I moved out, we hoisted his old futon over the back fence and he moved into a room above his favourite pub and then later, up north. Dad was restless, but resilient. He could get through this.

By the end of the weekend, we'd made a plan. Dad would go to his brother's house in Sydney, spending a month or so in the room where his own father drank himself to death. He'd get on waiting lists at detox units, and once he'd completed a program, he could talk to Kate about coming back. Maybe, she said, maybe if he was clean.

It was a big maybe. But when I saw him three weeks later, he'd halved his daily intake and was at the top of a hospital waiting list. He went into detox on his sixty-fifth birthday, the day before my thirty-third. I hugged him goodbye. He felt a little more solid in my arms. And he lingered longer there, too, even though he'd never been much of a hugger.

I felt an overwhelming sense of awe, watching my father step boldly into a radically other kind of life. *We never stop*, I thought. *We are never finished growing up*.

Retirement happened to Dad. It wasn't something he planned, and he wasn't ready for it. 'At this stage, Briohny, I'll work until I fall over,' he'd told me, repeatedly, even after his penultimate redundancy.

This was what one did, of course, right up until the nineteenth century when, in 1889, German Chancellor Otto von Bismarck invented pensions as a way to stave off the Marxist groundswell. Before that, there had been minor stipends for soldiers in some places and times, such as Ancient Rome and in sixteenth-century Britain, but nothing like what we call retirement today. While private pensions became available for some professions in the United States in 1875, Social Security payments were introduced much later: it was a way to get older workers out of jobs during the Great Depression. In the United Kingdom, the first pensions arrived in 1908, but it was no huge cost to the public purse. You had to be seventy to qualify, and at that time the average life expectancy was only forty-seven. Despite reforms in 1921, pensions were not available to British women until 1940, just nine years before my parents were born. In Australia, we had a small old-age pension paid to men over the age of sixty-five from 1901, and women from 1910, in order, ostensibly, to keep the elderly from starving.

Modern retirement depends on longer life expectancy, and suggests the right to comfort in old age. It has been funded since the mid- to late twentieth century in most developed countries through a combination of government pensions and individual investments. But this idea was concocted during times of plenty, with lower populations. Retirement as we know it is young, and fragile.

Dad's claim that he'd work until he dropped was not motivated by zeal for the job. In his heyday, he loved journalism, but as the trade changed, he grew weary of the office politics and the monotony. 'Oh, I don't wanna,' I remember him saying in the mornings, as he pottered about and prepared for work. But he didn't know what else to do, and so, when retirement was forced upon him after his content-producer job, he did nothing much at all.

Kate worried. He should work as a consultant, she suggested. He should get a part-time job in PR. He should volunteer. Do yoga. Join a fishing club. Write a weekly column. Write a memoir. Travel. Join a band. Teach community college. Mentor. Learn a language. Could I help? Perhaps we could work on something together? I brushed her off. Her suggestions were exhausting. I was too busy, I reasoned, and anyway, after forty years of full-time work, I thought Dad deserved a bit of nothing much. Reading books, watching midday movies, playing the guitar, and pottering in the yard. Isn't this what retirement is for?

In 1972, Simone de Beauvoir wrote, 'The reason that the retired man is rendered hopeless by the want of meaning in his present life is that the meaning of his existence has been stolen from him.' I don't think Dad would be comfortable with this statement, but in many ways, it fits. Work was the activity that gave him a solid identity. When work stopped, 'nothing much' turned into a whiskey-sweet oblivion.

'I used to work and drink, and then I just drank,' Dad told his detox counsellor.

The counsellor made him write a list of the things he liked to do. He handed it over and she nodded significantly. Did he notice anything about it? she asked. He did not. But when she joked that it made for a very lonely weekend, he realised that every activity he liked was best done alone. Reading. Writing. Photography.

'Is there anything wrong with wanting to be alone most of the time?' he asked me.

He'd finished his first detox and come to see me in Melbourne before heading north to find out if he still had a home there.

'I don't know,' I said. I felt awkward. That could be my list, too, give or take.

I thought, not for the first time, about how I come from a family of loners – my mother, ten years older than her siblings and shipped off to boarding school early, and my father, ten years younger than his brother, who remained behind when the family emigrated a second time.

Dad always venerated solitude. He taught me to love all the other lone wolves. Philip Marlowe. Dirty Harry. Mad Max. Randle McMurphy. Cool Hand Luke. The Dude. They were all men, all living in a fantasy world custom-built for one. It took half of my twenties to realise how little my own world corresponded. I learned to value relationships, and realised that as I aged, though there might not be more people in my life, I had access to different kinds of relationships. I had been a student, then a teacher. I had been cared for, and cared for others. I had maintained passionate relationships with texts and put texts of my own into the world, and they created new relationships beyond me. They opened my life outwards, even while I still had trouble doing this in the day-to-day. I knew, too, that relationships were always in flux. The meaning of the word *daughter*, for instance, was very different at three and at thirty-three.

'I mostly want to be alone, too,' I told Dad. 'But I don't want to be totally alone. I mean, I don't want to be isolated.'

'No.' He stubbed out his cigarette in the lid of the pack and sighed. He looked overwrought and weary, like a dog that has been tied up so long he's stopped barking. 'No, I don't want that either.'

There is too much emotional legacy passed from parent to child. You carry their ways of being into worlds that outlast and outcast them. Part of maturity, I suspect, is identifying these legacies, dusting them off, and discarding the ones you don't value.

Dad and I walked on through the streets of Carlton, the boozy haunt of his youth. We passed all the places we usually stopped at. Jimmy Watson's Wine Bar, where Dad usually drank several glasses of pinot and retold several stories about the 1970s. Percy's Pub, now closed, where Percy had sat at the bar until the end, nursing a pot of draught.

'I suppose that was the last real pub in Carlton,' Dad said sadly as we passed by, walking towards the cinema.

'So, what do you think you will do?' I said again, despite the impossibility of the question.

'I don't know, Briohny,' he said.

'Will you move?' I persisted.

'If I have to.'

Where would he go, though? He didn't own a house. What was left of the redundancy payments and his superannuation was enough to boost his pension for a few years, he told me, but what about after that? Rent on a studio apartment in most capital cities would total more than half his pension. And that would be a tiny room to smoke and read in. *Depressing*, I thought. *Enough to drive a man to drink*.

I realised that this must be a fairly common problem for older people. Renting in the inner city is insecure and expensive, and it's often impossible to get repairs. Add the needs of older people to this, and it becomes untenable.

Shane from the Housing for the Aged Action Group confirmed to me that older renters are subject to even worse treatment than other renters. Landlords, he explained, get pissy about adhering to universal design principles, such as installing walk-in showers and stair rails. Older renters are afraid to ask for repairs in case it lands them with an eviction notice. He had horror stories about squalid conditions, or decades-old rental agreements between a landlord and an older tenant dissolved when the landlord dies, and hungry inheritors come on the scene. 'And as mobility decreases, it's difficult to even look at rental houses. The older you are, the harder it is to move every six months. Financially, but also logistically,' Shane said.

Homelessness is an increasing risk for older Australians. On the census night in 2011, as Dad tried to remodel my marital status, there were at least 14,851 homeless people over the age of fifty-five filling out that form, and 18,740 people the same age had received help from homelessness services in the past year. That's only the number that had the chance to do the census, but it's a figure that Homelessness Australia expects to increase as the average age of the population does. There are going to be more old people over the next fifty years. McCrindle Research suggests that the population pyramid, of which older people were once housed in the tapering tip, will be inverted by 2020. This will increase pressure on aged, health, and housing services. This is reflected in the United States, too: in 2016, *The New York Times* reported that people over fifty make up 31 per cent of the homeless population, a jump of 20 per cent since 2007.

'I'm thinking about a Kombi van,' Dad said, rehashing a last-resort plan I'd heard many times over the years.

Finally, though, it seemed like an actual option – joining the grey nomads in an endless trip around the country. In fact, Dad was anticipating something that has already become a trend in the United States, where older workers – retirement savings decimated by the Great Recession – have lost their homes and moved into campervans. These 'workampers' are a growing underclass of grey-haired itinerants. They travel the country, boondocking in free campsites or Walmart car parks. They work seasonally at corporations such as Amazon, or harvesting sugar beets, or maintaining state parks.

'Workampers are plug-and-play labor,' journalist Jessica Bruder wrote for *Harper's* in 2014, 'the epitome of convenience for employers in search of seasonal staffing. They appear where and when they are needed. They bring their own homes, transforming trailer parks into ephemeral company towns that empty out once the jobs are gone. They aren't around long enough to unionize.'

Bruder described a vital community that relished their freedom and were grateful for the chance to earn minimum wage. These were people over sixty-five who described themselves as retired, but were still working hard. 'Some geriatric migrants I met already seemed one injury or broken axle away from true homelessness. Vans and trailers don't last forever. Neither do bodies,' she observed.

Dad had a reasonable amount of super. Enough for a while, if he moved into a van. And he put a good spin on it. (He could spin anything. He had even spun detox: they had made pizza, and the Narcotics Anonymous people had stories that made him look like a choirboy.)

But the Kombi plan worried me. It reawakened dormant fears I'd fostered when I first left home: Dad dropping off the radar, getting sick and not telling me, freezing to death on a park bench. These fears became worse. They seemed less like the occupational hazards of a committed drinker and more like gross injustice for an old man. I understood retirement in a modern sense. After a long life, there should be some comfort. There should be love and security. Even Dad admitted that there were things to dislike about the image of an old man alone in a caravan park. Australia is bigger and less populated than the United States. If there was a community for people like him, Dad might find it – or he might just get lost in that great expanse.

This conversation was the first of many talks like this between us. The established power dynamic sloughed off like an old snakeskin, and beneath we were both raw and sensitive.

We realised we had to get to know each other all over again, and there wasn't much time, not half as much as we had already spent. I noticed that sober, Dad was not as quick to crack a disparaging joke. He was gentler, and needed gentleness in return. He flinched when I said something abrasive and glib, and I realised that I had to find a new tone and pitch. I thought about the things I liked least about myself. How easily I get frustrated and snap at people, or make blunt jokes like reflex kicks. How much of this was learned, a response to making myself heard in a lifelong dialogue with my father, half jacked-up and itching to spar? At night, my head swam with a complicated mess of worry. How could I help Dad to find his feet when I had barely found my own?

One thing was clear, though. Our situations demonstrated that those so-called adult milestones – financial independence, family, home, and career – are not permanent states or insurance policies. Using these things to define adulthood underscores a paternal story where only the economically self-sufficient are grown-ups, with the right to make choices about their lives. We see this in the rhetoric about choice in old age. Old people who refuse to go into aged care are being difficult or selfish, despite the lack of services to help them make the transition.

Annie told me how her grandmother had rehearsed a speech until it was almost all she could say: 'I know there will come a time when I have to go into care, but that time is not now.' She didn't want to leave her garden, and at the independent living facility where she resided, they had promised she could get a pet. She wanted a budgie. She hated the idea of missing out on this small joy.

'Why can't she have a budgie and a garden plot in hospice care?' I asked.

Annie didn't know.

Ageing is not something we talk enough about. Or, rather, we define it in alarmist discourse. The ageing population is an apocalyptic-sounding narrative. We talk about anti-ageing, and positive ageing, giving the impression, as writer Melanie Joosten points out in her essay collection A *Long Time Coming*, that the correct way to age is to stay young. Ageing is regarded, for the most part, with fear and distaste. The ageing body is hidden. We are not used to seeing the old out and about. We exclude them. We are shocked by old age — a ridiculous thing, given its inevitability, for the lucky at least.

Schooled in decline narratives, we start practising our dread of ageing early. At sixteen, I thought twenty-three was past it. At thirty, the narrative of decline asserted itself again: thirty-somethings complaining about their inability to recover from a big night, their lack of energy, or suddenly-hard-to-ignore back problems.

I remembered Dad joking with me at seven, when I got my first real headache. 'It's all downhill from here, mate,' he said.

When Cassady was in her final years of life, we could not walk to the shops without inspiring pity. I tried to march through the side glances, but I was defensive. Sure, her hips were wonky. Sometimes, one of her legs was stiff, and her gait became unsteady. Her snout was a furless reminder of radiation treatment. Her muzzle was grey, and her eyes cloudier than they had been as a pup. But she still loved the beach, to play stick, to cuddle and stroll and growl at smaller dogs and noisy children.

I loved her more than ever. It was an almost unbearable love in those later years, having watched her recover from illness, witnessed her immense reserves of stoicism and trust. And in old age, she was so sweet: easier to please, less volatile. I'm probably anthropomorphising inexcusably, but she really did seem wise. It's hard to write about, this precious time, because thinking of her as an old dog reminds me how little time she got to be old. A dog can age fourteen years in eighteen months, it's estimated, while the luckiest of humans might be old for decades, pension willing. Cassady's old age was lovely, but fleeting. We deserved to take a walk in the sun without comment.

I snapped rude retorts at *tsk*ing busy-bodies. I found their enthusiastically proffered perspectives insensitive beyond belief. 'The poor old thing,' they exclaimed, and 'Oh, no,' and sometimes, shockingly, 'She's past it.'

Children would ask shy questions. 'What's wrong with her?' they wanted to know.

'Nothing is wrong,' I tried to explain, as patiently as I could. 'She's old, but she's quite happy.'

The parents nodded and smiled, as though we were conspiring on a myth, as though a happy old age was just a lovely story for children, like the frog that wants to go to the stars.

Even among friends, the consensus seemed to be that I should 'put her down' to avoid the indignity of being old. Whose indignity? I thought. Certainly not Cassady's. She had never been much for dignity. She scuttled across the floor to drop a spitty tennis ball in my lap. Took a nap on top of a plot of daisies.

'Living things want to live,' I began to recite to these well-meaning friends. I sounded like a Christian, but was there no space between a God-filled fervour for life and a mercenary insistence on death as soon as one's capability was reduced? What did these people think that life was for?

Our distain for ageing is a key component in a narrative of decline through which the human lifecycle is reduced to an assessment of utility. We are obsessed with productivity, an inhuman imperative, which discounts the reality of our embodied, imperfect, fragile lives. There must be a way to craft a counter-narrative. Can we think about ageing phenomenologically, and look on with curiosity and respect as we grow old? I remembered Iris Marion Young's work on the subjective experience of pregnancy, her efforts to underscore its phenomenology as an antidote to its medicalisation. Young regarded her new materiality with curiosity, interest, joy, and sorrow. Is such a framework possible with ageing? And if so, whose work is it to do? I suspect that the undertaking needs to be intergenerational. As I read Joosten's essays, I found a desire for this kind of approach in her persistent question 'what does it feel like to be old?' It's a question that at first sounds impertinent, but is actually fundamental.

My parents couldn't answer this question, of course, because they were still young. They were part of one of the first cohorts for which retirement was not synonymous with old age but rather an extra phase of adulthood, a time in which one is free, once more, to determine the shape of life beyond the dictates of work. Mum belonged to the first cohort of professional female retirees. That is, she was part of a new demographic, a generation of educated, middle-class women who worked professionally for the majority of their lives, retiring and receiving benefits as independent workers rather than spouses. She described the experience of her last months at work as 'very emotional. There is an awful lot to feel.' She spent much of the time in her office, shredding documents and listening to Vivaldi.

There are an increasing number of self-help books on this time of life for Mum to add to her library. Their titles are telling: *Not Your Mother's Retirement* and *Smart Women Don't Retire — They Break Free*. When we think of retirement stereotypes, we think of men fishing, or couples settled or travelling. We don't think so much of older single women in positions of repose. Even in writing that phrase, I realised I had no idea what such a position looked like.

Neither did Mum. In some sense, she faced similar pressures to me. Though she had a career behind her, for an adult of her age she still lacked many of the proper accoutrements. She had no husband. There were no grandchildren running around. She worried, as she prepared to finish work, about being productive and useful, two words she often used that made me feel uncomfortable. Can we never be rid of these words?

In the eighteen months after she left professional work for good, Mum learned another language, spent nine months in Italy, and started writing a weekly gardening column in a local paper. She joined the sixty-five-plus demographic that make up 31 per cent of our volunteer workforce, taking on a role as a counsellor for refugees. When I asked her about relaxing, she quipped that she was breaking some of her previous rules, 'like no reading for pleasure before four o'clock'.

I wanted to tell her to chill out. Calm down. Stop it. Or to repeat the phrase she used on me when I was small: *I think you are working yourself into a bit of a tizz.* But that would be insensitive and wrongheaded. Worse, to say these things would be to participate in the logic that insists old age signifies a new childhood where we do not know what's best for us. Besides, Mum's work after retirement existed in defiance of the ageist and sexist rhetoric that sought to curtail her life. Beyond her economic role, she would be central, not marginal.

Despite their different positions, Mum's and Dad's respective retirements did have common characteristics. Approaching her two-year anniversary of retirement, Mum started to worry and express regret. 'I really should have worked for longer,' she fretted. 'It's just that I was so exhausted and sickly. I really thought I was coming to the end. But since I've stopped working, I have all this energy, and I realise I might live a lot longer than I thought. A lot longer than I budgeted for.'

Both my parents also professed no fear of death, though they were terrified of ageing past the ability to support or care for themselves. 'Drop me off at the edge of the cliff with a brick and a note that says "Jump",' Dad said, while Mum had been extolling assisted-suicide plans since her late forties. It was only recently that she softened the agenda from 'pills in the drawer and you can help me take them' (usually accompanied by a comic throat-slitting sound produced in the back of the soft palate) to a living will that removed my power of attorney and ensured that no doctor could intervene to keep her alive through anything worse than a bad cough. ('I have asthma. A bad cough is really bad.') This, she claimed, was a document of last resort. Mum hoped she'd have the resources to do herself in before setting foot in a hospital.

We had these conversations so regularly they transmuted into a grim bit.

'The only help you will get from me is companionship on a journey to somewhere Nordic and liberal,' I joked.

'Oh, no! Pleeeeease, Briohny, won't you kill me?'

'I'll take you out to lunch and drop you off at the clinic. Then I will go and see a black-metal show. It's my last offer.'

'Pleeeeease, Briohny. Kill your mummy.'

My mother is a vegetarian. She doesn't smoke and hardly drinks. She lives alone in a small city. Every day, she takes brisk constitutionals on the hill that presides over her street. Her house glistens with solar panels and water tanks. She has two patches at the community garden. She could survive the apocalypse out there, but drawn-out, humiliating dotage is never far from her mind.

'You might find that as death draws near, you become quite

attached to life,' I said as I initialled each page of her living will. She'd laid out cheese and wine for the occasion.

'I won't!' she said, in her mock girlish tone. Then she switched to a more macabre mode. 'Lots of things can go wrong, you know. If you overdose, you have to be sure you do it right, or you end up in a hospital, incontinent, with renal failure and all the rest of it. That's where the living will kicks in,' she said, patting the contract between us protectively.

I signed and dated the final page.

'Thank you, my darling!' she said, giving me a theatrical hug. 'Now! This is an unpasteurised brie from France. And these Black Russian tomatoes were picked from the garden today especially.'

Despite everything Freud had explained, I didn't want to kill my mother. I understood that it was selfish, but I didn't even want to hear about her suicide plans. I couldn't see a way to live easily in the aftermath of such an event. Mum's fixation on assisted suicide intensified in the years after she neglected to help her own mother by 'putting a pillow over her head'. According to Mum, Grandma 'should have had a plan', and therefore shared the blame for this protracted expiration. She would not be so remiss.

As I looked on at my parents' transition into retirement, I thought about what this time of life would look like for me. I should have stayed off the internet but couldn't: I was only three years past my freaked-out thirtieth, and suddenly sixty-five looked too close for comfort. I found out I should be saving 9 per cent of my income for retirement. I should be automating my financial life. I should be making voluntary super contributions and have insurance and build equity – and then spam windows started popping up for Sportsbet and some kind of pornographic interactive anime and a program to make a lazy grand from home every day and then I remembered that I had not even paid off my student debt and I didn't know if I would have a job next year, so actually there was no point getting into this loop at the moment. I closed the windows to let in some fresh air, conjuring an image of a stylish old lady in huge black sunglasses driving a fast car along an ocean-snaking road.

Good. Done. Retirement planned.

But of course that's just another adult fantasy; the reality is not so simple. People my age who work in aged services or social research have a bleak vision of the future. 'I don't expect there to be any public housing or a pension by the time we are retirement age,' Shane said. In fact, he expected a future for himself much like that experienced by most of his clients. 'They are stressed, depressed, and socially isolated by the time they see me. But it's definitely a structural problem, and dealing with it on a case-by-case basis is insane.'

Kirsten, an architectural researcher, studied development responses to the ageing population. Property developers, she told me, were trying to rebrand independent-living facilities as luxury apartment blocks in order to ease the stress of downsizing. They wanted to make assisted living into an aspirational product. But this solution was only for the rich and reluctant. Kirsten said her work, though interesting, had amped up her thirty-something real-estate panic. 'No one can afford to spend 80 per cent of their pension on rent. It feels like hype sometimes, but the ability to own your own house is actually more crucial than we realise,' she told me.

In Australia, the current government is aiming to pass legislation to raise the pension age to seventy by 2035, my fifty-second year. Proponents of this measure argue that it's a good thing – that because we are living longer, it makes sense to work longer, both in broader economic terms and for our own emotional and financial wellbeing. These claims condense groups with diverse needs, as if the average longer life expectancy might cancel out the varied realities of millions of older individuals. And if our generation works longer, won't our children's generation have even less opportunity than we did?

Meanwhile, the news is peppered with stories of the middle-aged and out of work. One forty-five-year-old woman told *The Age* how a recruiter informed her frankly that 'most employers preferred to employ those under forty'. As I read such stories, I thought once more about the Universal Basic Income and the mitigating effect it might have for this vulnerable group. Another article reported the case of a fifty-five-year-old man who found himself unable to get work in hospitality management, so he withdrew his super and moved to Thailand. 'If I can't get a job at fifty-five, what is supposed to happen? Do they want me to sit on the dole until I turn seventy?' he asked a Fairfax reporter. 'I'm an economic refugee.'

While political refugees and asylum-seekers came to Australia with soon-to-be-dashed hopes of safety and security, our older people are headed in the other direction, starting a grey economy built on cheap offshore labour. Some of Dad's friends had taken this route in retirement. It was one of the things we talked about, as we bandied around plans. But neither of us felt comfortable with the idea. It conjured up steamy, unseemly scenes from literature: lecherous white men in linen suits, happy to leverage gross inequality in favour of their own comfort. This was not the picture Dad had of himself in old age.

In an ideal world, we would all, as Joosten asserts, have the right to be old. Housing and the pension would be adequate, and we could prepare for our twilight years not by stressing about money, but as de Beauvoir thought best, by living 'a fairly committed, fairly justified life so that one may go on in the same path even when all illusions have vanished and one's zeal for life has died away'.

De Beauvoir's claim aligns with the continuity theory of ageing, which is all about preserving one's sense of self well into retirement and old age. This may be a luxury that many cannot afford, but even for those who can, it still takes work. Mum was well trained in this respect, partly because, as a single woman whose only child left home at the beginning of high school, she was forced to build a strong, engaged life outside work and the family, and to justify herself and her choices continually. Dad, who was validated by his work and ensconced in the drinking culture that came with it, was not having such an easy or rewarding time.

The concept of continuity ageing is useful for younger adults, too. Inspired by my parents' experiences, I wrote my own list of things I love to do: writing, television-drama marathons, cooking, seeing live music, going to the cinema, helping to re-home abandoned dogs, reading, and talking about books and ideas. Sure, some of these were lonely tasks. I could see that I needed to add a few more that connected me to politics, the environment, and the community. But I could also see, when I looked over my list, that everything on it could and probably would continue into old age. These activities have defined the shape of my adult life, and with luck, they always will. They had 'generative meaning'. I was reminded of a close friend of mine who beat cancer at thirty-eight and had, in confronting death, realised with relief that all she wanted was more time to read and watch movies and eat meals with friends. Although she had reached hardly any traditional adult milestones, she had no other aching desires or fierce regrets. Knowing this, it seemed to me, should be a source of pride, not shame or anxiety.

Moreover, as I stared at the page, I realised that my list did not describe a childish life. Not a selfish one either, but an engaged one. The other things — a house, a wedding, a career — they were additions. They were not at the core of who I am and will be, no matter what the statistics and news reports asserted. It was what the psychologist had been pointing me to with the funeral exercise. Better yet, this was the still-alive exercise, the one that, if I was lucky, there would be lots of time to do again.

'Society cares about the individual only in so far as he is profitable,' de Beauvoir wrote. 'The young know this. Their anxiety as they enter in upon social life matches the anguish of the old as they are excluded from it.'

I read this line over and over in the months after Dad finished detox. But if our anxiety and anguish lies in an understanding of how the world is, as de Beauvoir argues, how are we, mere individuals, to work our way through it?

For once, Dad had no more answers than I did. We humoured each other as we traded plans about an acre of bush in the cheapest beachside location in Australia, or a Kombi van that an old man could live in happily for decades, needing nothing, blowing in the wind.

'Would you get a dog in the Kombi?' I asked Dad.

'I'm thinking about it,' he said. 'Would have to be a pretty old dog.'

'Those are the best kind.'

It's our atomisation from the very beginning of life, de Beauvoir insisted, that leaves the old disconnected and alienated. As long as we view ourselves as sources of labour and capital, and define our identities through our economic roles instead of living committed, collectively rich lives, we will continue to age out of society, ending our lives hidden away, locked into a fate of depression and decline.

The solution? De Beauvoir warned that it could only be radical: 'Change life itself.'

10
CHANGE LIFE

It was cloudy on the night of the supermoon, but we went out looking for it anyway. A few dogs streaked the oval, following their instincts towards sticks and balls and one another. We climbed to the highest patch of ground we could find. Nothing. Endless grey skies broken only by the streetlights.

'This is bullshit. It's Halley's Comet all over again,' Serge said.

I laughed. I'd forgotten all about Halley's Comet. It was a big deal when we were kids.

'I was obsessed with it,' Serge confessed. 'I learned everything about it. It's a 15-kilometre ball made of dust, ice, and gas that you can only see when it gets close to the Sun, which only happens once every seventy-five years; the rest of the time it's just orbiting through space. It goes further out than Pluto. I was so excited. I couldn't believe I was going to get to see it.'

'Cute,' I said, squeezing his hand. Stories like these clearly conjured an earnest, overbearing, imaginative child, and I loved him, along with the adult he'd become.

'It was the first time I got a sense of my own mortality,' he said.

'Oh, yeah? Did the vastness of space make you feel small and unimportant?'

'Of course, but that's not the point. It was super cloudy, we couldn't see shit, and I'd already worked out that because Halley's Comet is only visible once every seventy-five years, if I didn't see it then, I probably never would. It was the first time I had a sense of my life as a duration of time, with an ending, in which a limited number of possibilities existed.'

I hugged him. 'You must have been pretty upset.'

'I was inconsolable.'

I squinted up at the clouds. We are all inconsolable, I thought. We are inconsolable and we build things. We are inconsolable and we speak, listen, hold each other. We head out searching for the sublime, but end up craning our necks to some patch of dirty clouds, saying conciliatory things, going back inside where it is warm.

But there is a difference between being an inconsolable mass, all together, getting on with things, and being inconsolable and unsupported, broke, and alone. After a century of entrenched individualism across much of the globe, we don't want to feel responsible for one another, but we are. If people are unsafe, homeless, sick, and abandoned, we are responsible, even though the economic system we have set up shirks this responsibility. There is a name for a time without responsibility – it's called childhood. We aren't children, but we have created a childish politics, prone to loud tantrums where everything gets smashed. Perhaps that's why we continue to value the job and the kids and the marriage and the mortgage above all else – even when we can see, clear as a supermoon, how fragile these things are. Because we know that right now, outside these spaces, there is often no safety net, no space of home, no responsibility taken for what happens to us.

How far the normative description of adulthood feels from your own life depends, to a large degree, on your health, your ability to work and access money, who you love, and how you describe yourself to others. When I first began interviewing people for this book, I asked Rose, a twenty-six-year-old trans woman, student, and business owner, if she felt the pressure of the age-thirty deadline. Did she want marriage and a house?

'I'm not that concerned.' She shrugged. 'But I might feel differently if I was with some dude.'

'Because then you'd be doing *the thing*?' I asked.

'Yeah – *the thing*! I could have *that* life.'

She snuffed, a cute kind of half laugh. We were sitting in the flat she shared with her girlfriend. The space doubled as a beauty salon, and the dubious-looking devices of feminine composition surrounded us: a yellowing plastic massage table, miniature vats of dripping wax, powder pots in an unnameable variety of colours. I saw a saucer with some dark-red stained fluid, and what looked like pieces of sliced kidney floating in it, perched on the arm of a couch. It was a place of everyday assemblage for grown-up women.

I remembered another interview, with Amy, a woman in her late thirties who had done *the thing* right on time. In her twenties, she had a husband, a baby, and a mortgage. She spent her life around dinner parties: 'Going to dinner parties, preparing dinner parties, cleaning up after fucking dinner parties.' None of it felt right, though. Her life lacked meaning. She tried everything she could think of. She volunteered. She donated her eggs. She moved, and changed jobs. Eventually, she felt she had no choice but to blow up her life. She took her daughter and started something radically new. She decided to take precarious work and, as a consequence, lived in a poverty that 'offended some people'. 'I'm always accused of dragging my kid around with me, and I'm like, yeah, that's called being exposed to the world.' She decided she didn't care what people thought about her choices; they felt right to her.

Rose made this decision too. 'I thought that maybe failure could be a point of solidarity because it's a common thing, this sense of giving a bad performance. I know that I can be an abject failure and writhe around in it,' she said, adding, 'It's hard to want to buy in when the world is trying to push you out.'

Both Amy and Rose were being at least partly ironic, of course. But it was revealing irony. I felt sympathy for Rose's exclusion, and solidarity too, and I was glad that they had managed to find themselves in opposition to expectations. But I was also caught on a question that had reoccurred to me continually as I wrote this book: why does it all have to be so hard-won? Maturity, when people talked to me about it, seemed to come at the cost of such struggle. It was the consequence of poverty and its accompanying traumas, or of being forced out of or into a job or a living arrangement, or of struggling with the responsibilities of caring for others, or of realising, suddenly, that nothing in life mattered, in any fundamental way, to the individual who lived it. The moment of adult reckoning, it seemed to me, was not a part of the human developmental cycle, but a consequence of trying to be a person in an inhuman apparatus. Do we, as a society and a culture, feel okay about the consolation that Rose takes in writhing around in her *failure*? Do we feel resigned about Amy having to live in *offensive* poverty in order to pursue a life that is meaningful to her? Do we feel all right about the suicidal twenty-nine-year-old who sat in his therapist's office, doing the funeral exercise because he was *just kind*, not married or on a career path, and therefore felt he lacked intrinsic value?

For crafters of dream boards, or the readers of books like those on my mother's shelves, changing life is a question of mindset and initiative. But changing life is beyond the purview of the individual. Simone de Beauvoir insisted it was a question of ethics, of acknowledging that our freedom is predicated on the freedom of others. It is both obvious and wondrous to me that we live interdependent lives constructed not only through our own experiences but also through the connections we have to one another and to environments, which are always also political. Because of these connections, we need to insist — endlessly, continually, in the face of inhuman economic and social policies that infantilise us or leave us for dead — that we want to take responsibility for one another. Because we are adults, and we can claim this title as more than an economic role. Is it too optimistic for me to hope that, if we can adopt this stance, we might be able to train a culture over time in much the same way you train a large and difficult dog: by gently insisting on the same thing, over and over, in many different situations?

Governments could hasten this change. A welfare system such as the Universal Basic Income, which addresses poverty without continually forcing vulnerable people to prove their worth; educational institutions that are realistic about their role in the life course; and property laws that protect people's right to shelter instead of investors' drive to profit would all help. If we adopted these measures, who knows what kinds of adult lives would flourish? Whatever their character, I suspect they might just usher us, collectively, towards a new maturity.

I finished the penultimate draft of this book in 2016, a year defined by blame and recrimination. It was a childish year, I think, but maybe also a sobering one. After an extended adolescence of sparring with Dad on the couch, before our realities crumbled together, I've become convinced that generationalism is an attempt to make sense of the dehumanising effects of neoliberalism by ascribing character defects to the young, or immoral greed to the old, and abdicating responsibility for everyone. This was underscored by the Brexit vote and the US election result that delivered a tyrant to power, when intergenerational sledging reached fever pitch. 'Here is how the vote would have gone if the younger generation had their say …' went the first wave of compensatory think pieces. These ended abruptly when it was pointed out that, in fact, the maps showing progressive millennials did not represent hope for the future but the dismal state of the present, given the markedly low voting rates of those under thirty-five in both countries. Young adults were not participating in democracy, such as it was. Apathy! screamed the next round of think pieces. Irresponsibility!

At first, I felt indignant about this. My first voting year corresponded to the September 11 attacks and the beginning of the War on Terror. Ever since I had a say, political discourse, locally and internationally, focused on smeary threats to assets and traditions I could neither relate to nor access. The lives of young people were addressed as problems needing prescriptions, if they were addressed at all. Naturally, conservative politicians have no incentive to engage those whom the polls suggest would vote against them but, as we have seen, candidates and commentators on the Left lose when they play by the same rules and ignore young adults, or patronise them – seriously, Katy Perry *as a strategy*? No wonder so many feel disenfranchised. When I was eighteen, I remember looking at politics in my country and thinking, *Why bother. No one listens to you. No one cares.*

Now, I am well aware of how such thoughts evoke a two-year-old tantrum, or a thirteen-year-old's slammed bedroom door with the 'keep out' sign on it. But it was how I felt in my early twenties, and its echo rang into my thirties, too. The more I thought about it, though, the more wrong-headed and lame it seemed. It is childish to feel that the real world lies beyond you, and that you dwell, gloriously, irresponsibly, in some other space, whether neon or dank.

The aspiration for a meaningful adult existence should go beyond generationalism. Each generation is described as being uniquely reticent, uncooperative, and lazy. It's really just code for being young. Part of getting older is 'getting over one's self', so to speak.

So perhaps we need to resist the seductive powers of statistics that purport to provide evidence for our own deeply held suspicions about others, or headlines that induce our sense of outrage or entitlement at the expense of our need for solidarity. Beyond the small indulgences of everyday judgement, blanket claims about generations must sell magazines and whip up web traffic, or people would stop making them. Someone should conduct another study, about the kind of thrill (Dopamine! Adrenaline! Rhododendron!) we get when we read a headline such as 'Why [Insert Generation Here] Can't Grow Up', or scan blog posts for attack words such as lazy, immature, and shallow.

In the first decade and a half of the twenty-first century, the hapless young adult who lives metaphorically or literally in their childhood bedroom has become a cliché. When *Gilmore Girls* rebooted, Yale-educated journalist Rory moved back to her small town amid taunts that she had come home to join 'the thirty-something gang', a group of barely-young adults who, as her neighbour explained, had 'been to college but the real world spit them out like a stale piece o' gum and now they're back in their old rooms – like you!' Popular films such as *Sisters*, *Juno*, *Knocked Up*, *Laggies*, *Trainwreck*, *Failure to Launch*, *Friends with Kids*, and pretty much every comedy Vince Vaughn has ever made, feature childish protagonists, not ready for marriage and children, eking out their living from occupations that appeal to kids, such as car- and video-game design, or theme-park management, and depending too much on their platonic best friend.

As I wrote this book, I watched and re-watched these films with masochistic glee. They resonated uncomfortably, and they made me laugh. But I was also looking for something. I wanted to see if any of these immature idlers would be permitted to blossom into a mature anti-hero. Was there a way to end this story without a windfall or a wedding?

I was always disappointed.

As in *Big*, at the end of each film, the life cycle was put to rights. The lagging kiddult gave up adolescent things. The sexually voracious woman embraced monogamy. The ex-rocker dude accepted life as a corporate creative and head of household. The slacker stubbed out their joint in a soiled nappy. This giving up of childish things was framed as growing up. It frustrated me endlessly. Why were rebellion and maturity continually represented as incompatible?

I think I have worked out the answer. Because if rebellion is the dominion of the young, it is presented as something you should grow out of. Because a mature rebel is harder to dismiss. Because framing adulthood as synonymous with passive conformity excuses adults from an engaged notion of civic ethics, hooks them into compensatory consumption, and provides the young with a reason not to listen. That's why the women from *Sex and the City* can't buy a brownstone together, and any movie about a single, childless person in their late thirties has to also be about dysfunction.

Against the tidy endings of the genre, I have no big wedding finale or surprise happy pregnancy. Despite some accomplishments of which I am proud, my life is much the same as it was on page one. I'm inconsolable, but busy. Moving forward through time. Not plum crazy right now, though I know I might be again soon. It does not surprise me in the least that, when Jeffrey Jensen Arnett asked his twenty- and thirty-something subjects whether they felt like adults, the answer was almost unanimously ambivalent. We all know there is no destination called adult. That is part of what makes us so anxious about it. But adulthood can still be a useful concept to define what troubles us as cultures and societies.

My editor, Julia, helped me to organise my thinking on this subject into something that could be shared. Like me, she was intrigued and irritated by the way adulthood as an aspirational concept is set up and policed.

'Every day there is another article on why Gen Y can't do this or that.' We shared a mutual eye-roll. She gestured at the early draft sitting between us in the café. 'I think you're addressing this idea well, but I think there's something missing, and, it's, well, it's an emotional response,' she said. 'Have you thought about that at all?'

I think about my emotions all the time. Isn't that one of my generational attributes? I stalled, sipped my coffee.

'The thing is,' I replied, carefully. 'I feel embarrassed by my emotional response.'

Julia fixed me with her comprehending gaze.

'I mean, every part of my logical self is like, fuck this noise, move on, live your life. But it does affect me. Sometimes it's totally paralysing.'

'I know what you mean,' she said.

If we were making a film, there'd be an overlay in post-production – a clip would show the last paragraph of the heavily marked pages that sat between us. A seven-thousand-word rant about what the word 'adult' could fathomably mean today, chopped down to a tiny moment, a mere fleeting question amid the joy and sorrow and struggle of life, to which she had appended the note: 'You go from here …'

Ellipsis descending into the blinding white of the screen.

FURTHER READING

BOOKS

Adler, Renata, *After the Tall Timber: collected nonfiction*, New York Review Books, New York, 2015.

Ariès, Philippe, *Centuries of Childhood: a social history of family life*, Vintage, London, 1965.

Arnett, Jeffrey Jensen, *Emerging Adulthood: the winding road from the late teens through the twenties*, second edition, Oxford University Press, London, 2014.

Brokaw, Tom, *The Greatest Generation*, Random House, New York, 2001.

Carey, Kevin, *The End of College: creating the future of learning and the university of everywhere*, Riverhead Books, New York, 2015.

Coontz, Stephanie, *Marriage, a History: how love conquered marriage*, Penguin Books, New York, 2006.

———, *The Way We Never Were: American families and the nostalgia trap*, Basic Books, New York, 2016.

Côté, James E., *Arrested Adulthood: the changing nature of maturity and identity*, New York University Press, New York, 2000.

———, *Generation on Hold: coming of age in the late twentieth century*, New York University Press, New York, 1995.

Davis, Mark, *Gangland: cultural elites and the new generationalism*, Allen & Unwin, Sydney, 1999.

de Beauvoir, Simone, *The Coming of Age* (trans. Patrick O'Brian), W.W. Norton & Company, New York, 1996.

Edelman, Lee, *No Future: queer theory and the death drive*, Duke University Press Books, Durham, 2004.

Egan, Jennifer, *A Visit from the Goon Squad*, Alfred A. Knopf, New York, 2010.

Faircloth, Charlotte, *Militant Lactivism?: attachment parenting and intensive motherhood in the UK and France*, Berghahn Books, Oxford, 2013.

Ferrante, Elena, *My Brilliant Friend: the Neapolitan novels* (trans. Ann Goldstein), Text Publishing, Melbourne, 2013.

Gullette, Margaret Morganroth, *Aged by Culture*, University of Chicago Press, Chicago, 2004.

Harris, Malcolm, *Kids These Days: human capital and the making of millennials*, Little, Brown and Company, New York, 2017.

Hil, Richard, *Whackademia: an insider's account of the troubled university*, NewSouth Publishing, Sydney, 2012.

Joosten, Melanie, *A Long Time Coming: essays on old age*, Scribe Publications, Melbourne, 2016.

Kipnis, Laura, *The Female Thing: dirt, envy, sex, vulnerability*, Vintage, New York, 2007.

Lyotard, Jean-François, *The Inhuman: reflections on time* (trans. Geoffrey Bennington and Rachel Bowlby), Stanford University Press, Palo Alto, 1992.

Mintz, Steven, *Huck's Raft: a history of American childhood*, Belknap Press, Massachusetts, 2006.

———, *The Prime of Life: a history of modern adulthood*, Belknap Press, Massachusetts, 2015.

Nunez, Sigrid, 'The Most Important Thing', in Daum, Meghan (ed.), *Selfish, Shallow, and Self-Absorbed: sixteen writers on the decision not to have kids*, Picador, New York, 2015.

Penny, Laurie, *Unspeakable Things: sex, lies and revolution*, Bloomsbury, London, 2014.

Rousseau, Jean-Jacques, *Emile, or On Education* (trans. Allan Bloom), Basic Books, New York, 1979.

Solnit, Rebecca, *A Field Guide to Getting Lost*, Canongate Books, Edinburgh, 2006.

Whitehead, Alfred North, *The Aims of Education and Other Essays*, Free Press, New York, 1967.

ARTICLES AND REPORTS

Al Sherbini, Ramadan, 'Egypt Youth in Perpetual State of "Waithood"', *Gulf News*, 17 November 2015, http://gulfnews.com/news/mena/egypt/egypt-youth-in-perpetual-state-of-waithood-1.1620733

Bari, Taposh, et al., 'Millennial Moms: spending implications from a new generation of parents', Goldman Sachs, 11 May 2015.

Bruder, Jessica, 'The End of Retirement', *Harper's*, August 2014, http://harpers.org/archive/2014/08/the-end-of-retirement/

Buchholz, Todd G. and Buchholz, Victoria, 'The Go-Nowhere Generation', *The New York Times*, 10 March 2012, www.nytimes.com/2012/03/11/opinion/sunday/the-go-nowhere-generation.html

Buia, Carolina, 'Why Multiple Generations of Families Choose to Live Together and Why It's Not Such a Bad Idea', *Newsweek*, 25 April 2015, http://europe.newsweek.com/why-multiple-generations-families-choosing-live-together-324614?rm=eu

Cadwalladr, Carole, 'Students Used to Take Drugs to Get High. Now They Take Them to Get Higher Grades', *The Guardian*, 15 February 2015, https://www.theguardian.com/society/2015/feb/15/students-smart-drugs-higher-grades-adderall-modafinil

Calhoun, Ada, 'The Secret to Staying Friends in Your 30s', *New York*, 21 April 2015, http://nymag.com/thecut/2015/04/secret-to-staying-friends-in-your-30s.html

Carnevale, Anthony P., et al., 'Failure to Launch: structural shift and the new lost generation', Georgetown University Center on Education and the Workforce, September 2013, https://cew.georgetown.edu/cew-reports/failure-to-launch/

———, 'The Online College Labor Market: where the jobs are', Georgetown University Center on Education and the

Workforce and McCourt School of Public Policy, April 2014, https://cew.georgetown.edu/

Cooke, Richard, 'The Boomer Supremacy', *The Monthly*, March 2016, https://www.themonthly.com.au/issue/2016/march/1456750800/richard-cooke/boomer-supremacy

Cosslett, Rhiannon Lucy and Hanson, Michele, 'A Millennial and a Baby Boomer Trade Places: "I can't help but feel a stab of envy"', *The Guardian*, 12 March 2016, https://www.theguardian.com/world/2016/mar/12/millennial-baby-boomer-trade-places-stab-envy

Davies, Lizzy, et al., 'Marriage Falls Out of Favour for Young Europeans as Austerity and Apathy Bite', *The Guardian*, 26 July 2014, https://www.theguardian.com/lifeandstyle/2014/jul/25/marriage-young-europeans-austerity

Dow, Aisha, '"Ghost Tower" Warning for Docklands after Data Reveals High Melbourne Home Vacancies', *The Age*, 12 November 2014, http://www.theage.com.au/victoria/ghost-tower-warning-for-docklands-after-data-reveals-high-melbourne-home-vacancies-20141111-11kkxz.html

Doyle, Briohny, 'Greedy Landlords Should Show Renters More Respect', *The Age* and *The Sydney Morning Herald*, 8 December 2015, http://www.smh.com.au/comment/value-of-renters-should-be-recognised-20151207-glhx3c.html

Honwana, Alcinda, '"Waithood": youth transitions and social change', *Development and Equity: an interdisciplinary exploration by ten scholars from Africa, Asia and Latin America*, Brill, Massachusetts, 2014, pp. 28–40.

Hopper, Briallen, 'Relying on Friendship in a World Made for Couples', *New York*, 26 February 2016, http://nymag.com/thecut/2016/02/single-ladies-friendship-romantic-fraught.html

'Japan's Solo Weddings: "I want a wedding, not a groom"', *Marie Claire*, July 2015, p. 90.

Jericho, Greg, 'Working Past Retirement Age: for Generation X, putting the feet up seems a distant dream', *The Guardian*, 4 April 2016, https://www.theguardian.com/business/grogonomics/2016/apr/04/working-past-retirement-age-for-generation-x-putting-the-feet-up-seems-a-distant-dream

Khazan, Olga, 'The Luxury of Waiting for Marriage to Have Kids', *The Atlantic*, 17 June 2014, https://www.theatlantic.com/business/archive/2014/06/why-poor-women-dont-wait-for-marriage-to-give-birth/372890/

Kirchgaessner, Stephanie, 'Pope Francis: not having children is selfish', *The Guardian*, 12 February 2015, https://www.theguardian.com/world/2015/feb/11/pope-francis-the-choice-to-not-have-children-is-selfish

Livingston, Gretchen, 'Childlessness Falls, Family Size Grows Among Highly Educated Women', Pew Research Center, 7 May 2015, http://www.pewsocialtrends.org/2015/05/07/childlessness-falls-family-size-grows-among-highly-educated-women/

Malik, Shiv, 'Mario Draghi: "reducing youth unemployment is a priority for everyone"', *The Guardian*, 11 March 2016, https://www.theguardian.com/world/2016/mar/11/mario-draghi-reducing-youth-unemployment-is-a-priority-for-everyone for a Cheaper Country', *The Sydney Morning Herald*, 8 June 2014, http://www.smh.com.au/national/struggling-pensioners-opt-to-leave-australia-for-a-cheaper-country-20140607-39pui.html

Martin, Peter, 'Housing Crisis Report Says Backyards for Children Vanishing as Oldies Stay Put', *The Sydney Morning Herald*, 2 November 2015, http://www.smh.com.au/federal-politics/political-news/housing-crisis-report-says-backyards-for-children-vanishing-as-oldies-stay-put-20151028-gkl3eh.html

McCrindle, Mark, 'Australia in 2020: a snapshot of the future', 2008, http://mccrindle.com.au/ResearchSummaries/Australia-in-2020-A-Snapshot-of-the-Future.pdf

Nagourney, Adam, 'Old and on the Street: the graying of America's homeless', *The New York Times*, 31 May 2016, https://www.nytimes.com/2016/05/31/us/americas-aging-homeless-old-and-on-the-street.html?_r=0

Oliver, Amanda, 'What Every Millennial Wishes You Understood About Student Loan Debt', *The Huffington Post*, 19 December 2015, http://www.huffingtonpost.com/amanda-oliver/what-every-millennial-wis_b_8845084.html

Reeve, Elspeth, 'Every Every Every Generation Has Been the Me Me Me Generation, *The Atlantic*, 9 May 2013, https://www.theatlantic.com/national/archive/2013/05/me-generation-time/315151/

Schmidt, Lucinda, 'A Matter of Degrees', *The Sydney Morning Herald*, 30 May 2013, http://www.smh.com.au/national/education/a-matter-of-degrees-20130530-2neo9.html

Siegel, Harry, 'Why the Choice to Be Childless Is Bad for America', *Newsweek*, 19 February 2013, http://europe.newsweek.com/why-choice-be-childless-bad-america-63335?rm=eu

Steinmetz, Katy, 'Help! My Parents Are Millennials', *Time*, 26 October 2015, http://time.com/help-my-parents-are-millennials-cover-story/

Tortorici, Dayna, 'Those Like Us: on Elena Ferrante', *N+1*, issue 22, Spring 2015, https://nplusonemag.com/issue-22/reviews/those-like-us/

Tsang, Emily, 'Build Hostels for Young While They Save for Costly Housing Deposits: think tank', *South China Morning Post*, 25 November 2014, http://www.scmp.com/article/1648543/build-youth-hostels-young-people-who-cant-afford-homes-says-hong-kong-think-tank

Weale, Sally, 'English Children Among the Unhappiest in the World at School Due to Bullying', *The Guardian*, 19 August 2015, https://www.theguardian.com/society/2015/aug/19/english-children-among-unhappiest-world-widespread-bullying

Young, Iris Marion, 'Pregnant Embodiment: subjectivity and alienation', *Journal of Medicine and Philosophy*, vol. 9, issue 1, 1984, pp. 45–62.

Zhou, Christina, 'Melbourne's Rental Squeeze Forcing More People into Homelessness', *Domain*, 26 February 2017, https://www.domain.com.au/news/melbournes-rental-squeeze-forcing-more-people-into-homelessness-20170224-guk9gl/

ACKNOWLEDGEMENTS

This book was written on Wurundjeri land, where I live and work, with thanks and respect to elders past and present.

I am indebted to all the people who let me interview them, even when I couldn't explain what I was writing. I won't blow your cover; you know who you are. Without you, this book would not have been possible.

Julia Carlomagno helped shaped this project from two pieces of paper and a notion to an actual thing in the world — it would not have happened without her enthusiasm, understanding, and hard work. I relied, too, on my incomparable literary confidants Rach Crawford, Sam Cooney, and Nina Gibb, and my in-house production consultant, Eve Gill. Thanks Jennifer Down, Amy Gray, Ben Law, Emily Maguire, and Anna Spargo-Ryan; I am so proud to stake my allegiances with the community of Australian writers of which you are each an important part. There is another community I need to thank, too — animal rescue groups such as Victorian

Dog Rescue, who work tirelessly to find homes for abandoned animals, often with little by way of recognition or legislative assistance.

Finally, heartfelt gratitude to the people in my life who not only allowed but also unflinchingly encouraged me to write about them: Mum and Dad; my partner; and my three oldest friends Annie, Lyndal, and Olivia – you are as brave as you are cool, and you are all so important to me.

THE MISSING BARBEGAZI

H. S. NORUP was born in Denmark and lived in the US, the UK, Austria and Switzerland before moving to Singapore. Now, she has returned to Switzerland with her husband and two teenage sons. This is Helle's debut novel and very much draws on her love of the Alps, her passion for skiing and her belief that magic is all around us – particularly in the love, trust and companionship found in families.

THE MISSING BARBEGAZI

H.S. NORUP

PUSHKIN CHILDREN'S

Pushkin Children's
71–75 Shelton Street
London WC2H 9JQ

The Missing Barbegazi was first published in
Great Britain by Pushkin Press in 2018

1 3 5 7 9 8 6 4 2

ISBN 13: 978 1 78269 181 5

Designed and typeset by Tetragon, London
Printed and bound by CPI Group (UK) Ltd, Croydon CRO 4YY

www.pushkinpress.com

For my three favourite skiers

CONTENTS

MONDAY, 26TH DECEMBER

—1—

Tessa aimed her binoculars at the white blanket of new snow, searching for a barbegazi. The T-bar lift pulled her uphill, along the boundary of the ski area, as she scanned the mountains on the far side of the gorge. Her skis wobbled over a bump, and the eyepiece knocked against her cheekbone. She winced, but kept her eyes fixed on a crevice, from where small chunks of snow were rolling down the smooth white slope. Had they been loosened by a barbegazi?

She itched to ski beyond the prepared slopes to get closer. But that was impossible. A blizzard had raged over Christmas Day, and the avalanche warning was high. Today, not even the craziest skiers braved the dangerous off-piste. Yet.

Tessa's view of the crevice became a grey blur when the lift dragged her into a cloud. Annoyed, she lowered the binoculars, and let them dangle from their strap. Everything beyond the red trousers and green jackets of her ski-club teammates on the T-bars in front vanished in the mist. The clamminess chilled her, and she pushed her long brown plaits back, snuggled into her soft fleece and thought about the barbegazi. If only she could find their caves in the snow, and see them surf on avalanches.

When she emerged above the cloud, stray snowflakes glittered in the sun, filling the air with magic gold dust. The brightness blinded her. She tugged down the goggles on her helmet until they protected her eyes.

Empty T-bars swung back and forth where the other two eleven-year-old girls from the racing team waited. While dismounting the lift, Tessa tried to jam the binoculars into her pocket.

"Looking for fairies again?" Maria called out.

"They're not fairies," Tessa mumbled through the glove she had in her mouth, while she closed the zipper on her bulky pocket. She hoped Coach wouldn't notice. "They're—"

"Whatever." Maria exchanged a glance with Lisa. "It's not like anyone's ever seen one. Or will."

"My opa has." Tessa pointed with her ski pole towards the gully, on the other side of the T-bar lift. "It rescued him down—"

"Nobody believed your grandfather."

Her throat tightened, at Maria's harsh interruption.

“Everyone knows they’re extinct, Tessa.” Lisa’s tone was friendlier than Maria’s. Perhaps she was also remembering Opa’s funeral.

Not trusting her voice to sound steady, Tessa just shook her head.

“Oh my God, Tessa.” Maria waved her arms wildly and pointed towards the mountainside beyond the gully. “Look! Quick.”

Was something moving up there again? Tessa couldn’t help turning.

“I thought they were extinct. But, no, I see one. It’s a...” Maria drew a long, deep breath. “A-a-a... T. rex!”

Both she and Lisa exploded into fits of giggles.

“Very funny,” Tessa muttered. Hidden behind the goggles, tears welled up in her eyes. “Don’t wait. I need the loo,” she said, trying not to sound choked up, and she started gliding over to the mountain hut.

Still giggling, Maria set off, and Lisa followed her new best friend.

The lump in Tessa’s throat grew. She didn’t need the toilet, and she didn’t really care what they thought. She missed Opa so much her chest hurt. The pain pulsed into her heart as if all the blood in her body was trying to fill an Opa-shaped hole. No wonder Oma was ill, if this kind of pain was attacking her weak heart.

Tessa stopped and looked back to where Maria had pointed for her dinosaur prank. Above it, by a rocky outcrop, a small movement caught her eye. She gasped. Something white was bouncing up the snowy slope, then disappeared behind the rock. It definitely wasn’t a skier. Could it be a barbegazi?

Without taking her eyes off the outcrop, she fish-boned her way back up the slope, past the swinging T-bars and the top station of the lift. Here, on the crest of Kapall, orange netting barred the way out onto the ridge and the untamed part of the mountains. Tessa tried looking through the binoculars, but the outcrop obstructed her view of where she'd seen the creature last. If she could just get a bit nearer...

A ski-route-closed sign warned of alpine danger. Tessa checked to make sure that none of her teammates were looking. If anyone saw her ski off-piste in these conditions, Coach would ban her from training, and Mum would lock her skis away for ever.

And she wasn't going to ski off-piste. Not really. The first stretch of the ski route, through the gully and into the gorge, was almost flat, and she'd turn back as soon as she'd had a peek behind that outcrop.

With a last glance back, she squeezed through a gap between the nets, and out into the deep snow.

The wind had blown most of the snow away from the top of the ridge, and Tessa glided effortlessly along the flat surface. More of the crevice behind the outcrop came into view. To gain a better perspective, she planted her poles into the snow and stepped nearer to the edge. She looked through her binoculars.

There was a blurry spot on one of the lenses. Without taking off her glove, she rummaged in her pocket for a tissue, and one of the lens covers fell out. Instinctively, Tessa leant down to grab it.

Under her sudden, shifting weight, the ground beneath her right ski disappeared, as the snow overhang she had edged onto broke apart. A reflex sent both her arms outwards, to help her balance. The binocular-strap jerked at her neck as she let go of them. Tessa threw all her weight onto her left ski, but it was sliding sideways towards the drop... then stopped with a screech, on a flat rock that was sticking out of the snow.

Tessa's breaths came in sharp gulps. She balanced on her left leg. It shook with the effort.

Stupid. Stupid. Stupid. How many times had Opa told her to watch out for overhangs after a storm?

Below her hovering right ski, the bulk of snow she'd released was now tumbling down the mountainside, gathering speed and volume, and growing into a mini avalanche.

When she lowered her right leg, only a narrow strip of the ski rested on solid ground. She'd not slid far, but her ski poles were beyond reach. What could she do?

If she jumped the drop and landed on both feet, she could ski down the steep slope. She'd done it before with Opa. Though not from this height. Not with this much new snow. And never alone.

Instead, with the carefulness of a tightrope walker, she shifted her weight to the right ski, testing its hold on the rock. It held. In slow motion, she lifted the left ski a tiny bit and pushed it left. She balanced, shifted her weight and continued, lifting one ski at a time, very slowly inching away from the edge.

When she had made it to the other side of her ski poles, she collapsed on the snow, sobbing. Her whole body quivered. Only now did she dare to think what might have happened if both her skis had been on the overhang.

After Tessa stopped shaking, she hauled herself back to the ski area. By the barrier nets, she paused and looked back at the outcrop. Had she imagined the movement earlier, or really seen a barbegazi?

As she turned round, she collided with a tall man in a white ski outfit, a white helmet and mirrored goggles, who was pushing through the gap in the nets. He grabbed her arm.

"Watch where you're going," he snarled, his teeth gritted below a pale wispy moustache, which was so thin it looked like a pair of frowning eyebrows.

"Sorry." Tessa wrenched her jacket out of his hold.

The man skied along the ridge, past the breach Tessa had made in the overhang, before he disappeared down the steep decline into the gully.

All in white. How stupid. No one would ever find him if he got caught in an avalanche.

—2—

Gawion was too hungry and too warm to wait for the avalanche any longer. He left his sister below the most unstable-looking snow cornice, and traversed the steep mountainside to their cave entrance. After wrapping his long beard round his neck three times, he dived down into the hole and propelled himself through the narrow snow tunnel. His enormous foot got stuck when he forgot to twist it at a bend, but two paddling kicks soon enlarged the tunnel and freed his foot. He arrived home, sliding on his belly.

"Ahh, it is awfully nice and chilly in here," he said. His eyes adjusted to the dim light, and he hurried over to the huge chunk of glacier ice in the centre of the cosy cave. Pointing his feet outward, he leant his whole body against it to absorb the coldness. Papa sat on a smaller cube of ice around the other side, with Liel on his knees. They both stretched their furry hands towards the blue ice. Gawion had once sneaked down to the village after dark and seen humans sit in exactly the same way in front of flames.

Next, he lay down on his back and shuffled the soles of his long feet up to the glacier ice cooler. Only the claws on the ends of his toes stuck out above it.

"Gawion!" his mother screeched. "You have soiled my newly snowed floor."

"Sorry, Maman." He began picking up the pine needles and moss that had come off his fur and dirtied the floor.

With a swish, Maman swung her long beard over her shoulder, so she would not stumble on it, and marched back into the eating cave. Gawion followed her, hungry as always. This smaller cave was closest to the rock face, and the cascading icicles of a frozen waterfall decorated the back wall. He threw the dirt into a crack between the snowy floor and the gleaming ice.

Gawion scooped a handful of snow out of the wall next to the waterfall—his favourite flavour of snow inside the cluster of linked caves—and stuffed it into his mouth. The tiny crystals prickled his tongue. He munched and sucked on them with loud smacking noises. This snow had the delicious taste of a particularly icy snowstorm.

"Are there any raspberries?" he asked.

"Stop talking with your mouth full." Maman sighed. She looked tired, and her eyes had a faint, sun-coloured tint around their sky-blue centre. "We are out of raspberries. You can have one blackberry."

She carefully removed the shard of ice in front of their berry store, picked a large one from the tiny pile inside, and popped it into his mouth. Gawion savoured it, sucking on the hard, frozen lump until it dissolved into the tart juice of a not-quite-ripe forest blackberry.

"Where is Maegorodiel?" she asked, glancing over his head into the other cave.

"Waiting for an avalanche," Gawion said. "Only, I was hungry..."

"How could you leave her? There might still be humans about!"

"Maman, we are one-hundred-and-fifty-four years old."

Just then they heard a shrill whistle. A loud rumble followed it, and flakes fell from the ceiling. Finally, the avalanche he had been waiting for. And he had missed it.

"Potzblitz! Why is Maeg always lucky?" As usual, he should have listened to his twin sister.

Maman had closed the berry store, so he returned to the main cave, where Liel nestled into Papa's beard.

Gawion could not be bothered getting fresh snow for the floor, so he swept his foot sideways, hiding the remaining pine needles, while he looked over his shoulder to check his mother was not watching.

"Papa, tell the story of how you escaped from the zoo," Liel murmured, half asleep.

From somewhere outside, three piercing whistles could be heard. The third whistle was cut off and lacked the urgency of the first two, but left no doubt this was a desperate cry for help.

"Maeg!" Maman screamed.

Papa sprang up. Liel toppled over, hit the ice cooler and began wailing. Gawion scrambled through the tunnel behind Papa.

Outside, the trail of a huge avalanche stretched out below them, all the way into the gorge the humans called "Schöngraben". A few times they had dug human corpses out of avalanches there, and he had wondered why naming a place something that sounded like "beautiful grave" had not been sufficient warning.

Gawion chased his father down the mountain, surfing on the snow. They swerved on overhangs, hoping they might start new avalanches to carry them downwards even faster. Where they reached the end of the avalanche's long tongue, the ground flattened. An assortment of boulders lay scattered in front of it, like gigantic, frozen blackberries spat from the mouth of the gully. They whistled for Maeg while they searched underneath and around each one. The snow posed no danger to Maeg, but if she had somehow hit her head on a boulder... That was what Papa said, at least. Gawion wondered how Maeg could have whistled the emergency signal if she had been knocked out, and how she could have been knocked out in the first place. She was even better than him at surfing the avalanches.

Papa's whistling calls moved farther away from Gawion as they continued their search. Gawion had no problems seeing in the dark, but, trying to look everywhere at once, he stumbled into a hollow in the snow.

He sniffed, smelling all the different snow types the avalanche had carried. There was a whiff of thawing spring snow too—the sweet scent of Maeg.

"Maeg, where are you?" he called, and began digging.

But then his large nose caught something else. A pungent stench that gave him a scalding, trickling sensation down his spine. The snow around him reeked of iron.

He whistled for Papa to come, while he groped around in the loose snow. When Papa appeared, he had just found a handful of barbegazi fur.

Without speaking, he handed it to his father.

Papa gasped and said, "She has been taken, I fear."

FROM *HABITS & HABITATS: A HISTORIC ACCOUNT OF ALPINE ELVES* BY PROFESSOR, DR EBERHART LUDWIG FRITZ BAHNE

Barbegazi are mountain elves, although humans often mistake them for dwarfs, due to their short, stout stature. A mature barbegazi of approximately three hundred years in age can reach a height of 1.2 metres, roughly the size of an average seven-year-old. Fully grown, they weigh around ten kilograms—less than half that of a similar-sized human child.

This lightness and low density, combined with their enormous feet, enable them to "surf" on avalanches.

TUESDAY, 27TH DECEMBER

—3—

Tessa had forgotten to get her skis serviced. Again. So she began the training session with Coach on a bad note.

If him yelling "Those skis'd better be like new tomorrow or you can take them down to the sawmill, borrow a chainsaw, turn them into splinters, make a bonfire in your garden and forget about the race on Saturday!" without taking a breath could be called merely a bad note.

Tessa just stared at the ground. The race meant nothing to her any more. Yesterday, when Aunt Annie dropped off some homemade goulash soup, she'd overheard her talking to Mum about Oma. Mum had cried. From the gap left open by the kitchen door, Tessa had glimpsed Mum's thin, convulsing shoulders as she was embraced by Aunt Annie's pudgy arms.

"What if she gives up?" Mum sobbed. "This article I read said if one spouse dies, the other might lose the will to go on. Especially around Christmas."

Aunt Annie murmured something that Tessa couldn't hear because blood was pounding in her ears and surging towards her chest. The thought of having two holes to try and fill in her heart made her run to her room, and hide in the soft fluff of her pillow.

"Your turn, Miss My-head's-in-the-clouds," Coach yelled. "And stay active. Bend your knees. Don't sit like you're at a tea party."

Tessa nodded, without looking up, and got into starting position between the long stakes that marked the beginning of the training course. She planted her poles into the snow and leant back, flexing her knee and hip joints, tensing her muscles. On the piste in front of her, giant slalom gates were positioned in a colourful zigzag.

"Three, two, one, go!"

At "Go" Tessa catapulted herself forward and pushed off with both poles three times. Then she crouched, and, shifting her weight, raced through the maze of red and blue gates.

"Knees, Tessa!" Coach shouted from behind.

The dull metal edges of her skis had little hold on the snow, and she slid sideways in the turns. Cold air slipped under the rim of Tessa's helmet, whistling in her ears. If only she could hear a barbegazi whistle. Opa had told her they whistled warnings, signalling avalanches.

A figure in green stood waving their arms just ahead of her. Tessa canted her skis, sending a shower of powdery snow over Karen, the assistant coach, who'd stopped her in the middle of the run.

"Wake up, Tessa! The U12 competition will be tough this year. You need to up your game. Like Lisa and Maria." When Karen shook her head, fine white dust fell from her striped, knitted hat.

After crossing the finish line, Tessa zoomed in and out between hesitant tourists and caterpillar-like ski-school groups, to the lift. She arrived just as Lisa and Maria got on either side of a T-bar, whispering and giggling.

On the next run, she botched the start, didn't find her rhythm, and missed a gate. At the top of the course, Coach swore. She conveniently overlooked Karen's waving arms.

The rest of the morning was like climbing a mountain of ice. Blindfolded. Wearing slippers.

Heavy clouds pressed down on the Alps, concealing the peaks and becoming one with the snow-covered slopes. The lift rides were a complete waste of time—everywhere Tessa pointed her binoculars showed the same grey blur. Besides, the avalanche risk had gone down, and today tourists crowded the off-piste. The barbegazi had to be in hiding.

After her final run, Felix slid up beside her in the queue, and they shared a T-bar back to the top. They were second cousins, but he was almost like a brother to her. Felix was also the best skier in the team.

"Did you see that?" he asked, while they settled on the orange bar. "What a save! My approach to the last red gate was all wrong, but then I took the turn on my inside ski and threw my weight forward and knocked the gate away with my shoulder."

"Cool," Tessa said. She hadn't seen his run.

"And my catapult start... I wanna do it exactly like that on Saturday. Still three more training days left before the first race, and I'm ready!" Felix pushed his sleeve up to look at his sports watch. "Yes! My pulse is already down. D'you have something to eat? I'm starving. I hope there's still some of Mum's goulash left over."

"Don't count on it. She brought that over for me and Oma yesterday. But I doubt you'll starve." Aunt Annie—who wasn't actually Tessa's aunt, but married to Mum's cousin Harry—was known throughout the whole village for her delicious food and cakes.

"What's that? Is it chocolate?" Felix poked at her bulging pocket.

"Just my binoculars."

"You're not still looking for those...you know... Great Uncle Willy's barbie-fairy-thingies?"

"Not barbies. A barbegazi. One saved him after an avalanche. Right down there." Tessa jabbed her pole towards Schöngraben. "Opa said he'd show me, but now he's gone, and—" She stopped speaking before the lump in her throat could choke her voice.

They'd been picking berries in the gully when Opa pointed and said: "The barbegazi dug me out of the avalanche over there. Come December, I'll show you." Munching on blueberries, she'd glanced up from the bush for a second. Had he planned to show her a barbegazi, or just the spot?

Tessa speared a clump of snow with her pole, making it crumble. "And your grandfather didn't even believe his own brother."

The track turned bumpy on a steep stretch. Tessa concentrated on her skis not crossing, and they glided side by side in awkward silence.

After a while, Felix said, "One of our guests, a regular, was in an avalanche down there yesterday afternoon. It was weird—"

"Did they save him?"

"Who? Those barbie-things? Come on, Tessa. But it was so weird. He never talks to anyone, and he's only interested in the avalanche report. A fanatic off-piste skier. Has all the coolest equipment. Even that new electrical avalanche airbag..."

She knew just the type. A young guy with multicoloured ski overalls, perhaps a ponytail. Probably Scandinavian.

"...Then last night he's all chatty, telling me about the avalanche, and afterwards, going up the stairs, he whistled!"

"He whistled? That's what they do, you know."

"Who?"

"The barbegazi. Before avalanches, they whistle."

"So now you think he's one?" Felix gave a quick shake of his head. They'd reached the top, and he sped off, shouting that he wanted a last run.

Yeah, right. He just couldn't get away fast enough. Coach had already been dismantling the course when they passed it on the lift. They'd both seen that.

Tessa slid down to help clear the training piste, red-green streaks overtaking her.

If only she could find a barbegazi and prove they weren't extinct. It would solve all her problems. And everyone would know Opa had told the truth. That was bound to make Oma happy.

—4—

They searched all night. Whistling, digging, probing, digging, whistling.

First, they sifted through the loose snow, where Gawion had discovered the barbegazi fur, and combed the rest of the avalanche trail, finding nothing.

"She cannot have been taken," Papa said again and again. "She must have had an accident. A blow to the head... A minor injury... We shall find her farther up the mountain."

But Gawion had not mistaken the stench of iron in the hollow where he found the fur. Unfortunately, Papa had neither smelt thawing spring snow nor iron, and Gawion cursed himself for having scattered the snow before Papa arrived, making the scents disperse.

Papa took him across the flattened, rippled snow that attracted flocks of humans during the day. A huge metal monster growled like a thousand angry dogs, and chased them up a steep slope with its light beams.

Fear made heat flash through Gawion and cramp the muscles of his sensitive soles. Terrified, he leapt over a sun-coloured net, escaping into a ravine.

"Maeg cannot be here," Papa said, wide-eyed and shaking, before they slunk back to Schöngraben.

Where the ragged peaks rose naked above the snow, Gawion and Papa explored nooks and crannies, and sniffed behind boulders, looking in places Maeg had never been to. Gawion slid down couloirs and gullies and crawled back up them, making sure he overlooked nothing. Papa followed him, double-checking.

They stayed outside, exposed, long after daybreak, until the strange mechanical structures began transporting humans up the mountains again.

After Gawion had dozed for a while, he was fully rested and impatient to continue the search. He crept through the tunnel and peeked outside. Low clouds blocked the warmth of the sun and made it easy to hide from the humans. He could not even see the nearest of their mountain transporters, although the wind brought a faint echo of its sinister, metallic noise and distant human yells. But, today, he was not allowed to leave the cave on his own.

Back inside, Gawion lay down, close to the ice cooler. Liel was playing with the feathers she had gathered before the first big snowfall, oblivious to the worry around her.

His parents' muffled voices travelled through the snow wall from their resting cave. Maman's sobs and occasional shrieks—"We should never have stayed, Aeglosben... do not belong here... carried those twins for nine winters... Home in Mont Blanc's sea of ice would have been safe"—were clearly audible above Papa's indistinct murmurs.

Gawion crept to the wall and pressed his ear against it. Papa had now raised his voice, saying, "Safe? Mont Blanc was never safe. They captured us there." This was a story he had told his children many times. It was also the reason Papa had been so quick to assume Maeg had been taken.

More than a century before Gawion was born, Papa, not quite awake after the summer sleep, had wandered into a trap. When his desperate whistles alerted Maman and her father, they tried to rescue him. But the humans had attacked them with iron chains, and captured all three barbegazi. After travelling for a moon in an iron cage on a cart, they had arrived at Schönbrunn Palace in Vienna. Here they were gifted to the Empress Maria Theresa and, as part of the imperial menagerie, treated like royalty. Imprisoned royalty.

"We are much safer here," Papa said, trying to persuade Maman that his initial fear of an abduction had been foolish. Maeg could not have been captured. No one could have taken her, because no one knew a barbegazi family lived in these mountains.

Well, that was not entirely true. The berry-human knew about them. And that was Gawion's fault too. Just like it was his fault Maeg was gone. Potzblitz! If only he had stayed and waited for that avalanche, then they would know what had happened to Maeg.

When Maman appeared, he sprang up and followed her into the eating cave.

"Are we going out to search now? I am hungry."

"Blueberry or blackberry?" Maman sounded tired. "I shall give you one of each. And no one is leaving until nightfall."

As she stooped to pick up the berries, Gawion saw that the bald patch at the back of her head had grown since he first noticed it a few days ago. She looked shabbier and even thinner than she did after sleeping for a whole summer.

"Give these two to Liel." She stroked his beard. "Papa and I have already taken our dinner."

That did not sound right. Maman and Papa had not been outside the resting cave all morning. And the last few days, his parents had always been doing something else while the children ate. Were they eating at all? Or was that another reason for Maman's exhaustion?

"Are the rest of our berries on ice somewhere?" He snuffled, trying to catch a whiff of berries that might be hidden under the snow.

"Do not worry about that," Maman said. "Just find Maeg."

But he did worry. The winter solstice had come and gone, without the anticipated gift of berries from the human he had once saved. There was nowhere to find berries at this time of year. Except in the village. No matter what Papa thought, they might soon have several reasons to go near the humans. Perhaps Gawion should seek out the berry-human.

"Go on." Maman took his hand and placed the four berries in his palm.

Gawion put the blueberry into his mouth with a cube of ice, attempting to dilute the flavour and make it last longer. He manoeuvred both lumps under his tongue, and fought the urge to swallow. His stomach growled.

—5—

At home after ski training, Tessa skipped down the wooden stairs to the granny flat, with the bread she'd bought at the bakery and Aunt Annie's plastic container.

"Omaaaa," she called, opening the door. A musty smell met her, mixed with the scent of camomile tea from the kitchen corner. The heavy curtains were opened, but the grey light from outside hardly made it past Oma's squishy armchairs, so Tessa switched on the ceiling lamp. At the far end of the room, the grandfather clock, next to the massive bookcase with all Opa's skiing trophies, ticked in rhythm with light snores from the sofa. Here, a magazine crossword puzzle covered part of Oma's pale face, and her glasses balanced on the tip of her nose. The chequered wool blanket had slid to the floor.

But it was too early for an afternoon nap.

On her knees, by the sofa, Tessa leant in to hug Oma awake. She put her head on Oma's chest and listened to her heart. It beat much faster than the clock, and it didn't sound particularly weak.

Oma stroked Tessa's hair and whispered, "How was the snow?"

Tessa smiled. Every lunchtime in winter that was always the first question Oma had asked Opa. But she used to be bustling around with pots and pans, preparing lunch for the two hungry skiers—or one hungry skier and one hungry schoolgirl—when she asked it.

She almost answered "Not worth getting out of bed for", as Opa would've on a day like today, though she'd never seen him stay in bed.

"Okay, I guess," she said, and rose.

In the kitchen corner, she emptied the goulash soup into a saucepan and heated it over a low heat, as Aunt Annie had instructed. By the time it bubbled, she'd set the table, sliced the bread, and helped Oma get up.

She gulped down two portions before Oma had swallowed more than a few bites.

"You have to eat," Tessa said in Mum's voice. "You love Aunt Annie's goulash soup."

Oma leant back and touched her lips with a napkin. "I must have eaten too much at breakfast."

That was a lie. There was only a teacup in the sink from this morning, but Tessa just nodded. She cleared the table, leaving the dishes for Mum to do when she came home between her lunch shift and dinner shift at the restaurant. Until then, Tessa would do her best to cheer Oma up.

"Do you want to play Rummy? Or I can get Scrabble from upstairs?"

Oma heaved herself up and shuffled back to the sofa.

"I think I need to lie down for a bit," she replied. "Why don't you tell me about today's skiing?"

Like Opa used to do. Tessa couldn't remember ever seeing Oma on skis, but, from Opa's daily reports, she knew the ski area better than most locals. They were dangerously close to talking about Opa. Was that a good idea? Mum had told her to avoid drama and anything that might be upsetting.

Tessa perched sideways on the edge of the sofa. Suddenly it seemed that every topic led to Opa. She couldn't say her skis needed service without both of them thinking how Opa used to sharpen and wax her skis. The avalanche yesterday had been near Opa's avalanche. Even her problems with the other girls were linked to the barbegazi, and from them, to Opa.

"What is it, dear?" Oma took her hand and gave it a soft squeeze. "I'm not made of glass just because my ticker's acting up."

"It's..." Oma might be the only person in the whole world who knew the barbegazi weren't extinct. Perhaps they could talk about them without mentioning Opa.

Oma's thumb stroked Tessa's hand, teasing the words out.

"It's the barbegazi. Nobody believes they still exist."

The thumb strokes stopped. "You mean, nobody believed your grandfather."

"Did you?" Tessa asked quietly.

"Of course I did. He survived an avalanche that flattened two rows of trees, and somehow he made it home on a broken leg. Your grandfather—rest his soul—had no patience for fantasy. He could never have imagined the barbegazi."

Oma let go of Tessa's hand. She found the handkerchief hidden in her sleeve and dabbed at her eyes, but she spoke with more force than Tessa had heard in a long time.

"Until that professor came, he didn't even know they were called barbegazi."

"What professor?"

"The author of that fairy book. Even mentioned Opa in the barbegazi chapter. The two of you were always looking at it when you were little. Don't you remember?"

Shaking her head, Tessa walked over to the bookcase, and scanned the heavy, dark-green and wine-red hardbacks.

"Try behind my knitting basket," Oma said.

On the bottom shelf, squeezed in after volumes nineteen to thirty of the encyclopedia, stood a thin black book.

Tessa prised it out. Seeing it, she vaguely remembered drawings of elves, and sitting by the fire upstairs, listening to Opa's story. She'd been too young to read, but he always showed her the section about him. This would be proof. Lisa and Maria could see for themselves that Opa had told the truth.

A bookmark stuck out in the middle, and her trembling hands opened it there. The font was small, and Opa's notes and a pencil-sketched barbegazi filled the margins. A big arrow pointed to the place she was looking for, and she read:

Over the years, several skiers caught in avalanches claim to have been dug out by something white and hairy. However, as the persons were unconscious when found by rescue teams, none of their stories have credibility.

As late as last year, a skier reported his miraculous rescue in the Arlberg region of Austria. Despite the fact that Arlberg is several hundred kilometres from any historical sightings of barbegazi, which were all near major glaciers in the Swiss and French Alps, this author travelled to the region to investigate. Unfortunately, the skier, Willy Berger, withdrew his story of the sighting, confessing to have suffered a serious head trauma, with resulting hallucinations, in the avalanche.

Head trauma. Hallucinations. This was all wrong. Opa had always told her a barbegazi saved his life. Why would he say something else to this author?

Tessa slumped into a squishy armchair, across from the sofa where Oma lay with her eyes closed. It didn't prove anything. But she still believed Opa. Whoever had written this book had misunderstood. She closed it and tried to decipher the name on the spine. The tiny letters there, once golden, had lost their colour and become dark shadows. Inside the cover, curly writing said: *Habits & Habitats: A Historic Account of Alpine Elves by Professor, Dr Eberhart Ludwig Fritz Bahne.*

What a strange name! She entered it in the search engine on her phone, and tapped the first result. It was from the Institute of Zoology at the University of Zurich. A long list of Professor Bahne's publications appeared. She scrolled down, stopping to read interesting titles, like *Animal Behaviour:*

Dying Elfish Customs and *On the Origin of Elves: Survival of the Least Humanoid* and *Secrets of the Glaciers: Proof Against Barbegazi Extinction?*

At that last one, Tessa jumped up.

Oma stirred. "Did you say something, dear?"

She wanted to do a happy dance, but stopped herself. Mum had said no drama.

"That professor believes they're alive," she replied, as calmly as possible.

Outside, on the snow-covered garden table, tiny flecks landed at irregular intervals. The clock chimed. Two thirty. Mum would be home soon.

"Sorry, Oma. I forgot... Tell Mum I went skiing with... Erm..."

"Mmm hmm," Oma murmured, with closed eyes.

For a moment, Tessa watched her still shape, reluctant to leave. She spread the blanket over Oma's stockinged legs, before she ran upstairs, hugging the book against her chest. *A-live-a-live-a-live*, her steps tramped.

Of course, the barbegazi had survived. And she'd find them, if she searched in the right spot.

FROM *HABITS & HABITATS: A HISTORIC ACCOUNT OF ALPINE ELVES* BY PROFESSOR, DR EBERHART LUDWIG FRITZ BAHNE

The name *barbegazi* comes from the French *barbe glacée*, meaning "frozen beard".

The white beards of grown males often reach the ground. Female beards are slightly shorter. Both females and males use their beards as scarves, but whether the beards have other functions as well is unknown.

Similar to other species of elves, barbegazi have pointed ears, iron intolerance and limited magical abilities.

—6—

Tessa dismounted the chairlift on the crest of Kapall, next to the barrier nets she'd slipped through yesterday. The ski route was open today, and the nets rolled back. On her way up, she'd thought about Professor Bahne. His email address was listed on the Institute of Zoology website. It was perfect. After she found a barbegazi, she'd write to him, then he could mention her in one of his books, and everyone would believe her.

Dark clouds swelled over the Arlberg pass, and snow fell in big fluffy lumps. The cold lift had frozen her bum. Tessa shivered. To get warm, she started out with short, quick turns—Coach would've been pleased. She sped past the deserted training area in tuck position, taking advantage of the empty piste, and stopped by the edge of the traverse path that led back to the chairlift. The place Opa had shown her, where he'd been rescued, was below the Törli couloir, near the mountain stream. At least, that's how she remembered it.

Half-erased tracks snaked their way down the white surface, disappearing into the clouds above Schöngraben. The off-piste skiers from this morning were gone—probably finishing their days with après-ski drinks and music, in mountain huts. That was both good—the barbegazi wouldn't need to hide—and bad: no one would be near to help if anything happened to her. No one even knew where she was, and, on its own, her avalanche transceiver was pointless.

Tessa hesitated. She searched the contacts on her phone for someone to tell where she was headed. Lisa: no, Felix: no, Coach: definitely no, Dad—he lived thousands of kilometres away—no, no, no. She wasn't allowed to ski off-piste alone. Mum would be livid, if she ever found out. Felix was a better option than the other contacts, and his dad, Uncle Harry, was a rescue patrol volunteer.

She tapped with her frozen fingers: I ski Schöngraben now :-).

After pressing send, she donned her gloves, and left the prepared slopes. The ski route began easy and flat, following the forest, above the treeline. Her phone beeped, but she didn't stop. She only paused to catch her breath, where the landscape changed and the slope steepened.

Every season, the first time she stood on the edge of this near-vertical drop, it unnerved her. Only the knowledge that she'd survived the descent in earlier years assured her she could do it again. Normally, the bottom of Schöngraben was visible, but today it was snowing so much the view was greyed-out.

Turning back was still possible. She only needed to backtrack up to the trail through the forest. A route she'd often taken last year with Lisa.

After a long look at the whirling snow above the shrouded gorge, she made up her mind. The barbegazi would still be there tomorrow. She turned and shuffled sideways, up towards the trail. The soft snow made it hard work, and she soon became warm and sweaty inside her ski jacket.

A piercing whistle resonated between the mountainsides.

Tessa stopped dead. The hairs on the back of her neck stood up. The strange whistle sounded again, from high up on the opposite ridge. A similar peculiar whistle answered, from deep below in Schöngraben. The penetrating whistles didn't sound like rescue whistles, or referee whistles, or the shrill tone from blowing hard in the top part of the wooden recorders in the music room, or anything else she'd ever heard.

In an instant, she changed her decision and skied back down the slope. After five turns, she'd passed the spot where she'd begun backtracking, and, on the steep drop, there was no turning back. The barbegazi would save her if she was caught in an avalanche, wouldn't they?

They didn't whistle again. Silence cushioned her, like cotton wool. The only sounds were the clanks of her skis, whenever they grazed each other, and her wheezing breaths. The ground flattened out. Her turns became effortless. She floated across the white blanket, almost without touching it, until something blocked her skis. They stopped abruptly and Tessa flew in a low arc, landing face down in soft, wet snow.

Both skis remained attached—the bindings were tightened for race practice. She got up and brushed the snow away. Huge, boulder-sized snow heaps surrounded her. The remains of yesterday's avalanche. It had come down through the narrow Törli couloir, the other ski route in Schöngraben. The only route Opa had forbidden her to ski. The route where an avalanche had once buried him.

Somewhere nearby, he'd met the barbegazi.

Tessa edged forward, taking care to avoid the snow-covered rocks, while she searched for something resembling a barbegazi cave entrance. Snow stuck to her goggles, blocking her vision, although she kept wiping it away. She couldn't see the end of Schöngraben, where two massive man-made earth mounds protected the village from avalanches. The place where she should cross the mountain stream must be close by. Was she too far to the right? Or had she crossed already? This was so stupid. What did she think she was doing, following the sound of whistles? They could've been anything. Anywhere. Echoes in the mountains often made sound appear to be coming from a completely different direction. Perhaps it had been the whistle from a train down in the valley. How silly to think she'd heard a barbegazi!

She'd lost her speed, and she had to push herself through the deep snow. Her sweaty thermal underwear turned cold, making her shudder. The falling fluff swallowed the sound of her hiccupping sobs. Tears gathered inside her goggles. She could see even less while crying.

Suddenly, the ground below her caved in, revealing a hidden hollow under the new snow. Tessa tried to scramble back, but it was too late.

The tips of her skis rose, while her weight tilted her back. Something in her stomach somersaulted. She screamed. Windmilling her arms and the ski poles, she seemed to hover, suspended for an instant. Then the tails of her skis hit the ground. Both ski bindings released, catapulting her backwards, and she landed, with a crunch, on her back protector. Her helmet touched down, bouncing once. She tried to breathe, but the air had been knocked out of her.

A quiet, "Help," escaped her. And then she just lay at the bottom of the hole.

Far above, snow whirled out of the dark grey sky.

—7—

They crawled outside before the noisy metal things stopped. A snowstorm was coming. Papa said none of the humans would be foolish enough to journey through Schöngraben with so poor visibility. Even Maman and Liel came out to search near the cave.

Gawion surfed over to the western forest. He bounded up the steep scarp, between two rows of fir trees. Bending his toes so his claws gripped, and bouncing his heels off the ground, he propelled himself upwards. Then he slid downhill between the next two rows. All the while, searching for signs of his sister. But he found nothing.

Papa wanted them to comb the forests on both flanks of the gorge, although the avalanche trail ran straight between them.

"If she is injured, she might not be able to dig herself out of the snow," Papa had said, as if that was what he really believed. "Perhaps she has even gone into deep sleep to preserve energy, and cannot hear us."

Gawion had tried to tell Papa that Maeg must be below the avalanche tongue, because it was clear from her first whistle that she had been surfing the avalanche. But Papa refused to see sense.

Despite the emergency whistle, the lump of her fur and Gawion having smelt iron, Papa refused to believe Maeg had been abducted. Which was like someone denying winter was ending when the mountain streams overflowed and patches of bright grass appeared in the snow.

They ought to search much nearer to the human habitats, but Papa had forbidden Gawion to pass through the human-made earth mounds at the end of the narrow valley. Perhaps he could sneak around them to the village instead.

Almost as if he knew what Gawion was considering, Papa whistled from somewhere above, in the eastern forest. A second check-up whistle sounded, before Gawion answered.

He zigzagged up and down, trawling the forest. The snowfall covered his tracks, so at least he need not worry about that. His stomach growled again and again. Might he find a few late blackberries under the snow on a north-facing stretch?

The mere thought of berries made his mouth water. He grabbed a handful of snow and sucked on it, hoping to satisfy his hunger. It was no good. The powdery snow lacked taste and density. It disappeared on his tongue without even cooling his mouth.

He reached the bottom again, close to the mountain stream. It gurgled deep below the snow. The pit he had dug was nearby. If only the berry-human had finally delivered the gift.

He was gliding towards the hole when he heard a scream. A scream, not a whistle. And a very soft, human "Help".

Helping humans did not interest him, right now. But if a human had captured Maeg, perhaps he should capture a human.

The idea was ridiculous. Humans could not survive in the snow half as long as barbegazi could survive non-freezing temperatures. Which was not very long.

When the deep hole he had dug for the berries came into view, he hurried towards it, then stopped. What if Maeg's abductor was down there? Perhaps it had set a barbegazi trap. Should he run and hide? Or let himself be captured to find out where it had taken Maeg?

Gawion inched closer to the hole.

—8—

Tessa swallowed gulps of air. She had stopped crying. Her situation was simply too scary for tears. Instead, she pushed her goggles up and wiped her eyes. She wasn't buried under the snow, but this was the next worst thing.

The deep, cave-like hole was roundish and several metres across. The gap in the overhanging snow above her was much smaller—Tessa-sized, plus the bit her floundering poles and skis had torn down. Rounded rocks broke through the bumpy ground. This place wasn't cosy, not like the barbegazi caves in her imagination.

Standing and stretching, she thrust one ski pole upwards. It barely reached the opening. Climbing up the soft snow wall seemed impossible. A gap in the wall, a sort of tunnel, led into the snow. It was dark and narrow. Perhaps she could worm her way through it. But where would it end?

She took her phone out. No connection. Not even a single little dot. Mum's old phone, and it was useless. The cracked screen showed two texts. One was from Mum: Home with Oma. Off to work soon. Have fun with Lisa. Mum xxx. The other was from Felix. U r crazy:-(:-0, it read. He'd sent it two minutes after she'd texted him.

A sob escaped her. Mum wouldn't worry, if she thought Tessa was at Lisa's. She'd just think the girls were having one of their sleepovers. Like they used to. When would Felix begin to worry and tell Uncle Harry? Would Felix worry at all? He'd probably be lost in a computer game and only wonder where she was when she didn't turn up for ski training tomorrow. She stifled another sob. No one would be looking for her!

She had to do something. Find a way out, or make some kind of sign. The piste patrol only supervised the prepared slopes, but if, against all odds, someone came this way, they would not detect the signal from her avalanche transceiver unless they searched for it. She picked up one of her skis, held it with both hands, over her shoulder, and threw it. The ski flew out of the hole and disappeared. She crossed her gloved fingers, hoping it had landed upright, sticking out of the snow like a signpost.

The other ski, when she tried throwing it, landed on the edge, ripping more snow down, before it crashed to the ground. That gave her an idea. Using the ski, she hacked her way round the rim, enlarging the opening. After a few minutes, she'd torn the overhanging snow down completely. With her ski boot, she kicked into the wall of snow, at the height of her knee, making a step. Then she dug other steps with her gloved hands, getting warm as she laboured over her task.

It didn't work. She could get up onto the first step, but she couldn't get any grip with her hands, to hold herself against the wall and advance farther. Her ski and poles were no use as supports either. In frustration, she threw the other ski out of the opening, and then she heard a high-pitched squeal.

Tessa held her breath. It had definitely not been a human sound. She whistled.

Nothing. Had she imagined it?

No. It had to be one of them.

"Please, barbegazi. I can't get out," she called.

Although she had wished for and almost expected it, the next thing that happened surprised Tessa: six fingers and a furry head appeared at the top of the hole. Two pointed ears and a rather large potato-like nose stuck out of the shaggy whitish fur. Beneath bushy eyebrows, a pair of ice-blue, beady eyes were staring at her.

FROM *HABITS & HABITATS: A HISTORIC ACCOUNT OF ALPINE ELVES* BY PROFESSOR, DR EBERHART LUDWIG FRITZ BAHNE

According to Foubergé's 1781 written account,* barbegazi have forty-two words for snow. This number most likely included repetition of several words in a variety of French and Swiss local dialects.

Barbegazi classify snow based on wetness, smell, taste, colour, season, the size of the individual crystals and avalanche risk factor.

Their love of avalanches prompted Foubergé to adopt the collective noun "avalanche" and hence describe an "avalanche of barbegazi".

* Foubergé, A.S. 1781: *Elves of the Central Alps*. Paris: Éditions Féerique, 24–26.

—9—

Gawion lay on his stomach and looked down into the hole, rubbing his arm where the wooden foot had grazed it. A numbing tingle spread from his shoulder to his fingertips. Beyond a doubt, those long pretend feet contained other materials than wood.

A human child, a baby, younger than Liel, peered up at him, without swooning or shrieking. It smiled. Had it said "barbegazi"? Was this a trap? The elf hunters of his daymares were grown and menacing, nothing like this.

He jumped up, sniffing and scanning the surroundings, but found nothing except a faint whiff of metal from the sticks in its hand and those unnatural feet.

"Help me, barbegazi! Please!" it screamed.

Good. It sounded frightened, and it was trapped. Gawion shoved his toes into the snow as anchors, lay down again, and stared at the human.

He had never observed a conscious one up close before. Two funny plaited beards poked out from under the raspberry-like shell on its head. The tree-trunk-coloured plaits hung under its ears, not, as beards normally did, under the nose. Did these side-beards have any special function?

"Please help me," the human said. Eyes the colour of ragged peaks stared up at him, while springs flowed from them and dripped onto the floor.

If Maeg was imprisoned somewhere, perhaps an exchange could take place. If he found Maeg and her abductor... Perhaps Papa could guard this human while he searched the village? But, no, that might take too long. It would catch its death in the cold. Bringing it home was no solution either—the glacier block cooled the cave, not to mention Maman's reaction.

"Please, barbegazi."

Should he help it out? No others would travel this route so late. Without an avalanche, a search party's appearance was very unlikely. The reckless creature was alone. And it had nothing to do with Maeg's disappearance, or he would have caught a trace of his sister's thawing-spring-snow scent.

The streams from the human's eyes dried up. Its mouth, unhidden by a beard or fur, formed a tilted new moon, exposing single rows of odd, square teeth. It looked so friendly.

Gawion's stomach grumbled.

"Have you brought the berry gift?" The words, spoken in the human tongue, flew out of his mouth. He wanted to stuff his whole beard down his throat to stop them.

"Berry gift? What's that?"

Oh, why had he spoken? This was not the right human. Gawion withdrew from the rim.

"Hey! Come back." The voice turned panicky again. "Please, barbegazi! I... I need your help. I won't tell anyone."

Humans were deceptive. He mistrusted it, but he had to help. That was what they did, when they found living humans buried in the snow. After marching ten paces away from the hole, he began shovelling with his enormous feet. The top layer of snow was light and fluffy powder, and the soundless digging required no effort. The cries of help behind him continued. When his claws hit a crusty layer of old snow, the scraping drowned out the screams. He took a moment to savour the chill and harvest an icy lump to suck on. Then his feet let loose again, cutting a horizontal tunnel.

Just before he broke through the thin snow wall, he paused to prepare himself. The shell on this one's fragile head troubled him, and he had not rescued anyone conscious in a long time. After considering the size of this human, he revised Papa's lessons about their anatomy and the best walloping spots.

Gawion shot out of the tunnel. Swirling in the air, he oriented himself towards it, his walloping arm outstretched.

"Tha—" The impact cut off its voice, and it sank to the ground, lifeless as an aestivating barbegazi.

Yes! Gawion pumped his fist in triumph. Now he just had to get rid of it, and prevent it from ever returning.

—10—

"Hey, kid, wake up."

Tessa opened one eye and saw a pair of heavy brown shoes, dark green socks and hairy legs below leather knickerbockers. She groaned.

"Take me home..." she mumbled, and hummed a few notes.

"What's that? You okay?"

With a huge effort, she rolled onto her back. A pimpled boy stood bent over her. His expression wavered between concern and irritation. A chequered shirt and a green felt waistcoat completed his outfit. Formal wear.

"Was that you whistling?" he asked.

The back protector riding up her neck, or something under her ski helmet, blocked her from shaking her head. The goggles. They had slid down in front and almost choked her. She groaned again. Warm light shone out of a glass door onto the porch where she lay. A wreath of holly and red berries hung above gold-etched text and a row of stars. Tessa knew she recognized the door, but the letters kept slipping out of focus, and the four, or maybe five, golden stars danced. Where had the hole in the snow gone?

"You can't lie in front of the hotel entrance."

Wasn't he the big brother of someone in her class? A trainee waiter?

He glanced inside, then back at Tessa before he opened the door. Bells tinkled. "Harry! Hey, Harry!"

Her head hurt. Perhaps she'd bumped it when she tumbled into that hole. But how did she get to the village? She remembered being trapped in the snow, desperate to escape, then misty fumes, like dry-ice, surrounding her, and now she lay here as if by magic.

"Harry," the waiter called through the open door. "You know all the ski kids, right?"

Why had he asked if she whistled? The barbegazi had whistled, long before she landed in the hole. The barbegazi. She'd seen one, hadn't she? It was real, wasn't it? How else had she escaped? She closed her eyes, recalling the details. The beady eyes, set deep in the thick fur. The tangled beard snaking round one of the three-fingered hands. If only she'd seen the feet. The barbegazi had said something. Something she understood...

"Tessa!" Someone in white, with a floor-length black

apron, squatted and shook her. "Are you all right? What happened?" Uncle Harry propped her up.

Her head spun. "I crashed..."

"Tell Mick to mind the mushroom soup. I'll take Tessa home. Won't be more than ten minutes."

"Yes, chef." The waiter disappeared, to the jingle of bells.

"Is Susi or Aunt Gertrude home?" Uncle Harry tugged at the goggles and pulled them up onto her helmet.

The dense fog in her brain cleared.

"Oma's always home," she said.

Where was the barbegazi? Did something move among the fir trees at the far side of the parking lot just now? Falling lumps of wet snow obstructed her view.

"What are you looking for?" Uncle Harry was following her gaze.

"The... My skis." It wasn't even a lie. Where were her skis? The poles, her new World Cup Lekis, stood in the snow below the porch.

"I can see something." Uncle Harry ran across the parking lot and came back carrying her skis, or rather, what used to be her skis. "What on earth did you do to them?"

Tessa blinked. Was she seeing double? No, both skis had been broken almost in half behind the binding. Only the metal edges held the halves together. Ragged wood splinters peeked out between the waxed black bottom and the enamelled top. Her new Atomic skis, ruined.

She slumped, sliding sideways.

In a haze, Uncle Harry drove her home. Afterwards, he helped Oma upstairs so she could watch Tessa until Mum came. He thought Tessa might have a concussion. Tessa thought he might be right.

She lay on the sofa all evening, dozing and humming a song that was stuck in her head, while Oma sat in the armchair with her crossword puzzle. Every time Tessa fell asleep, Oma woke her, just in case, like you're supposed to with concussions.

"I should be taking care of you," Tessa mumbled, but Oma just smiled and fetched water and cool cloths. Perhaps she was better at fussing over someone than being made a fuss of.

"The barbegazi must've carried me," Tessa said, when she began to feel less woozy, and asked if Oma believed she'd seen one.

"Of course, dear," Oma replied.

But would anyone else? They hadn't believed Opa. Not even Mum, who'd been away at hotelier school at the time. "Why didn't Opa care that no one believed him?"

Oma shrugged. "He'd have been just as sceptical if he hadn't seen the barbegazi with his own eyes."

Later, Mum rushed in the door, calling, "How is she? How are you, Mum? Are you both okay?"

She ran to the sofa, seizing Tessa, saying how sorry she was, how she would've come earlier—the restaurant wasn't even busy—but she'd forgotten her phone in the car and only seen Harry's message when she was on her way home.

"My darling girl," Mum said, over and over again. Her fussing was frantic compared to Oma's, but Tessa leant into the hard embrace.

Oma and Mum whispered for a long time in the hallway before Mum helped Oma downstairs.

"Could I have some hot chocolate, Mum?" Tessa sat up, discarding the wool blanket. The song in her head had stopped and the red digits on the oven, *23:41*, didn't wiggle any more. Everything seemed normal, except her journey from the snow, which remained a blur. And, of course, the barbegazi.

Mum brought her a steaming cup with a thick layer of whipped cream on top. She still wore her ankle-length *dirndl* costume—the waitress uniform—and she sat at the other end of the sofa, kneading her temples, without speaking for a while.

"So you fell into a hole in Schöngraben, got rescued by a fairy who delivered you to Hotel Lawinenfang, but ruined your brand new skis. That about right?" Mum finally said, in a matter-of-fact tone.

Tessa stirred her drink and nodded. "Barbegazi are actually not fairies—"

"I don't know where to start, Tessa..." Mum snatched the blanket from the floor and began folding it. "This obsession of yours has to stop. In what fantasy world would you ever be allowed to ski through Schöngraben alone? If that's what you did. And how could you ruin your skis? Your father sent money for those, and you know I can't afford—" She scrunched the blanket into a ball and threw it back onto the floor. "Perhaps I shouldn't let you ski at all, if you can't keep even the simplest rules. You never ski off-piste alone. Never."

Mum's voice had changed from shrill to choked, and she leant forward, placing her face in her hands.

"I'm sorry," Tessa mumbled. "I didn't mean to—"

"Promise me..." Mum straightened and turned to look Tessa in the eyes. "I want you to promise to never ski off-piste without adult supervision again."

Tessa hesitated. She had found a barbegazi. It wasn't something she'd imagined. But how would she ever find it again without skiing off-piste on her own?

In a tiny voice, she said, "I promise."

—II—

Gawion drew a breath of relief. The tall human who had fetched the broken wooden feet had looked so much like the berry-human that he had almost shown himself. At the last moment, he wondered at its lack of beard and noticed how it resembled the berry-human of decades ago, not the berry-human he had seen last winter.

The two humans disappeared in a vehicle, with a loud roar. All human mechanical inventions polluted the mountain silence: the wheeled vehicles, the contraptions for transportating humans up the snow-covered slopes, and, worst of all, the flying vehicles topped with rotating metal blades.

Sometimes, after avalanches, those machines flew above Schöngraben, close to the cave, making a whirlwind of powder snow. They scared Gawion. Maeg too, although she liked it when they dropped explosive devices to blast snow cornices and release avalanches. The loud bangs scared him even more, though he had not told Maeg. Life had been easier when the humans used horses and carts, and stayed away from the high mountains.

Gawion had not been so close to the village in decades, and he stared transfixed at the imposing human dwelling, while he inched backwards through the rows of fir trees. Nearby, dogs bayed.

Another vehicle arrived. Its light beams lit up the trees and millions of snowflakes. Gawion froze, standing immobile as a glacier. Two majestic firs cast long shadows beside him, but only a sapling grew between him and the vehicle. A dog barked somewhere. Turn off the lights, he prayed. Doors slammed, and human voices moved away. The lights still shone.

"You forgot the headlights again," a deep voice said.

One human returned to the vehicle. It stared right at him and said, "What *is* that?"

"Rrroowff! Rrroowff!" In one fluid motion, Gawion turned, got down on all fours, pretending to be a dog, barked and bolted. He kicked and shoved with his legs, sweeping piles of snow over the imprints of his long feet.

Howls and baying answered him, but he did not stop until pine branches slapped against him, blurring his vision, in the forest.

"Rooooowf," a bark greeted him from not far behind. It

translated into: "What's up, mate?", and a large dog slunk towards him.

Gawion panted, trying to catch his breath. He wanted to hide—dogs were as bad as humans—but he could not run any more. His own barks had been a survival instinct, born by the background noise of baying dogs. He realized now that he had barked, "Help. The humans are after me." Or something like that. He was uncertain of the local dialect, and, though elves spoke all languages, Dog was a whole new snowball game. Intonation played a key role. Meaning changed depending on where in the throat the sounds were initiated. Barbegazi necks are nearly invisible, so Gawion had little to work with. As did many dog races. Not this one though. Its long, broad neck rippled with thick folds of short-haired, tree-trunk-coloured fur.

"You okay?" the dog asked.

"Yes, thank you."

"Rraaooooo." The dog howled from deep in its throat. "Situation under control. Relax," rang out across the valley.

A chorus of distant yaps answered.

"Call me Brownie," the dog barked. It sat next to Gawion, stuck its pink tongue out and panted.

"Gawion."

"Are you one of those fancy dog types? I'm a Labrador myself." Brownie studied him with kind, starless-night eyes. They were glazed over, and Gawion got the distinct feeling Brownie's eyesight was poor. "Haven't seen anyone quite like you before." The neck stretched, growing even longer. A wet nose nuzzled him. Brownie sniffed. "Hmmm. Your scent is odd."

The wet dog stench overpowered Gawion, who leant away. He only knew the names of two dog types: Rottweilers and bloodhounds. The dogs that hunted innocent creatures. Maman's recollections of those horrifying monsters, chasing them as they escaped the zoological garden at Schönbrunn, gave him daymares, and he hoped he would never meet either.

"Have you no humans?" he asked, to distract Brownie. The village dogs he had seen from a distance were tied up or fenced in by their humans.

"Yeah, but I'm a free spirit. I go home when I need food and a warm hearth."

Gawion sighed. He longed for the morning, when he might curl up in front of the ice cooler. His sigh must have meant more in Dog, because Brownie turned his half-blind eyes towards him again, and said, "What's the problem, mate?"

"I fear humans have abducted my sister. I am searching for her."

"Does she smell anything like you?" Brownie snuffled again.

"I suppose so." Gawion did not know how to describe that sweet scent of thawing spring snow, in any language except his own.

"I'll have a sniff around. Ask my mates."

"Thanks."

"Meet you here tomorrow night," Brownie barked, and he padded off back towards the village.

No matter what Maman said about dogs, Gawion was not afraid of this creature. Perhaps he had even found a friend in the village. Someone he could trust.

He lifted his beard and sniffed where Brownie's nose had nuzzled him. Yuck! After rubbing it clean and rolling in the snow, he still stank of wet dog. If he did not get rid of the odour before morning, he would be in an avalanche of trouble.

FROM *HABITS & HABITATS: A HISTORIC ACCOUNT OF ALPINE ELVES* BY PROFESSOR, DR EBERHART LUDWIG FRITZ BAHNE

Hardly any information exists about the barbegazi's diet, but snow and ice doubtless feature high on their dietary plan.

However, when captured barbegazi were given ice cubes, it rarely sustained them for more than a few weeks. Experiments with feeding them moss, pine needles and cooked or raw alpine meats were equally unsuccessful in keeping the barbegazi alive.

WEDNESDAY, 28TH DECEMBER

—12—

Tessa dreamt about skiing and snow and barbegazi, waking often to untangle her sheets. Once, she woke with a pounding heart and vivid dream images.

In the dream, she had skied through a hole into an upside-down world, where loud music blasted from invisible speakers. A giant furry creature had taken her skis and bent them into circles. "Round as a berry," it said, and smacked its unseen lips. Then it shrank—or she grew—and the creature, now clearly a barbegazi, said, "Have a blueberry, Tessa." It threw a turquoise berry the size of a watermelon towards her. Tessa opened her mouth, which expanded, to catch the berry. When she swallowed, the world spun again, the music stopped, and she stood in the hole in Schöngraben, looking up at the barbegazi. It said, "Have you brought the berry gift?"

The berry gift. That's what the barbegazi had said. She remembered now.

The wooden beams of the roof creaked. She tried to imagine herself back in the hole, the barbegazi above her, instead of the ceiling, asking, "Have you brought the berry gift?" The words had been spoken in a clear, high-pitched voice. Definitely real, she thought, before she slipped into another dream.

When Tessa woke, bright winter light shone through a gap in the curtains. Mum had let her sleep in. The ski club would be training now. She wished she were there, racing, cold air prickling her skin. Then she remembered her ruined skis and pulled the duvet over her head, shutting out the light.

The berry gift! She jumped out of bed and grabbed the black book on top of her piled-up school books. Opening it, she flipped to the barbegazi chapter and skimmed the pages. The book contained interesting information about barbegazi fur and feet and iron cages, but no references to berries or gifts.

While she ate a late breakfast, she mulled over the mysterious berry gift. Mum was at home, folding laundry. She scolded Tessa for skiing off-piste alone, and nagged her about remembering to "live in the real world". Tessa only half-listened and nodded whenever Mum paused.

"Oma's dusting her cupboards and bookcases this afternoon," Mum said. "I offered to do it, now that I'm taking the day off anyway, but she wants to do it herself."

Tessa looked up. "That's good, right?"

Mum shrugged. "I just hope it's not too much for her. Perhaps she'll let you help."

"Okay," Tessa said. "She can't do the top shelves herself." She didn't need to add that Opa used to do those—Mum's eyes became glassy before she turned away, nodding.

Later, standing on the ladder, she wiped dust from Opa's trophies. On the biggest, a prize from the Austrian downhill championships more than forty years ago, an inset of shiny, red crystals—Tessa used to think they were rubies—sparkled like redcurrants after rain. Her thoughts wandered to the barbegazi dream.

Oma swept the duster over the grandfather clock. She appeared to have even more energy than last night. It seemed safe to ask.

"Did Opa ever mention a berry gift?"

"Him and his berries. The freezer's so full of berries, I could hardly find room for the Tupperware of leftover goulash soup." Oma dusted the long pendulum of the clock, and it skipped a few beats. "For years I suspected he gave them to Mrs Huber. The Hubers never had much, and after she was widowed... She was his childhood sweetheart, you know."

In a flash, Tessa thought of old Mrs Huber—brandishing her walking stick, her mouth tugged down in a constant look of disapproval.

Sniffing, Oma pulled an embroidered handkerchief out of her sleeve. After drying her eyes, she muttered, "I didn't speak to her for decades."

"But he gave them to the barbegazi?"

"Of course he did. And to the very last he spoke about it. 'Remember the berries on the twenty-first of December' he said, 'Remember to tell Tessa—'" Oma let her hand with the duster fall. "What date is it, dear?"

"It's after Christmas."

"Oh, Ohhhh..." Oma drew the sigh out. Like a balloon leaking air, she deflated and sank into the squishy armchair.

Alarmed, Tessa jumped down from the ladder.

Oma's face had turned quite white. Tiny beads of sweat appeared on her forehead. "I promised him," she whispered, clutching her chest, her breathing becoming ragged.

"Oma! Shall I get Mum? Your pills? Call the doctor?"

"Fe- fetch. Su- Susi. Pills," Oma stuttered, and Tessa ran up the stairs, calling for her mother.

Tessa helped Mum get Oma wrapped in her coat and out into the car. Before she closed the passenger door, she hugged Oma and whispered in her ear, "Don't worry. I'll bring the berries to the barbegazi," but she wasn't sure Oma heard.

—13—

The moment Gawion slid into the cave, on his belly, he regretted coming home. Maman screeched, Papa bellowed his name and Liel, scared of the noise, wailed, her nose turning glacier-blue. Papa whistled one of those whistles that is audible ten kilometres away in the right wind conditions. Gawion rose, edging back, until he stood against the snow wall.

"THE VILLAGE!" Papa bellowed. "HAVE I NOT TOLD YOU"—he paused to inhale—"under no circumstances, to get within a hundred barbegazi feet of the human dwellings?"

Gawion opened his mouth to speak, but Maman beat him to it.

"How could you? We are already worried sick about Maeg."

"But—"

"What is this?" Maman sniffed, then she pushed Papa aside—no mean feat—and strode towards Gawion. He forced himself not to duck. She snuffled with her large nose. "Your stench. That is not dog, is it?"

"DOG?" In one leap, Papa had landed on his other side, thrusting his boulder of a nose into Gawion's beard. Both of them sniffed at him as if they were dogs themselves, reminding him of Brownie. Gawion pressed his lips together to stop an improper urge to laugh.

"For the love of snow, tell me you have not been consorting with dogs." Maman spoke softly, her tone pleading. It wiped his sense of amusement away. He would have preferred it if she had screeched.

"A very friendly dog," he muttered.

With their long feet, his parents blocked him from moving, and their fur stood on end, tingling. He could sense them exchanging glances above his head.

"Oh, Gawion." Maman sighed. "Never trust a dog. They do the bidding of humans."

"Your maman believed the imperial dogs were her friends, in Vienna. Do you remember, *ma chérie?*"

"I shall never forget." In a gentle gesture, Maman twirled strands of Papa's beard around her fingers. "Those snarling, baying beasts, tracking us to the station, despite the snowstorm—"

"If the train had not departed right after we got Grandpère up on its roof, we would still be stuck in that iron cage as part of the imperial menagerie."

Keep talking, Gawion thought. The longer they talked, the calmer they became. Perhaps they would forget all about him.

"Yuck, yuckety-yuck. Why does Gawion smell so bad?" Liel, her nose a normal snow-colour again, had sneaked past her parents and now stood underneath Gawion's chin.

Papa swivelled on the spot. "Yes. Explain yourself."

Gawion took a deep breath, his brain whirling, trying to find a way to avoid being grounded and having to watch Liel while Maman searched with Papa.

He told them the whole story, from finding the human, who seemed to know what he was, in the hole, to his meeting with Brownie. Or, almost the whole story.

When Gawion explained how he had transported the human and her broken wooden feet to a big dwelling on the edge of the village, Papa tensed and said, "You moved into their artificial light? You could have been seen," and grasped his hand. "Good thinking, posing as a dog."

Gawion did not mention that he only pretended to be a dog after he was in fact seen.

Maman shook her head while he talked, mumbling "Never trust a dog" over and over. So he neglected to inform them of his meeting with Brownie tonight.

They did not ground him, but he had also not mentioned the worst thing. His biggest mistake. The crucial part missing from his explanation. The one thing he omitted, after careful consideration: that he had spoken to the human.

—14—

Back in Oma's kitchen, Tessa crouched to open the freezer. The drawers stuck, filled to the rim with berries in clear plastic bags. Oma usually wrote content and date and weight on frozen food. Nothing marked these bags—another sign they were meant for the barbegazi. But how could she deliver them without skiing off-piste?

Tessa wished she'd not been left at home. The ticks from the grandfather clock amplified the emptiness of the room. "Just go on ticking," she muttered, and ran upstairs.

She turned on the TV, flipping through reruns and cartoons, until she let the weather channel fill the house with sound and flickering light. After retrieving her phone from the charger, she curled up on the sofa, waiting for Mum and Oma to return.

Felix had sent three messages. The first read: u r as crazy as ur opa. The second, an animation of a stick figure snapping her skis in half, made her smile. And the third was good news: come by tmrw b4 ski to fit my old skis 4u. Only 2 x training until race! At least she could get up on the slopes tomorrow.

Returning to the elf book, she studied the barbegazi chapter again, and read snippets about limestone-cave goblins and mountain-spring sprites.

Later, Mum sent a message: Oma okay. Am driving her to hospital for tests. Go to Lisa's or there's soup in the fridge. Mum xxx.

If they were going to the hospital, it didn't sound as if Oma was okay.

The cosy kitchen and the homemade desserts at Lisa's tempted Tessa. But Maria would be there, or Lisa would be at Maria's. They'd boasted of their daily sleepovers. She didn't really mind leftover soup, and she wasn't even hungry.

But the barbegazi she'd seen might be hungry, craving the berries Opa used to bring. And if barbegazi ate berries, then she knew something that professor didn't. He'd be so grateful when she told him, he'd definitely mention her in his next book!

Opa had wanted Oma to tell her about the berries... Tessa bit her lip. Perhaps there was another way of reaching the barbegazi hole. She'd promised Mum not to ski off-piste alone. She hadn't promised not to go hiking alone. The nearest hospital was thirty kilometres away. Would that give her enough time?

As a precaution, she wrote two notes. The first, *I'm going over to Lisa's,* she fixed to the fridge with the Merlion magnet Dad had sent from Singapore. She placed the second on her pillow, where Mum wouldn't look unless she became worried. In scrawling letters she'd written: *If Lisa's not home, I'll walk up to Schöngraben.*

After pulling on thermal long johns and thick, striped socks, she rummaged in the attic until she found Mum's big rucksack—the one they used for overnight hikes in summer. Downstairs, she lined the rucksack with a heavy-duty blue plastic carrier bag, and filled it with the frozen berries. Less than half of them fitted inside, but going upstairs she swayed under the rucksack's weight. With her outdoor clothes on, she trudged outside and into the garage. Her ruined skis lay by the jumble meant for the refuse station. She shuddered. Breaking alpine skis required immense force. She'd always thought of the barbegazi as cuddly creatures. Perhaps they weren't quite as harmless as she'd imagined.

Although she searched, she couldn't find her snowshoes. Last season, after the final race, when ski training stopped, she'd often used them with Lisa. They would walk up the slopes, chatting, and sit on a bench in the sun, before running downwards, sliding through powder snow up to their knees. They always exited the forest on Jakobsweg, the old pilgrimage route through Europe which led all the way to Santiago de Compostela in Spain, then half-glided to Lisa's house, and drank hot chocolate in that cosy kitchen. The snowshoes were probably still at Lisa's.

Opa's snowshoes hung on the wall, above her broken skis. They looked like relics from the Stone Age. The wood, bent into the shape of elongated tennis rackets, gleamed. As usual, Opa had oiled them in the spring. The strings and the smooth leather straps seemed new, yet they had been old long before Tessa was born. They weighed a lot compared to her own high-tech aluminium snowshoes, but they were better than nothing. She strapped them onto the sides of the rucksack, and borrowed Mum's lightweight, adjustable hiking poles.

On her way through the darkening village, a ski bus rumbled past, its snow chains grinding on the gravel. A group of wobbly ski-boot walkers shouted après-ski song refrains. To avoid them, Tessa crossed the road. Behind the last houses, the road became a steep track. Sweat ran down her brow under the knitted hat. She huffed, and her shoulders ached.

Two sledges rushed towards her, their riders squealing and laughing. Tessa shrieked and jumped sideways to escape being hit. The toboggan run was open tonight, even though it was Wednesday—above her, on the track leading up the mountain, splotches of warm yellow light gleamed among the snow-covered trees.

Another group of tobogganists sped past. Tessa crept along the edge of the track until she crossed the bridge over the mountain stream and the sharp turn-off to the toboggan run. From here on, there would be no more sledges and no more light.

By the last lamp post, she secured her headlamp and tightened the leather straps of the snowshoes round her boots. When she was done, her breathing had slowed. She shivered and took a few tentative steps. Although she walked with her feet wide apart, the heavy things still clanged together. Her legs were too short to heave Opa's snowshoes far enough to lift their wobbly back ends. Should she take them off again and just walk on the hardened ski trails? No. If she accidentally stepped off those tracks, she might sink into soft snow.

"No falling into holes, today." She trudged forward, finding a slow rhythm. Pole in, lift opposite foot, drag forward, set down, pole in, lift, drag...

The two huge mounds, which marked the entrance to Schöngraben, and protected the village from avalanches, loomed above her. When she passed between them, the faint shrieks from the toboggan run died away.

On skis, the lower part of the gorge seemed flat, but it was steeper than most roads, and soon her whole body ached. Her shins cramped. She whistled—not a tune, just individual hoarse tones—but she lacked air. The thumping blood in her ears, and her ragged breathing, made it difficult to hear if anyone whistled in answer.

From up near the trees, on her right, came a faint swishing sound. There couldn't be tobogganists here. Or skiers, so late. Could it be a barbegazi?

Tessa stopped and turned. Her headlamp drew a dark green circle on the black forest. "Hel-lo," she called, her voice cracking. "Anybody there?"

Silence.

She continued her slow ascent, whistling and calling, "Hello bar-be-gaziii... I'm bringing the berry gift."

—15—

In the cave, the day had felt endless. Maman recited her terrifying dog-tales and kept repeating her "never trust a dog" mantra. Despite her scrubbing his beard with all kinds of snow, Gawion still stank. That set both her and Papa off whenever he neared their wrinkled noses. If it had not, he might have confessed and told them he had spoken to the human.

But what did it matter? He had only asked about the berry gift, and, after his memory charm, the human would have forgotten ever seeing him.

What he would not give for the berry gift! The blackberry he had shared with Liel, helped less in his hollow stomach than a snowflake trying to fill the crack in a glacier.

Outside in the pleasant evening gloom, they prepared to resume the search. Papa pointed him to the bare rocks above the treeline. The least likely place to find Maeg.

"We should search below the avalanche, Papa."

"Have you not already trawled the area from the avalanche to the earth mounds? Or did you neglect your duties, in your haste to go on adventures in the village?"

"I did not," Gawion answered, feeling blood pound all the way up to the points of his ears. Every snowflake of the scar left by the avalanche had been combed. And every boulder and lump of snow below had been turned during that first frantic night. Twice. First with Papa, and then again on his own. "How about beyond Schöngraben? In the village."

"Too dangerous. If Maeg has indeed been taken, she might be used as bait to lure us thither. That is how they captured Maman and Grandpère, when they tried to rescue me."

"I know, I know." Gawion stopped Papa before he got into his storytelling stride. He had heard about those particular events hundreds of times. They were a chapter of the cautionary tales told to keep him and Maeg away from humans. "But we could sneak around the village, listen to the dogs. They might reveal news of Maeg."

Papa rubbed his chin under its long beard, and sighed.

Gawion, sensing his uncertainty, pressed on. "She is not lying under the snow, Papa. She has been taken. It was your first instinct when we found the fur."

Papa stood with hunched shoulders, staring down at the village—his fear both obvious and contagious.

Dots of light littered the darkening valley, creeping up towards the surrounding night forests. From up here, where few trees grew, the lights seemed as distant and mysterious as the emerging stars.

After a long time, Papa said, "All right. I will go to the village. You must stay in Schöngraben."

"But, Papa—"

"There will be no discussion. Search the bottom part again, if you must, but do not cross between the human-made earth mounds. Understood?"

Gawion nodded. Brownie would have to come into Schöngraben.

Near the bottom of the gorge, they parted. Papa continued, hidden by the trees. Gawion passed the hole where he had found the human just yesterday. Its gaping emptiness neither surprised nor disappointed him. His stomach reacted, though, with a faint grumble.

He followed the mountain stream—the only area with no human tracks—stopping at intervals to kick at mounds in the snow. He had already searched here. If only he had been able to persuade Papa to let him go to the village!

He heard a feeble human whistle, coming from a strange light cone farther down the narrow valley. A voice called, "Berry gift."

Gawion sniffed. No, that could not be. His stomach growled in response. A smile spread below his beard. Finally, the berry-human had come. Excited, he surfed towards the light, careful to stay clear of its beam.

"Berry gift," the human called again. It stopped. The light was shining out from its head. The human dimmed the brightness until it cast an oval pale shape on the snow.

With a jolt, Gawion recognized the human he had found in the hole yesterday. How could it come back, when he had ruined its wooden feet? And how could it remember? His charm should have filled its head with that horrible noise.

The usual winter forest stillness seeped out from the shadows under the trees. Underneath the berry aroma, the air carried only the faintest tang of iron.

The human dumped a large pack on the ground, fumbled inside it and extracted a see-through bag. Even from this distance, Gawion could see the small blood-coloured balls, and hear the dull clicks they made when the human shook the bag. It used its teeth to tear the transparent material. The delicious scent of raspberries engulfed Gawion. His stomach rumbled and the human looked up, pointing the light beam to a place just in front of his toes.

It threw a handful of berries out beyond the light. Gawion hurried to sniff them out. The first four he swallowed without taking time to enjoy them. He had to stay alert. The rest he collected and dropped into the little pocket Maman had knotted in the middle of his beard. He would save them for her.

The human threw more berries, but this time they landed inside the light. One of them was just at the edge though. He might be able to snatch it, without the human noticing. Then again... The human stood completely still, probably staring at exactly that berry.

"I've brought the berry gift," it said.

Gawion could not leave without all those berries. Perhaps if he walloped the human and took them... But that was an impolite response to someone bringing food, and then it most certainly would not bring any more.

The light cone moved to the side. Now was his chance. His arm shot out and seized the berry, but the light returned too soon.

"I'm not going to harm you," it said. The human poured berries into the snow by its feet, dotting the ground with blood-coloured spots. "The berries are from my grandfather."

Was this really a descendent of the berry-human? He sniffed, inhaling deep through his large nose, but the sweet berries overpowered any particulars of the human's scent. He supposed it could be true. Why else would it bring berries?

"He broke his leg in an avalanche right up there, years and years ago." The human pointed. "One of you saved him and helped him home."

That *was* true. Gawion only hesitated for a moment more before he said, "To be sure, it was I."

—16—

In two leaps and a flurry of white powder, the barbegazi landed next to Tessa. Up close he—or she—looked even stranger than in Opa's sketched drawings. Like an upright, cuddly teddy-polar-bear, with the biggest feet she'd ever seen. She wanted to sing and dance and jump around, but, fearful of frightening it, she stood without moving while the barbegazi snatched the berries at her feet.

Most of them disappeared into a parting in the middle of its long beard, but it scooped one three-fingered handful of snow and berries into its mouth, and gulped down the mixture with loud smacks. Talk about craving berries. It must've been starving.

The barbegazi only reached her shoulder, and hedgerow-like eyebrows hid its eyes, so she tried to get down on her knees to look into its face. Her snowshoes clanked together. The barbegazi swirled its head towards them, then up at Tessa, like a startled animal. It stopped chewing and stared at her. Instead of trying to get down on her knees, Tessa slowly leant back until she was half-sat on the sturdy frame of the rucksack. She adjusted the beam of her headlamp, so it didn't shine directly on the barbegazi. The creature's ice-blue eyes followed her movements.

"I'm Tessa. What's your name?" Inside the mitten, she crossed her fingers, willing it to speak.

"Gawion." He bent his head in a formal bow. The gesture, worthy of a ballroom filled with royalty, was at odds with the yellowish, gleaming fur, which hung in clumps encrusted with ice.

Tessa gave a quick nod. How could she get it to talk?

Before she thought of a question, Gawion asked, "Where is your grandfather?"

The pitch of his voice—for she was certain it was a he, now—reminded her of those "Staying Alive" singers Mum liked, or someone speaking after inhaling from a helium balloon, but without the mirth.

"He died. Twenty-eight days ago." The familiar lump grew in her throat. This, the barbegazi, was what Opa had planned to show her. They should've been here together, and then told Oma all about it afterwards. She blinked to keep the tears at bay.

"Allow me to condole." Gawion bent his head. "That explains the missing berry gift."

"Did you help me out of the hole yesterday?"

A third bow, before he rubbed his belly, streaking his beard with red spirals.

"I apologize for the damage to your wooden feet."

Tessa shuddered. Not because she was scared, but because Gawion's bow sent an icy breeze towards her. It was as if he were radiating coldness. Despite the state of her skis, she wasn't scared at all.

"Why'd you break them?"

"I presumed it would prevent your return. Obviously, I was mistaken."

Tessa smiled.

"I wanted to find one of you. And I did. Now they have to believe me." She could even take a photo and send it to that professor. The whole world would know the barbegazi weren't extinct! "Will you come with me? So my friends can see you?"

The ice-blue eyes gazed deep into Tessa's, then Gawion shook his head, the long beard swinging from side to side.

"Please. You must come. I brought berries," she said. "I have more berries at home. You can have all of them."

He sighed. At least, it sounded like a sigh.

"Please. No one believes me. Everyone says you're extinct."

"It is better that way."

Hot tears welled up in her eyes. The barbegazi blurred around the edges.

"But why?" she asked with a sob.

"Your sort will want to capture us."

"My friends wouldn't do that," Tessa said. But others might, she knew. In school, they'd just finished their endangered species project, where they'd learnt about gorillas and pandas and snow leopards, and breeding programmes in captivity. In that light, some of the entries in the elf book took on a new meaning. Perhaps she shouldn't tell that professor she'd found a barbegazi.

"That's why Opa lied," she said. "He lied to protect you." Or maybe the professor lied in his book, to protect the barbegazi? Opa had never stopped talking about his rescuer, and the whole village had mocked him for it. The puzzle baffled her, but clearly someone had made an effort to keep the barbegazi's existence secret.

"Okay. I won't tell anyone about you," she promised. "And don't worry, no one even suspects you're still around."

"I fear that is not entirely true," Gawion said. "You see, my sister has been missing since the big avalanche." He nodded up towards the Törli couloir.

"Let me fetch a shovel and help you search," Tessa offered.

"You are most kind, but Maeg—Maegorodiel—is not here. Not under the snow. It is much worse."

"What's worse than being buried under the snow?"

"Being held captive in the village."

"But who?..." Few people had skied off-piste on Monday, when the avalanche warning was so high. On Kapall, she'd only seen the man in white. Then she remembered the whistling guest at Felix's house.

"It might be nothing," she told Gawion, "but I have an idea."

FROM *HABITS & HABITATS: A HISTORIC ACCOUNT OF ALPINE ELVES* BY PROFESSOR, DR EBERHART LUDWIG FRITZ BAHNE

Barbegazi aestivate, spending the months from May to October in a deep sleep, below one of Europe's ever-shrinking glaciers. Global warming and retreating glaciers* are therefore believed to be major contributing factors in their presumed extinction.

Statistically, the best time to capture barbegazi is in October. In several documented cases from Mer de Glace in France and Great Aletsch Glacier in Switzerland, the creatures have stumbled sleepily out of their dens, into traps set in glacier crevasses.

---

* Measured retreat of the Great Aletsch Glacier (the largest glacier in Switzerland) from 1870 to 1990 amounts to two kilometres, or close to ten per cent of its length. Since 1980, glaciers around the world have been losing mass at an accelerated rate.

—17—

"Let me help you with the berries first." The human, Tessa, got up. It was taller than Papa. As it tilted the big pack towards him, he saw the countless see-through bags, filled with berries, inside. Berries and more berries. Perhaps enough to feed them until the summer sleep.

"D'you want more raspberries?"

Gawion licked his lips. "Please." With so many berries, he could eat a few more without feeling bad.

Tessa smiled and poured raspberries into his cupped hand, spilling several, which Gawion snatched up from the snow. He scooped them into his mouth and closed his eyes, savouring the cold lumps.

"Good?"

He opened his eyes and nodded, trying to say "delicious", but only managed a grunt. His mouth had not been full of berries since he woke in the autumn. Maman, as usual, had risen days before the rest of them. She had gathered a whole mountain of berries, and her beard, which she knotted into a basket, was striped in colours of a sunset sky. As always, just after aestivation, Gawion had been allowed to eat as many berries as he wanted, and, starved as he was, he had eaten five whole handfuls.

Later in the year, they scraped snow away from brambles and found half-ripe and half-rotten berries underneath. Tessa's berries were much better, because they had been picked just when they were ripe. The raspberries dissolved in his mouth, and the tasty juice filled him with pleasure and energy. His belly gave a slow, satisfied growl.

Tessa made odd noises, like a small bird hiccuping. "You look like a vampire with blood running down your chin."

He finished chewing and gave the sort of courteous bow Maman had taught him to. "I am much obliged to you." He did not want to reveal that he had no clue what a vampire was. Probably some type of dog. Dog! He was supposed to be meeting the dog.

"Excuse me a moment," he said. Then he bayed, "Brownie?"

A distant howl answered with something he did not quite catch, perhaps about Brownie sniffing him out.

"What was that?" Tessa had begun to jump and do strange things with its arms. Almost as if it thought it could fly. Perhaps this human was a little bit peculiar.

"A prior engagement. Are you attempting to... to take to the skies?"

"You're so funny. That's not in the book." Tessa bird-hiccuped again and stopped moving its arms and legs. "I'm freezing cold."

"Aha. And you do not like that?"

"No. D'you want to borrow the rucksack to carry the berries?" Tessa lifted the blood-coloured pack with all the scary metal buckles. "It might be too big."

In stupefied shock, he saw how Tessa was swinging the thing towards him. A buckle struck the back of his arm. Gawion jerked away. Numbness spread up to his shoulder and down into his hand. Warm sweat broke out under his fur, and he felt momentarily dizzy.

"Oh, sorry. Did I hit you?" Tessa put the pack on the ground and fumbled inside. He did not think it had noticed how much the tiny amount of iron in the shiny metal had affected him.

"It is okay." He gasped.

"It's way too big for you. I can tie this with a rope, then you can pull the carrier bag." Tessa lifted out a sky-blue carrier with all the berries in it, and tied a short rope through the sun-coloured handles. "Should be able to hold. I've used one of these to carry ski boots."

Gawion saw to his relief that there was no metal anywhere on the carrier.

"What's up, mate?" The big dog padded into the circle of light.

"Brownie!" Tessa patted the head of the dog and rubbed behind his floppy ears.

Brownie gave his usual greeting: "Rooooowf."

"Good dog," Tessa said and rubbed harder.

"Nice, but stupid," Brownie barked to Gawion. "Why do they always say 'good dog' when I ask them how they're doing?"

Gawion made the kind of low growl that is the same as a shrug in Dog, before he barked, "Have you found my sister?"

"I might have a trace." Brownie leant against Tessa's legs. It had stopped rubbing him and was staring at Gawion with open mouth.

"You understand each other?" The human looked back and forth between him and the dog.

He nodded. "And Brownie understands every word you say."

"He does?" Tessa crouched and looked into the dog's starless-night eyes. "You do?"

Brownie replied with a short bark.

"I wish I could tell someone about this, but they wouldn't believe any of it." Two shrill beeps sounded, and Tessa looked at a small, square, metal thing. "Oh, gosh. Mum's on her way home. I'm sorry. I have to go."

It fastened the pack's metal buckles round its middle. A hot shiver ran down Gawion's back, and he instinctively hugged his own stomach.

"Can we meet tomorrow night?" Tessa asked. "Closer to the village?"

"By the big earth mounds?"

Tessa frowned, then, apparently realizing what he meant, nodded.

"When?"

Gawion thought for a moment. He would prefer to split up from Papa, before he met with the human.

"When the moon is above the last mountain in the east, on this side of the valley," he said.

"D'you mean Eisenspitze?"

Gawion stiffened at the name, which meant "Iron Peak", and he could barely nod. He had forgotten that there used to be iron mines on that mountain.

Tessa turned and walked away, the strange wooden feet clanking.

"What trace?" Gawion barked.

"At a tree, by the stream on the path towards St Jakob. I got a whiff of something there that smells like you do."

Could Maeg be there? Could the water have carried her outside Schöngraben? No. The surface was frozen and covered with snow. But whatever it was, he had to find out as much as possible. Even if it meant sneaking out of the gorge.

Brownie sat with his tongue out, panting.

Gawion ought to get the berries home. But not yet. He shovelled with his feet, hiding the sack of berries under a mound of snow. "Can you show me the place?"

Brownie growled, "Sure," and Gawion followed the lumbering dog, leaving Schöngraben.

—18—

As she ran home, Opa's snowshoes, fastened to the sides of the big rucksack, swung against Tessa's arms and hips, clanking noisily over her heavy breathing. But that didn't matter. The barbegazi weren't extinct, and she had talked to one of them. Gawion.

"Gawion," she said aloud.

The name rolled off her tongue, sounding fancy and French. And Gawion needed her help. Tessa's imagination raced ahead.

Together they'd find Gawion's sister. In the future, Tessa would bring berries every year. All the barbegazi would become her friends. Scores of barbegazi babies would dance around her while she fed them raspberries. Oma would be so glad she was carrying on from Opa.

She'd become a famous barbegazi protector... No, not famous. She'd become a *secret* barbegazi protector. And she wouldn't tell anyone but Oma about them—not even Mum—until the time came to hand over the responsibility of delivering berries to her successor. Perhaps her own granddaughter. She saw herself as an old lady with long white plaits, skiing ahead of a teenage girl.

At the sight of the dark house and the empty driveway, she slowed. If she wanted to keep the barbegazi a secret, then she had to start right now, by avoiding questions from Mum. Better let her think she'd been home all day.

She cast a glance at the sky. Stars twinkled. There were no heavy clouds. Good. Then Mum would park outside. The crescent moon was still far from Eisenspitze, and it was already after eight o'clock. She'd probably be meeting Gawion around nine tomorrow night, then. She giggled. Agreeing on meeting times with someone who didn't own a watch was a bit tricky, but it was all part of being a secret barbegazi protector.

After she dumped the rucksack with the snowshoes in the garage, she dashed into the house. She hid her hiking boots in the far corner under the entryway bench, and hung her damp ski clothes below several coats. Turning on all the light switches she passed, and pulling off layers, she raced through the kitchen, snatching up the note, and into her room.

When she heard the car, she stuffed her fleece and socks and the crumpled-up notes into the drawer under her bed.

"Tessa. I'm home," Mum called.

Panicked, Tessa grabbed a book from the pile on her desk and jumped into bed, pulling the sleeves of her thermal top up to her elbows and the covers up to her nose.

"Tes-saaa..." Mum drew her name out into a sigh as she entered the room. "I've told you a million times to turn off the lights."

"Sorry," she mumbled. "Where's Oma?"

Mum sank down on the edge of the bed and hugged Tessa, long and hard. When she let go, she frowned. "Why are you wearing thermals in bed?"

"I was cold." Technically, that wasn't a lie.

Mum touched her forehead and ran a hand down to the back of her neck. "You're all sweaty. Please don't tell me you're coming down with something."

"I'm fine, Mum."

Mum stared at the book. "Learning maths? In the Christmas holidays? You must be ill." She went to the dresser and pulled out a dry T-shirt and some leggings. Hugging the clothes to her chest, she just stood there like she'd forgotten where she was and what she was doing.

"What's wrong?" Tessa asked.

Mum threw the clothes in Tessa's direction and whirled around. "Coffee," she said, stomping out of the room, sounding as if she had a bad cold.

Clearly something was wrong. Tessa hurried to change into the dry clothes on her way to the kitchen.

Mum stood with her back to Tessa, making a mug of black coffee and a cup of hot chocolate. When she trudged to the table, her eyes were glassy. Tessa snuggled into the pile of cushions in the corner of the bench, feeling her own tears rising.

Mum took a big gulp of coffee. "Oma might need heart surgery," she said. "They're transferring her to the University Heart Clinic in Innsbruck tonight."

Tessa slumped back and leant her head against the wall. Her plan of making Oma feel better by keeping the promise to Opa was stupid. And Oma didn't even know she'd delivered the berries. She took a sip of her hot chocolate, burning her tongue, and watched blurry teardrops splatter onto her red knitted top.

"Maybe her heart is broken because Opa died."

"Maybe, sweetheart." Mum smiled through her tears. "Oma's heart is just a bit... The doctors need to fix it. They *can* fix her heart."

Tessa didn't know if Mum was trying to convince herself or Tessa. They sat in silence for a while.

"I'll be staying at Cousin Sonja's in Innsbruck for a few days, and I want to get there tonight. I talked to Lisa's mum on the way home—"

"No."

"Tessa..."

"We're not friends, Mum. I don't mind being home alone."

"Please, Tessa. Don't be difficult. You can't stay here on your own."

"Then let me come! I want to be with Oma."

Mum smiled, but shook her head.

"What about Aunt Annie and Uncle Harry?" It would give her an opportunity to spy on the skier from the avalanche...

What was wrong with her, she wondered. How could she think about that, when Oma was in the hospital?

"I'm sure Annie's busy. They're bound to be fully booked over New Year's."

"I can sleep on a mattress in Felix's room. And help Aunt Annie prepare breakfast. Please, Mum." Tessa leant across the table and took Mum's warm hands in hers. For a moment their roles seemed to have been switched. "Please. Then you don't need to worry about me at all."

Mum sniffed and wiped her tears away with a dishcloth. "I suppose I could ask. They'd want to know about my mum's surgery anyway."

It took Tessa two minutes to stuff the elf book, a toothbrush and some clean clothes into a duffle bag. Mum's choked voice, as she explained to Aunt Annie, came through her bedroom door.

At least she could let Oma know that she'd delivered the berries. She sat down at her desk and tore a piece of chequered paper from her maths exercise book. At the top, in red marker, she wrote, GET WELL SOON OMA, inside a heart. Below, in pencil, she drew a row of nine empty horizontal boxes, counting, while she mumbled the letters, "b-a-r-b-e-g-a-z-i." She had little time and now came the difficult part. Oma was so much better than her at crossword puzzles.

Tessa needed help, and she grabbed the Scrabble box and poured the tiles onto the table. On the board, she built her message: BARBEGAZI HAVE BERRIES PROMISE TO OPA KEPT. The words didn't cross as much as Oma's secret messages usually did, but it would have to do.

"Five minutes," Mum called.

Hurriedly, she copied the pattern of boxes on the paper and added hints: type of elf, really important verb, fruits in your freezer, something you say you will do, opposite of from, grandfather, past of keep.

Mum glanced at the piece of paper when Tessa gave it to her and said, "Oh, you've made her a crossword," before she folded it and slid it in between the pages of the novel in her handbag. "She'll be so pleased."

When Mum dropped Tessa at Felix's house before she drove to Innsbruck, Felix was already asleep—it was late and he'd done extra training in the afternoon—so Tessa would sleep on the sofa in the lounge this first night.

After tucking blankets around her, Aunt Annie pulled a chair over to the sofa, and she sat, her big bosom heaving, holding Tessa, enclosing them in a heavy lavender scent.

Tessa cried a bit. Aunt Annie sobbed violently and blew her nose, using half a box of tissues. It almost made everything worse.

When she had been pretending to sleep for a while, Aunt Annie shuffled out, leaving Tessa alone with her silent tears.

FROM *HABITS & HABITATS: A HISTORIC ACCOUNT OF ALPINE ELVES* BY PROFESSOR, DR EBERHART LUDWIG FRITZ BAHNE

Similar to polar bears, barbegazi are covered in an insulating underfur, topped by long guard hairs. Each hair shaft is transparent, with a hollow core that reflects and scatters light.

Combined with the barbegazi's ability to blend into their snowy surroundings, their hair transparency has led to legends of barbegazi being invisible.

Despite their diminutive size, barbegazi possess brutal strength, and elf researchers should at all times carry iron chains.

THURSDAY, 29TH DECEMBER

—19—

Aunt Annie believed in the "healing powers of the great outdoors", so she sent Tessa to ski training. Also, she argued, it would take Tessa's mind off things.

Although she didn't care about the ski race any more, Tessa was glad to get away from Aunt Annie's chatter and fussing. It was too much. Luckily for Felix, Aunt Annie had a house full of guests to mollycoddle. Tessa wondered how he managed off-season.

Felix had left early to help Coach set the course, and by the time Uncle Harry had adjusted the bindings on Felix's old skis to fit her boots and weight, she was already late.

Icy air prickled her cheeks, as she dragged herself from the bus to the lift station, puffing and exhaling white clouds. Felix's skis were heavier than her own, or perhaps her arms and back and thighs were just sore from yesterday's walk. She blamed Opa's snowshoes.

Thoughts of Opa led directly to Oma. She squeezed her crossed fingers together, hoping the puzzle had helped, and sniffled in the chairlift.

"Just ski, Tessa," she muttered, as she set off from the top.

"Aha. Lady Tessa graces us with her presence," Coach yelled, at the start. "One hour late! Why am I standing here, if you can't be bothered to get up in the morning?"

"Sorry," Tessa mumbled. Explaining would mean tears.

"New, old skis? What happened to your Atomics?"

"Chainsaw."

Coach exploded in a roar of laughter and the queue behind her chuckled.

"Good one, Tessa," Felix called.

She got into starting position.

"What d'you think you're doing?" Coach yelled. "Glide through and inspect the course first. Take those other two latecomers with you. Explain the double gate to them."

Great. Coach had grouped her with Hans and Helmut, the two most annoying and chaotic skiers in the club. Skiing with them was like running through the village in nothing but your undies. Tessa stemmed her skis, snowploughing in slow motion down between the red and blue gates. Loud giggles from the T-bar lift told her Lisa and Maria had seen her with the two little monsters in tow.

She sped up after the course ended. Behind her, Hans and Helmut jumped on bumps and shouted and laughed. When she stopped by the lift queue, they sprayed her with snow, just as Hans skied into Helmut—or Helmut into Hans—felling the three of them. She disentangled herself from the rowdy mass of green arms and red legs, to disapproving noises from two German women in metallic jackets and a tall white-clad man in the queue.

At least she got her own T-bar, but the rude shouts at Bambi-legged tourists, from Hans and Helmut, embarrassed her. She hadn't brought her binoculars—she didn't need them any more—so she watched her teammates. Felix raced between the gates, almost lying on his side in every turn, sometimes touching the snow with a hand. He skied much faster than everyone else, with effortless up-down movements. No wonder he'd won the regional championship last season.

When she neared the top, she looked out into Schöngraben. Ski tracks snaked their way down all reachable sides of the gully. She hoped Gawion and the other barbegazi were safely hidden in their caves.

Tessa skied to the start of the run, with the two monsters hot on her heels.

"Okay, missy, I'm sending Hans and Helmut with you, so you'd better give it your all." Coach increased the volume. "You hear that, boys? Get her. Three, two, one, go!"

Tessa pushed off.

"Knees, Tessa! Arms, Helmut!"

She bent further down with her knees. Her aching thighs burned. The thought of the monsters behind her spurred

Tessa on. Finding a rhythm, she focused her eyes on the next gate, before she even finished her current turn. Air whistled round the rim of her helmet, but she kept her focus on the course. After the finish line, she continued at full speed to the lift. Hans and Helmut hadn't caught up.

At the start, Coach stood with thumbs up on both hands, beaming at her. "See! See!" he bellowed. "That's what happens when you take your head out of the clouds."

Tessa nodded. She didn't really know what had changed, she just knew that those monsters catching up or, even worse, passing her, would've been the ultimate humiliation.

Coach gave her thumbs up on five runs before it was time to clear the piste.

The new experience of getting praise at giant-slalom training made Tessa glow inside. Perhaps things weren't completely hopeless. She had found the barbegazi. And if she could learn to race, then nothing was impossible. The doctors might even fix Oma's heart.

She couldn't help Oma, but she could at least try to help Gawion. And she knew just what she'd do when she got back to Felix's house.

—20—

Brownie's nose had caught the scent of thawing spring snow, and now Gawion had proof. Real proof that Papa could not dismiss, and confirming their worst fears.

Gawion had spent the rest of the night transporting the berry gift home. The incident with the metal buckle on Tessa's pack had given his arm a numbing weakness that not even a handful of berries could dispel. Despite the pain, he managed to drag the full sky-blue carrier up to the avalanche. From there the couloirs were too steep.

Surfing downhill on the snow, even carrying an unconscious Tessa to the village, was no problem. Ascending was something else entirely. It took five trips up the steep incline, to bring all the berries to a hiding place he dug close to their cave's entrance.

He had wanted to storm inside and show Maman the gift, but stopped himself. First, he needed a plan for how to tell them. And while he lugged the heavy load up the mountain, he speculated.

Normally, he would start with bad news, then sweeten it with good news. But his bad news was much worse than when the resting cave ceiling collapsed. Perhaps if he switched the news around, making sure everyone had a full stomach before he told them what he had discovered about Maeg... But how could he pretend food helped, when he knew the truth?

Still trying to decide, he propelled his way into the cave.

"What is this about a human helping us?" Papa asked, before Gawion had even got up off the ground. "Your whistled ramblings last night made no sense, son."

"A human! Helping us? Have you gone quite mad, Gawion? First the dogs, now this." Maman, one hand on her forehead, fanned herself with her beard. "Have we taught you nothing?"

"Never, ever, ever trust humans," Liel sing-songed, from her nest in the living cave. She played with her toy barbegazi, making it dance through a forest of bird feathers. "Never, ever trust humans, Baby," she said to the bundle of fur tied around sticks. "No, Maman," her toy answered.

"Some humans can be trusted. You trusted that human child in Vienna," Gawion said.

"That was different, son. We had known Anne since it was a mere babe."

"Well, I trust this one. Tessa is the grandchild of the

berry-human. And I have a surprise for you. Wait here." Gawion scurried outside.

Behind him, Maman shrieked, "Is he bringing a human here?"

He uncovered the sky-blue carrier and snaked his way backwards through the tunnel, keeping a solid grip on the handles of the sack.

Back inside, he whistled triumphantly.

"It brought the berry gift!" Bowing, with a flourishing movement of his hand, he split the carrier open with one of his sharp claws. Clear, see-through bags tumbled out, revealing the abundance of berries.

Maman looked in wonder at the growing mountain of wild strawberries, blueberries, blackberries and raspberries. There were even some of the large cultivated strawberries that Gawion loved.

"Nourishment," she said. "We are saved." The desperate gleam in her eyes made Gawion wonder just how close to starvation they had come.

After they had stuffed themselves with berries, contentment and calmness settled in the cave.

"The human told me they believe we are extinct," Gawion said.

A strange noise, like rumbling thunder, filled the cave as Papa exploded into a bellowing laugh.

"That is the best news I have heard in a long time," he howled.

Even Maman smiled.

"No, Papa," Liel said, her voice teary, "If we are extinct, how can I find a papa for my babies when I am a grown-up?"

"Stop being silly. We are not extinct," Gawion said, feeling exasperated.

"Come here, sweet icicle." Maman held her arms out towards Liel. "You know, a little bird tells me how your Mont Blanc uncle and the rest of them are doing, every year before the melting starts."

Liel smiled.

"I like Gawion's human, it is just as nice as yours," she said, and licked a large strawberry. "Tell me about Anne again."

Maman gave a little chuckle.

"Oh, I remember that little human. From the moment it could walk, it followed its father around the zoological gardens. During the nine pregnancy winters it brought me the finest berries. When I vowed that my babies would not be born in captivity, Anne promised to help."

Gawion hated to ruin the mood. Brooding, he weaved the end of his beard around his berry-coloured fingers. Perhaps if he waited with the bad news until nightfall...

"Gawion," Papa said. "What have you not told us?"

"I talked to the dog," he began. Of course he could not keep something so important secret from Papa, who was always watching him, waiting to point out his mistakes. Out of the corner of his eye, he saw Maman shaking her head. "It had tracked Maeg to the mountain stream below Schöngraben, close to the village."

He had expected shrieks and moans at the revelation, but Maman only whimpered and said, "I knew it."

From under the sacks of berries, he extracted the lump of Maeg's fur that Brownie had helped him retrieve.

"Bits of this clung to branches of the trees along the stream." He gave the lump to Papa. "Higher up than Maeg would be able to reach from the ground."

"The dog told you? The exact height?" Papa glared at him, almost as if he knew how Gawion had jumped and jumped to pluck the fur. "Because you did not cross the boundary last night, did you?"

Gawion swallowed. "I..." He nodded slowly, staring down at his speckled beard.

Papa took a deep breath.

"So someone carried her. Could she have placed the fur herself?"

Gawion shrugged. "Perhaps."

"Maybe Maeg also met a nice human," Liel said, but even she seemed to sense the fear reigniting in their home.

"The berry-human's grandchild will search in the village. I am meeting it in the evening, by the earth mounds."

"For the love of snow, you are too trusting." Maman shook her head again. "The human might contrive to capture you."

"It would never do that, Maman," Gawion said, with a certainty he did not quite feel.

—21—

Tessa trudged after Felix, from the bus stop. They walked in silence past hotels and pensions displaying red *Fully booked* signs. She sagged farther and farther behind until Felix waited by the corner of the long, steep driveway up to Berger's Bed and Breakfast.

"Take these, I'll take your skis." He held his poles towards her. "Just don't expect me to do it again, noodle-arms."

Tessa was so tired she didn't argue.

"So what really happened to your own skis?" He heaved both pairs of skis onto his shoulders and walked on. "Dad said he'd never seen anything like it."

"Chainsaw." Tessa made an odd-sounding fake laugh.

She needed time to think. She couldn't tell Felix about the barbegazi, but she didn't want to lie to him either.

"It wasn't one of your barbie-fairies?"

"I thought you didn't believe me."

"Whatever." Felix shook his head.

"Is that skier from the avalanche still at your house?"

"I guess. Mum lets the rooms for the whole week in high season."

They rounded the bend, and the house rose above them. With its thick layer of fairytale snow frosting, the oversized roof sparkled in the sun. Car-shaped white mounds stood in a row along the driveway and on the track up to Schöngraben.

"Which room is it?" Tessa asked, searching the dark windows below the garlands of snow.

"Which room is what?"

"That skier's."

"It's on the other side. The corner towards Schöngraben. Why?"

"No reason."

Inside, the house was silent. No sounds came from the guest rooms upstairs. With the sun shining in a clear blue sky, the guests—tourists who skied for fun, one week a year—would spend the whole day on the slopes.

Aunt Annie had left them a note—that she was visiting Aunt Margit, one of the numerous relatives living in the valley—and a homemade lasagne. They didn't bother heating the food, but gulped it down with large glasses of blackcurrant cordial.

After lunch, Felix wanted to do his knee bend exercises and rope jumps, and play on his computer. Tessa said she'd relax on the sofa for a bit. As soon as his bedroom door was closed, though, she sneaked upstairs, where the guest rooms were, and along the narrow corridor, her stockinged feet making soft swishing sounds against the carpet. She whistled, hoping the tune didn't mean anything offensive to a barbegazi, and listened for an answer. Nothing. After knocking, she tried a few doors, but they were locked.

Aunt Annie ruled her kingdom from the kitchen. That's where the master key would be. Tessa went downstairs, tiptoeing past Felix's door, even though she could hear the rhythmic stamps of his exercises. In the kitchen, she opened cupboard after cupboard until she found one with a neat row of empty numbered nails. At the end hung a key with no number. The master key.

Her fingers hovered in front of the key before she snatched it from the nail.

"What're you doing? Are you crazy?" said Felix, who'd entered the kitchen, and wrestled the key from her.

"Please! Just let me peek into his room. I won't even go in."

"Why?"

"It's a long story." She really wanted to keep the barbegazi a secret, but if Maeg was here, she might need Felix's help. If Maeg wasn't, she needn't tell him anything. "I'll explain after."

"I'm not supposed to use the master key when there are guests," he mumbled.

"No one will know."

"Promise you won't go inside." Felix held the key towards her.

Tessa tried taking it, but Felix clutched the key until she said, "Promise."

"Be quick. I'll whistle if anyone comes." He sat down on the bottom step of the staircase. "It's the last door."

Upstairs again, her heart pumped as if she was in the middle of a ski race. She lay both palms and her ear against the door, listening. After knocking again, her shaking hand guided the key into the lock and turned it. Blood hammered at her temples as she pushed the door open.

"Hello... Maeg?" she said, and whistled a single tone.

A sliver of sunshine came through the drawn curtains. At first glance, from the doorway, the tidy room seemed empty, except for a closed suitcase on the bench. The only clutter was on the desk, where a ski helmet with silvery goggles perched. Tessa had wanted those goggles for Christmas, but Mum said they were too expensive. Dad would've bought them, but she hadn't asked him. The trendy goggles confirmed her suspicions—this guest was one of those cool off-piste skiers.

Something shiny on the chair reflected the light, but, in the gloom, she couldn't see what it was.

"Tessa?" Felix called from below.

She had to see what was on that chair. It might be important. She wouldn't touch anything, and neither Felix nor the guest would know she'd been in the room. "Just a moment."

After casting a glance back down the vacated corridor, Tessa tiptoed into the room and eased the chair out from underneath the desk. Icy prickles tingled on her back. A heavy, metal chain and a sharp iron poker lay on the seat.

Skiers had no use for metal chains and pokers, but people hunting barbegazi did. This was evidence.

Tessa rushed to open the wooden wardrobe. Ironed shirts and trousers hung above stacks of folded pullovers and socks.

Otherwise it was empty. She opened the bathroom door and looked behind the shower curtain. She got down on all fours, searching under the bed and the desk. Nothing. The suitcase was locked. She shook it. From inside, came the sound of clanking metal. Where could Maeg be?

Felix called again, but she ignored him and opened the desk drawer. On top of a stack of papers was a worn terrain map. A scatter of black circles and red crosses marked spots on the clustered contour curves. It was a map of Schöngraben.

"Tessa! Get out!" Felix banged his fist against the door frame. "You promised."

"Look at this." Tessa pointed to the chain and poker.

Felix sneaked closer and stared at the metal objects. "So what?"

The stairs creaked.

"Someone's coming," Felix hissed, already by the door. "Quick."

Tessa slid the chair back into place, and stuffed the map up under her knitted top. Turning to leave, her foot got stuck behind the leg of the chair. She stumbled and fell flat on the floor.

Before she could get up, a shadow from the corridor grew on the carpet and something crashed to the floor.

In slow motion, and with a sense of dread, Tessa rose.

Aunt Annie stood in the doorway, a laundry basket spilling folded towels by her feet. Tessa had never seen Aunt Annie's face turn purple before. And her eyes were popping out of her face.

"Tessa!" she screeched. "Get out at once! Felix! What on earth are you doing?"

Felix threw the towels into the laundry basket and pulled it out of the room.

"Kitchen. Now." Aunt Annie shoved them towards the stairs before she locked the door, leaving the laundry basket on the corridor floor.

Tessa's cheeks burned like she'd just come in from the snow. The stolen map burned even more, hidden awkwardly under her top. She pushed it down into her striped long johns and moved it round to her hip.

"Never in my life... I'm disappointed in you, Felix. You know never to go into occupied guest rooms." Aunt Annie had stopped screeching, but there was an unknown sternness to her usually jolly voice. "What were you thinking?"

"It's... we–" Felix began.

"Tessa, you've had a trying week with Oma and hitting your head and everything... Perhaps you should go and lie down, have a rest." It wasn't a question. Aunt Annie looked out of the window. "Felix, get the soft brush and sweep the snow off the cars. All of them. Afterwards, tidy your cave so there's room for Tessa."

Tessa scampered out of the kitchen after Felix.

"I trust you didn't touch anything in the room," Aunt Annie called behind them.

The map felt like a blinking burglar alarm.

"I'll help you," Tessa said to Felix.

"Don't. Even. Bother." He ran downstairs and slammed the door to the ski room behind him.

FROM *HABITS & HABITATS: A HISTORIC ACCOUNT OF ALPINE ELVES* BY PROFESSOR, DR EBERHART LUDWIG FRITZ BAHNE

Over long distances, barbegazi supposedly communicate with each other by whistled signals. Whether whistling, talking or non-verbal communication is used when they are close together is unknown.

Recent reports of mountaineers in the high Alps hearing shrill whistles in advance of avalanches, has led to rumours that the barbegazi might not be extinct.

These claims are supported by the unearthing of polar-bear-like fur, by this author, in a crevasse on the glacier hiking trail between Jungfraujoch and the Konkordia Hut in Switzerland.

—22—

Tessa lay on the sofa, staring at the knots in the wooden ceiling. This time, she'd really messed up. And for what? A map owned by every hiker in the area, for sale at the tourist information, and a chain to lock up skis. How had she ever imagined she could help Gawion find his sister?

Her phone rang. It was Mum. For a moment, she considered not answering, but then Mum would just call Aunt Annie. After the fourth ring, she picked up.

"Hi, sweetheart, how are you?"

"How's Oma?"

"Oh, you know... The doctors are very competent," Mum said, and gave a long explanation of tests and outcomes, trying to sound upbeat.

"Did she solve my puzzle? Can I talk to her?"

"She's a bit too tired to talk or do crosswords at the moment."

"Please get her to do it, Mum. It'll make her feel better."

Mum ended the call with, "I hope you're being a big help to Annie."

Tessa hadn't thought she could feel any worse.

She went to the window. Blankets of winter snow still hid half the cars, and a cloud of powder surrounded Felix. It was unfair only he got punished. Perhaps he'd cooled off by now and would let her take over.

Outside, the sun had disappeared and the temperature dropped.

Felix greeted her with a "Go away", without even pausing in his work.

"I want to help."

"You'll just scratch the cars."

Frost bloomed like flowers of ice on the windscreens of the cars Felix had already uncovered. Tessa shuddered, remembering dark mornings, driving to school in the car when Mum had left it outside during the night.

Of course! She almost laughed out loud. You couldn't keep a barbegazi inside a house. They'd never survive the heat. But in one of these frozen cars...

As inconspicuously as possible, she ambled up along the row of visible cars, whistling a few notes. At each one, she ducked behind them and made peeking holes on the windows with her warm breath, before examining the interior. One car had a white sweater on the backseat, and she took so long to be sure it wasn't Maeg that Felix had walked up to her and poked her shoulder with the brush.

"Stop touching the cars. What're you doing?"

"Looking for the car of that guest."

"Okay, Tessa, I'll play along in your spy game. Just tell me why."

It wasn't a game. If Felix knew what was happening, he wouldn't be so condescending. He'd be helping her search for Maeg. But she couldn't tell him without betraying Gawion's trust.

"Show me the car first," she said.

"It's not here."

"You're sure?"

Felix rolled his eyes.

"First of all, it's not a car, it's a white van. The coolest van ever. With tinted windows, four-wheel drive, four-litre engine." He counted out these facts on his gloved fingers. "I haven't seen it since he arrived. Probably scared of the other guests denting it."

Tessa's mind whirled. Maeg had disappeared on Monday. A van was an even better hiding place than a car. But it could be anywhere: on a lift station parking lot, on a forest track, by a hotel or post office or supermarket in one of the nearby villages. How would she ever find it? She didn't even know what to look for.

But Felix did. She needed his help, and she owed him an explanation. Even if it meant trusting him with the secret of the barbegazi.

While he swept snow off the last cars, she told him everything that had happened in the last two days. She didn't mention Brownie. Talking with a dog might be too big of a stretch for Felix.

Afterwards, Tessa sat on his bed while he tidied his room, telling him barbegazi facts she'd learnt from her elf book. Felix collected a jumble of clothes and shoes and comic books from the floor, and stuffed everything into his wardrobe. Signed posters of seven World Cup skiers hung on the walls. Two monitors, keyboards, a steering wheel and other electronic stuff crowded his desk. Using a T-shirt, he dusted his biggest skiing trophy, before he positioned it in front of his other shiny trophies, on the top bookshelf.

"I don't know, Tessa," he said, pulling on the T-shirt over his long thermal top. "If Dad hadn't told me about your broken skis..."

"But you saw the metal chain and poker, right? And the map—" Tessa drew the map from the inside of her long johns.

"You took that from the room? Are you insane?"

"Sorry. But look! He's marked all these places in Schöngraben." She pointed to the circles and crosses after unfolding the map. Seeing it in the light, she noticed that some of the circles had handwritten notes.

"That's funny," Tessa tapped a circle. "This one's where I fell in the hole." They both leant over the map, trying to read the tiny scribbles.

"Willy Berger sighting," they said together.

"But that's Opa. That's where Gawion rescued him."

Felix stared at her, then he began nodding.

"Okay. I think I believe you. Let's find that van."

After he printed a photo of a similar van from the internet, they got dressed and jogged down to the huge lift station parking lot. It was late afternoon and only a few cars remained there. No white vans. They walked along the busy main road to St Anton and back through the village, splitting up to check side streets and carparks. They didn't find the van.

Tessa's tired legs protested. Now that Felix believed her, she almost didn't mind the exhaustion. But how could they search the whole valley?

By the time they returned to the house, hunger pangs competed with her aching thighs. Aunt Annie was off on another family visit, delivering a homemade apple strudel, based on the mouth-watering smell in the kitchen. She hadn't left any of the dessert for them, but a meagre plate of bread, cheese and salami waited in the fridge.

Felix frowned. "Mum's really mad this time," he muttered.

"At least you get to meet a barbegazi," Tessa said, chewing on a wedge of Emmental.

Roughly an hour before the moon would be above Eisenspitze, they mounted lightweight aluminium snow-shoes—borrowed from Aunt Annie's stuff-guests-might-need closet—and hiked up the track along the mountain stream, towards the avalanche protection mounds and Gawion.

—23—

A sickle moon hung low over the dreaded mountain, when Gawion surfed down towards the earth mounds, with his stomach in a knot of worry. The steep eastern gullies, with their hoof marks from agile mountain goats, remained untouched by humans. But at the bottom where Schöngraben widened, tracks from wooden feet created a detailed pattern of ridges. Hard ridges. During the day, the sun had warmed the top layer, before the rippled surface froze again. Gawion stubbed his toes on the ripples, and he whistled in pain.

"Slow down and keep your claws out, or lift your toes," Papa called.

Papa had insisted on coming with him. He mistrusted the human, and he planned to hide among the nearby trees, ready to help Gawion if needed.

It was an unnecessary precaution. Gawion did not fear Tessa, only what it might have discovered about his sister.

A shrill, human whistle rang out ahead. It had no meaning.

"Gawion," Tessa called.

Gawion sped up, then slowed as he saw that not one, but two, humans waited below in a circle of light.

Papa grabbed his arm, stopping Gawion abruptly.

"See that?" he whispered, pointing with a shaking finger. A metal chain dangled from the hand of the second human. "It is just like at Mont Blanc."

"Are you even sure it is metal, Papa?" he whispered, although the way it glinted in the light from Tessa's head and clinked when the human swung it around, left no doubt.

Papa sniffed with his large nose. Gawion just stared at Tessa. Had it deceived him? No, he refused to believe that. It had brought berries. It was a descendant of the berry-human. And that chain...

"Gaaawiiiooon," it called again.

"Fairly low iron content and rather slim," Papa said, in a low, bleak tone. "But one well-placed swipe would immobilize you long enough for them to carry you out of the gorge."

"Tessa would not do that. It wants to find Maeg."

"Who chose to meet so near the village, son?"

"But why bring us berries?"

"To gain our trust."

Gawion edged closer, trying to hear what the humans were saying. If only his hearing was as good as his sense of smell. Tessa faced away from him, and he could not make out its words.

The other human swung the scary chain faster and faster. Raising its voice, so they heard every word, it spoke with an angry undertone. "D'you know how many barbarians I could've killed while we're standing here? If that barbegazi isn't coming, this is a complete waste of time. Capture it on your phone. Or bring it to the house and hide it in the shed."

Gawion stopped breathing. The forest stilled, as if the trees were listening. As if like him, they were trying to understand the strange language. Trying to find an explanation that was not the obvious meaning of those words. But there was no other explanation. The new human talked about killing, and hiding him in a shed, and capturing him on a phone—whatever that was.

Tessa stomped. Its feet clanked. The wooden feet it had used to walk on the snow surface yesterday were gone. Tonight it wore metal feet. Metal feet primed to paralyse him with a single kick.

How could he have been so gullible? He had liked Tessa and believed its promise to help them. And here it was with an elf hunter by its side.

Papa sighed. Gawion refused to look up at him. From under his bushy eyebrows, he saw Papa shake his head.

"Come, son." Papa tugged at his arm. "I was much older than you, when humans captured me. Show me where you found the bits of Maeg's fur."

After casting a last glance at the two humans, he led Papa up through the forest, giving the earth mounds a wide berth. Behind them, Tessa continued to whistle and call his name.

Gawion swore that he would never, ever again trust a human.

—24—

"Why do boys always have to kill things in stupid computer games?" Tessa stepped on the spot, trying to keep warm. The snow shoes clanked. She whistled for the millionth time.

Somehow, the excitement of the afternoon had fizzled out on the way up into Schöngraben's gloom. The hike had begun with Felix asking questions about the barbegazi, which she answered. But she'd already told him everything, and soon Felix switched topic to the ski race and the pressure of being last year's seasonal champion. Tessa tried to understand, she really did, but secretly she wondered why he couldn't simply be happy about winning last year, and enjoy his collection of trophies. So they'd been standing without talking for a while when Felix lost patience and exploded into his computer game tirade.

"I play lots of games without killing," he said.

Tessa raised her voice: "Gaaawiooon!"

A long silvery chain attached Felix's house keys to his ski trousers, and he played with it, swinging it in vertical circles, making the keys jingle. "He's not coming," he muttered, and looked at his watch. Again. "It's half past nine and the moon's already on the other side of the valley."

Tessa wiggled her fingers and toes to avoid them turning numb with cold. "Please. Let's wait a bit longer." She turned her headlamp up, enlarging the reach of the light. Rotating slowly, she stared into the shadows and repeated her call.

Felix swung his keys faster and faster. "Come on, Tessa. I want to start this season with a win, and tomorrow's the last training."

Where was Gawion? Had something happened to him? What if he'd also been taken?

"It's just a ski race," she told Felix.

"Just!" Felix rolled his eyes.

For a while, they stood in silence again. Tessa stomped her feet and swung her arms, opening them wide, then hugging herself. The chill seeped up through the thick soles of her boots. Felix just swung the chain.

"I can't play your fairy game any more," he said eventually.

"It's not a game."

"Right now the barbarians in *Civilization* seem a whole lot more real than your barbegazi."

"They are real. I brought them berries."

"I never saw any berries. Besides, there's a hundred ways to dump a load of berries up here."

Tessa stamped harder. Why was Felix so annoying again?

"You saw the map," she said through gritted teeth.

"For all I know, you could've drawn circles on that map yourself."

Angry tears threatened, and her voice rose, turning shrill: "I didn't. You know I didn't. I found it in the room."

"Whatever. I'm not risking the race for your crazy fantasies." Felix began walking.

"Please! Wait! He'll come."

"Maria's right. You're absolutely loony," he said, without pausing, without turning, without looking at her.

Tessa's stomach clenched, like she'd been hit in the solar plexus. A chill that had nothing to do with the temperature spread from there. The light from Felix's headlamp disappeared behind the first of the avalanche mounds, and it was as if the stars had been turned off.

Felix had believed her, and now suddenly he didn't. He thought she was loony. Everyone did.

Why would Gawion trust her? He needed someone to help save his sister, and Tessa couldn't help anyone. She couldn't help him and she couldn't help Oma.

How could she have thought a silly crossword puzzle would make any difference?

Warm tears splashed down her cheeks as the last of her resolve melted away. She sobbed into her gloves and slumped until she sat on her knees, the snowshoes forcing her to angle her feet awkwardly. Her knees grew colder and colder, prickling until they turned numb, and then she didn't feel them at all. If only the pain inside could disappear as easily.

The blood flowing towards her chest would never be enough to fill two holes in her heart.

FROM *HABITS & HABITATS: A HISTORIC ACCOUNT OF ALPINE ELVES* BY PROFESSOR, DR EBERHART LUDWIG FRITZ BAHNE

Barbegazi have elfish abilities for languages and can speak in whichever tongue they are addressed, as documented in Foubergé's transcriptions from 1779.*

To the frustration of more recent elf researchers, barbegazi refuse to talk in captivity. In the only successful case of getting a response, the scientist used a modified replica of "the rack" found in the Tower of London, to stretch the feet of the barbegazi, until it screamed: "Zooterkins! Gadzooks! Potzblitz! Gadsbudlikins!"

After the demise of the creature, a linguist read the transcripts, believed to be gibberish, and explained that these were perfectly normal swear words from the Renaissance period.

---

* Foubergé, A.S. 1779: "An Examination of the Usage of Language by Subhuman Creatures" from *Philosophical Transactions*, Vol. 69. London: Royal Society, 721–748

—25—

Gawion glided in front of Papa, on the narrow track between the mountain stream and the forest. Next to Brownie's deep paw prints, large indents, not much deeper than their own shallow marks, made a pattern in the snow—the footprints from Tessa's and the elf hunter's surface-walking metal feet.

They stopped, and, after crawling up on Papa's back, Gawion snatched a lump of fur from a branch.

Papa sniffed it, inhaling deeply while shaking his head.

"I refused to believe it," he said. "I hoped she was merely injured..." Then he ordered Gawion to go home, while he searched near the human habitats. "Await my whistle, when the brightest stars of Ursa Major are above Polaris," Papa called, on his way down the track.

Gawion was so downcast he did not even protest. He shuffled up between the trees, staying in the forest high above the earth mounds. He wondered what he was supposed to do if Papa did not whistle at the agreed time: Search for him or hide?

Through the dark, needle-covered twigs, he saw a faint light shining. At least Tessa had stopped whistling and calling his name. A weird gurgling sound—a cross between a bubbling spring and an animal in pain—reached him. It was unlike anything he had ever heard, and it seemed to be coming from the humans.

Curious, he crept nearer, promising himself to stay in the shadows.

The elf hunter had disappeared. Rolled up like a coloured snowball, Tessa lay on the ground, convulsing, and emitting the strange loud gurgles. It must be very cold after so long in the snow. Suddenly it howled like a wolf. The howl meant nothing in Wolfish, but it was clearly a cry of pain. Had the elf hunter attacked Tessa? Or was it all another trick, to trap him with?

Gawion inhaled, filling his nostrils with night-forest air. His nose only detected a weak metallic taint. Much less than the smell from that chain. The human had saved them from starvation—he could not just leave it to die in the cold.

He circled Tessa widely, sniffing, ready to scamper at any sign of danger. Not daring to approach, in case it kicked him with those clanking feet, he called its name.

Three times he called, before it reacted. The light from Tessa's head travelled over the snow until he felt the slight tingle of its feeble warmth.

"Oh. Gawion. Where. Were. You?" Tessa said, between bouts of the weird gurgles.

"Where is the elf hunter?"

"In the village. We haven't found Maeg yet."

"Why did you bring it here?" Gawion spoke with Papa's sternness.

"The elf hunter? Here? No. You misunderstand. That's Felix. He's helping us. He was, anyway..." Mountain springs streamed down Tessa's cheeks.

Perhaps trusting a human was naive, but he could tell this sadness was real. Gawion lumbered closer.

"You thought I'd brought the elf hunter? To capture you? You don't trust me?" Tessa's speech ended with another howl, as piercing as that of a vixen he had once heard, after one of her cubs had been killed by a human vehicle.

"No, no. I do trust you," he said, "Only my father was with me and... and we thought the... the metal chain." It seemed silly, now, to have been scared of this baby human.

"...And my Oma's in the hospital and her heart's broken, and I don't know what to do." It gurgled again.

He stroked one of its plaited side-beards. Slowly the streams became trickling springs and the only sounds were wet sniffs from its pointy nose.

Tessa got up, wiping its eyes.

"The elf hunter is staying in Felix's house," it told him. "That's why I needed his help. Will you come with me?"

Gawion hesitated. They had talked about bringing him to a shed. Was this all part of a plan?

"If we run, we might catch Felix before he gets home."

"I have a better idea." The faster they caught this Felix,

the farther they would be from the village. "If you leave the metal feet here, I can carry you."

With one pull at a strap by each ankle, Tessa let the metal feet drop to the ground.

"Cool! I don't remember last time you carried me."

When he scooped Tessa up, it gave a small shriek. Its warmth burned in his arms. Gawion leapt forward to gain initial speed, then surfed over the rippled surface, remembering to lift his toes. The bundle he carried made new bubbling noises, with no sadness to them.

Outside the earth mounds, Tessa directed him east of the mountain stream where he had just been. He hoped Papa was far away by now.

Near an illuminated human habitat, a light bounced ahead of them, and Tessa called, "Feeeliiix!"

"What?" The beam swirled towards them. The other human stood transfixed until Gawion stopped next to it with a sideways skid.

It gaped so much he could see the human's single row of teeth, its raspberry-coloured tongue, and, worst of all, the inside of its throat. It really ought to hide that view behind a beard. Gawion averted his eyes.

Tessa slid down from his arms, saying, "You still think I'm loony?"

"What... It's... I... You're real," it sputtered, and finally closed its mouth.

Perhaps it was a less intelligent human than Tessa. It was certainly not scary.

"Sorry, Tessa," it said.

"Gawion, meet Felix," Tessa continued. "Felix, put your

key chain away, it's made with iron, and barbegazi don't like iron."

Still staring at him, Felix folded the frightening metal chain and hid it in a flap in its clothes.

"Felix lives right there." Tessa pointed at the glare behind the trees. "I found a map and some iron tools in the elf hunter's room, and I'm sure he's got Maeg in his van."

Van? Gawion ran through a list of meanings for the word. A bird's wing. A vanguard. None of them made sense.

"May I ask what a van is?"

"It's a big car. A vehicle. Look," Felix said, and pulled a strange flat image out of a pocket. "This one's white, with tinted windows so you can't see what's inside."

"I see," he said, rather relieved that the cousin could speak in full sentences and keep its mouth reasonably closed. "And where is this van?"

"We don't know," Tessa explained. "We've been searching all afternoon."

"My father and I can continue the search. But extracting Maeg from a metal vehicle might require your assistance."

"If you find the van, we'll think of a way of getting your sister out," Tessa said.

"Just come and get us. Throw something at my window to wake us up," Felix said. "I'll show you."

Both humans turned off their lights and ran to the last tree before the house, a huge pine. They crept under its prickly branches. Gawion followed them.

Felix pointed. "The window on the corner is my room." It rummaged in the darkness and found one of the hard ovals Liel loved to play with. "Can you hit it with a pine cone?"

It was not a snowball, but Gawion and Maeg had often thrown them at each other, whenever the snow was too wonderfully cold to make snowballs. He took the oval, crept out of the den under the tree, brought the thing back over his shoulder and sent it off with a spin.

It hit the dark square with a clank.

Felix whistled two shrill tones. It sounded almost as if it whistled "hot glacier", which made very little sense. He was about to ask Felix what it meant, when a human appeared by the entrance to the habitat. Artificial light spilt out on its snowy hair and new-snow coloured garments. Gawion ducked back under the sheltering twigs. The human rounded the corner, and stared at the dark square Gawion's oval had hit. Then it turned towards the mountains, towards the trees, towards them.

"It's him," Felix whispered.

Tessa leant forward.

"I think I've seen him before."

Gawion had seen that particular human before. Several times, in fact, over the past decades. He had walloped it once. Now he wished he had never dug it out of the avalanche. He knew it by the tilt of its shoulders and the length of its legs, but most of all he knew it by its scent. A scent that now had a distinct flavour of Maeg.

"The elf hunter," he hissed.

"I thought he was much younger," Tessa whispered.

The elf hunter turned back, climbed up to the entrance, and disappeared into the dwelling.

"No," Felix said, "that's him. That's Professor Bahne."

FRIDAY, 30TH DECEMBER

—26—

Gawion stood on an outcrop in the forest above the village, gazing up at the Great Bear in the sky. It hung upside down directly above Polaris.

Papa ought to whistle soon. Gawion could not wait to speak with him. Papa would be astonished, when he learnt how Gawion's human friends had tracked down the elf hunter, and worked out where it kept Maeg captured.

Waves of heat prickled under his soles, when he remembered how the elf hunter had just appeared out of nowhere, while he stood next to that big tree, exposed. He had wanted to rush after it, into the human habitat, and force the monster to reveal where it held his sister.

Tessa had seemed to be as shocked as he was, while Felix had taken charge and held Gawion back.

"Professor Bahne?" Tessa had repeated. "But..."

"Professor Bahne is the elf hunter, and he's here. That means Maeg's here. Somewhere. We'll find her," Felix had said, patting his shoulder, calming him.

Tessa's eyebrows had scrunched together, rippling its forehead.

"Take the printout. And wake us when you find the van." Felix had rolled the strange flat image of the vehicle into a hollow cylinder, and Gawion had dropped it in his beard pocket.

Tessa had nodded slowly, but still said nothing, while he agreed with Felix to return the following evening, if they did not find the van during the night.

When Gawion had set off, bouncing from foot to foot up through the forest, there had been a new lightness to his step. Felix had made it sound as if it was only a matter of time before they found Maeg. Perhaps it was. They only needed to locate the vehicle. Papa would be so relieved! He might even admit that he had been wrong to doubt Gawion's judgement.

Finally, Papa whistled. He was in the same forest as Gawion, farther down in the valley, and it did not take long to find him. But the moment Gawion said he had talked to the two humans, Papa exploded in a stream of hissed reprimands. Rebukes for not going straight home and for talking to humans and dogs segued into a general scolding for trusting humans.

"I suppose it is our own fault for living in a place with no other children," he hissed.

"I am not a child," Gawion said, before he told Papa about the elf hunter, and showed him the image of the new-snow-coloured vehicle.

Papa frowned and shook his head, muttering: "A human has abducted your sister, and you want me to trust human children?"

At least he did not send Gawion home.

Staying by the edge of the forest, they glided past villages and empty fields, far down into the inhabited valley. They stopped and sneaked closer to investigate, whenever they saw clusters of human vehicles. But their search yielded no result. The only vehicle they discovered that resembled the flat image was as dark as a starless night.

When dawn broke, and they returned to the cave, Gawion's hope of finding Maeg had shrunk to something smaller than a blackberry at the bottom of a gorge.

Throughout the morning, Maman kept nagging him. And Liel, with her constant background chant of "never, ever trust a human", really got on his nerves.

"You know nothing of humans," he finally shouted, and kicked the big ice cooler, knocking a third off it. "Potzblitz! I cannot wait to get my own cave. I am sick of—"

Papa whistled so piercingly then that lumps of snow fell from the ceiling, and the tunnel entrance to the cave collapsed.

"You can build one right now," he bellowed. "And take your sesquicentennial hormones with you."

Seething with anger, Gawion marched into the resting cave.

"And this!" Papa sent the piece of broken-off ice cooler spinning across the floor after him. Gawion jumped out of the way, and it continued into the soft snow, making a barbegazi-foot-deep hole.

"Thanks for the help," he muttered.

Behind him, Maman said, "Oh, Aeglosben, the humans might have heard that whistle."

For the rest of the day, Gawion worked hard. He started by digging a long, long tunnel from the resting cave. Next came his very own exit. He needed to get rid of the excess snow, and he shovelled it up to the surface with his feet. Papa surely had not considered that he would now be able to leave unnoticed, he thought, when he broke through the surface into a downpour of wonderful white pellets.

Every time Gawion scooped powder snow out, he hoped to see the sky had darkened, so he could return to Tessa and Felix.

—27—

Aunt Annie's anger evaporated while they helped her slice cucumbers, and carry jugs of milk and juice, for the breakfast buffet. She believed their hasty explanation of wanting to get to training early, and they left when the first guest appeared in the breakfast room.

Outside, only a single pine cone lay below Felix's window—Gawion had not returned. Hidden behind the same large pine tree that had concealed them last night, they folded printed photos of a van similar to Bahne's.

"I still can't believe Professor Bahne might be the elf hunter," Tessa said.

"Might be?" Felix crammed the printouts into his pocket. "The evidence is clear."

"Hmmm. And I can't believe you never told me he was the skier in that avalanche."

"And I can't believe you never told me who'd written that book." Felix mimicked her voice in a mocking tone.

Tessa's helmet dangled from her arm, but she wore her normal boots. Her ski boots lay by her side, unbuckled, ready to put on if Bahne appeared in his skiing gear.

"Sure you don't want me to come?" Felix asked, for the millionth time.

Tessa nodded.

"Just tell Coach I have a stomach bug, and hand out those photos. Promise the finder a full baking tray of Aunt Annie's brownies." That ought to get their teammates interested in searching for the van. "Anyway, you need the training more than me." She winked.

Felix punched her shoulder.

"Text me," he said, before picking up his skis and setting off.

She waited impatiently, stamping her feet and blowing fake smoke signals in the frozen air. Guests stumbled out of the house, balancing skis and poles and children, and slid towards the ski bus. No matter how many times she turned it over in her head, Tessa couldn't grasp that she'd been deceived. When no one except Oma believed her, Bahne's book had given her hope. She'd planned to write to him, *trust* him with her knowledge of the barbegazi. And she refused to believe she'd been hoodwinked. There had to be another explanation.

When Bahne finally left the house in his white outfit, he wore normal boots, and he didn't bring skis. He stared at the mountains surrounding Schöngraben before he turned and strode down the driveway. Tessa dumped the helmet next to her boots and skis, and followed him.

After crossing the road, he paused by the bus stop. Tessa hid behind the bustle of people waiting for the bus to the lifts. Before he walked on, he glanced back over his shoulder. She ducked, although he wouldn't recognize her if he saw her in the crowd.

No one looked less like a crazy off-piste skier than the professor. In fact, he resembled an elderly gentleman, a village doctor, in one of Oma's TV series. He certainly didn't look like a barbegazi abductor. And maybe he wasn't one. Maybe they'd come to all the wrong conclusions. What evidence did they really have? A scent in the air, detected only by Gawion. An iron chain and an old map—part of the research for his latest book, perhaps.

Without looking back, Bahne turned down Tessa's own street. Shadowing him, she tried to act like a tourist. A boring grey jacket and round retro sunglasses from Aunt Annie's stuff-guests-might-need closet served as her disguise.

Bahne strode right past her house, with its unlit fairy lights around the black windows, and turned left down a bend in the road. Her stomach knotted. Would Oma be having heart surgery today? She crossed her fingers on both hands, whispering, "Please, let Oma be okay."

By the garage, she stopped and peeked round the corner. The street turned a sharp left, downhill, and ended in the small parking lot by the Matthis Bed and Breakfast. Expecting

Bahne to come driving up the hill, Tessa stayed hidden next to the garage. She checked the time on her phone and inspected the photo Felix had sent of the van.

If only she could find another explanation. What if someone else had also been in the avalanche? What if Professor Bahne was hunting the elf hunter? Perhaps he was another secret barbegazi protector. So secret, even the barbegazi didn't know of his existence.

After five minutes, Tessa traipsed back to the corner. With nowhere to hide, she practised things to say if Bahne confronted her on the road. Things like "I'm staying at Matthis's. I forgot my lift card." It was stupid. He didn't know her, and he had no reason to confront her.

Six cars, blanketed in snow, stood in the parking lot. No vans. Bahne had disappeared.

Was he in the house? Had he booked two rooms? Not likely. Mrs Matthis would've told the whole village, if an even remotely interesting guest stayed with them. Where had he gone? If she'd lost him, Felix would be really impressed...

Then she saw a white figure, hurrying along the trodden trail that crossed the snow-covered fields. She hid behind a low wall, got her binoculars out and had an instant close-up view of the frozen valley. No ray of sun reached the bottom of it between early December and the end of January, and the air remained still and icy during those months. It was the perfect place to stash something in sub-zero temperatures.

Bahne crossed the main road and vanished down the hiking trail. Tessa clambered over the wall, and sprinted after him over the fields and across the road. Half-skidding, she followed the steep trail under the railway overpass, to the wooden bridge crossing the river.

The track up to the sawmill was partly hidden by towering stacks of planks covered in fluttering tarpaulins. On the far side of the bridge, the cross-country ski trail ran alongside the rushing water and a steep hiking route led up into the forest. Above her, a train whooshed by.

There was no sign of the professor.

Paw prints and footprints and markings from ski poles surrounded the trail. Pine needles lay scattered on some, and others had a half-erased, day-old look to them. She chose a set of fresh footprints to follow, and jogged towards the sawmill.

When she passed the dark office building, she paused to glance at a closed-for-the-holidays sign, with a sprig of holly attached to it, on the main door, before she continued through the maze of sheds and silent workshops. Between stacks of timber, Tessa caught a glimpse of movement. She sneaked along the heaps of wood, until she saw it. A van, exactly like the one in the photo, was parked behind an old shed, and, hidden by long rafters covered in snow, she crept closer. Close enough to hear a muffled, deep voice and metallic clanks.

What was Bahne doing in there? She wanted to text Felix, but her phone had no reception in the sheltered valley.

Try as she might, Tessa failed to find an innocent explanation for Bahne's van being parked in this remote location. Had it been any other vehicle, she could've imagined the professor confronting the elf hunter inside. But it wasn't. It was Bahne inside Bahne's van in a very cold, isolated place, and Tessa finally stopped doubting he was guilty.

One of the upright doors at the back of the van opened. Bahne crawled out backwards, saying, "—get you to talk," before he slammed the door. Orange lights blinked when he locked the van with a beep. Striding past Tessa on the other side of the rafters, he mumbled to himself about some kind of rack.

She waited several minutes after he'd gone before she dashed round the shed to the van. Hiding behind it, in case Bahne returned, she tried the doors. Locked, of course. She knocked on a window. "Maeg," she said, as loud as she dared. "I'm a friend of Gawion's."

From inside came a moan and a quiet, squeaked, "Help."

FROM *HABITS & HABITATS: A HISTORIC ACCOUNT OF ALPINE ELVES* BY PROFESSOR, DR EBERHART LUDWIG FRITZ BAHNE

No accounts exist of barbegazi surviving longer than three days in temperatures above ten degrees Celsius, and they only thrive in sub-zero temperatures. Because of this heat sensitivity and their severe intolerance for iron, the recommended environment in which to keep barbegazi in captivity is an iron cage inside a glacier cave—or, these days, a ventilated, industrial freezer.

—28—

Back near the road, Tessa's phone beeped as soon as she had reception. A list of messages and two missed calls from Felix appeared on the cracked screen.

What's happening? at 10:21.

Where r u? at 10:47.

U ok? at 11:03, 11:18 and 11:36.

It was almost noon now. Ok. Found Maeg, Tessa texted.

Meet at bus stop, he wrote back.

Tessa waited for a few minutes before Felix jumped out of the ski bus. Walking up the steep driveway to the house, Tessa had just begun telling him about her morning, when he shushed her. Bahne was walking towards them, skis on his shoulder, eyes hidden behind silvery goggles.

Tessa froze, but Felix pushed her.

"Act normal," he hissed. Then he spoke louder: "Snow's good today, Professor. Off-piste, as usual?"

"Probably." Bahne slowed, but didn't stop. "Schöngraben allows me to do what I enjoy most."

Tessa clenched her teeth. Like hunting barbegazi, she almost said.

"Just stay away from those avalanches," Felix said.

Bahne snorted. His thin moustache curled.

"How can you chat with him," Tessa said when he was out of earshot, "as if he's normal?"

Felix shrugged.

"Just thinking ahead. Perhaps we need to... I don't know... get him to talk or something."

"There you are," Aunt Annie called through a kitchen window. "Food's ready." Luckily, she turned her back before she noticed Tessa wasn't wearing the green ski-club jacket and didn't have any of her ski equipment.

After discarding their outdoor gear, Tessa and Felix entered the kitchen in their thermal long johns and knitted tops, as if they'd both just come home from training. They wolfed down spaghetti and meatballs. Tessa finished her account of the morning in whispered bursts whenever Aunt Annie, who was baking, fetched something in the pantry or turned on the mixer.

"Was the car key in his room?" Felix whispered.

Tessa thought back, trying to remember if there'd been any keys in the drawer where she found the map. She shook her head. "He could've been using it."

"We won't get the master key with Mum here anyway. I've got another idea." Felix raised his voice to be heard over the din of the mixer. "We're going out, Mum."

"Where–" The closing door muffled the rest of Aunt Annie's question.

"Get dressed," Felix said in the hallway, "I'll get a coat hanger."

"A what?" Tessa asked, but Felix was already gone.

Outside, Felix placed a wire coat hanger against his chest before he zipped up his jacket.

"What's it for?"

"Opening the van. I saw it in an online video. Tried it once on Dad's car."

"It worked?"

"Yeah, kind of, but the alarm went off." Felix shrugged. "With Maeg inside, I'm guessing the professor has disabled his alarm."

They jogged all the way to Bahne's van. Soon Maeg would be free! Tessa couldn't wait to bring her to Gawion. He'd be so happy. And Tessa would truly become a secret barbegazi protector.

They tried the van's doors, knocked on the windows and called Maeg's name.

This time there was no answer.

"You're sure she's in there?" Felix asked.

"Still in there, you mean."

"Yeah, yeah. Anyway, with Bahne skiing, this is probably pretty safe." Felix unbent and straightened the hanger, before he attacked the passenger door.

"Perhaps she's sleeping," Tessa muttered.

After a few tries the lock sprang up. No alarm sounded. Tessa opened the door, and crawled inside and between the seats to the back.

A large cage, with rusted iron bars as thick as her wrists, filled half the space. On the floor, in the furthest corner, lay a lifeless furry bundle.

"Maeg!" Tessa tore at the locked hatch. She stretched her hand in through the bars, but the opening was too narrow for her elbow, and she couldn't reach the barbegazi. "Maeg!" she called again, a bit louder.

The bundle didn't stir.

"Let me try." Felix had joined her, and he nudged Maeg with the ex-coat-hanger before Tessa could stop him. A jolt, like an electric current, ran through the barbegazi's small body, then it stilled again. Maeg moaned.

"At least she's alive," Felix said. The lock on the cage had an old-fashioned keyhole, which he failed to open with the coat hanger. Two modern padlocks on massive iron chains further secured the hatch. "Pro stuff! No chance opening these with any of Dad's tools. We need the keys."

"I promise, we'll save you, Maeg," Tessa whispered, as she crept out of the van.

They trudged between locked sawmill buildings and stacks of planks, the gushing river swallowing the sound of their footsteps. Scenarios for rescue missions flitted through Tessa's mind, but none of them were realistic. She discarded them faster than they took to appear.

Halfway home, they sought cover from an icy drizzle under the wide eaves of a house. Here, Aunt Annie couldn't overhear them, and so they leant against the wall to think up a plan. A few times one of them began a sentence with "What if?...", only to end it with "...Forget it."

Eventually the streetlights flickered on. Sleet pounded on the roof. Tessa's bum was numb with cold when an idea finally took form.

"This might sound really crazy..." she said, "and we would need Gawion's help. And lots of luck."

Without delay, she told Felix her plan.

—29—

After closing the door, Bahne turned the key twice and tested the handle. He surveyed the room. His locked suitcase, with his tools and fur samples, lay at the exact angle he had placed it before going out. Everything seemed to be in order, unlike yesterday.

Yesterday, an unfamiliar scent had lingered in the room, and his suitcase had been moved. When he confronted Mrs Berger this morning, she denied that anyone had been inside, but there was something shifty to her eyes. Perhaps, he thought, he should leave this place earlier than planned.

At home, in his laboratory, he had an industrial walk-in freezer and the necessary equipment to force the barbegazi to talk. A local builder had replicated the modified rack, based on a sketch from the historic archives in Geneva. His own narrow feet tingled, at the mere thought of stretching those hairy barbegazi pads.

"But how can I keep it alive?" he muttered. Even after years of trawling through ancient texts, their dietary needs remained an unsolved mystery. He emptied the contents of his backpack. Moss, bark, pine cones, pine needles and grass from deep below the snow in Schöngraben scattered onto the plastic sheet on top of his bed. Despite trying to feed it a variety of native plants, the barbegazi in his van was weak from lack of sustenance. So far, it had rejected everything he offered, except a few ice cubes. Whatever the barbegazi needed, he knew it must be available here and now in these mountains. And so, instead of leaving early, he might have to extend his stay.

While he showered and changed clothes, he took deep breaths, and reminded himself that despite his failure to get any human words out of the barbegazi, his trip was an immense success.

All the miserable Christmas holidays he had spent in this B & B, with its chatterbox proprietor, had finally paid off. After years of marking barbegazi tracks on his map, he had known the most likely places to be rescued by one of them.

"Rescued," he scoffed. As if he needed to be rescued. His new avalanche airbag had worked like a charm. It had kept him afloat on the surface of the sliding snow. Both skis were gone, as expected, but he would rather lose them than risk breaking a leg. And he had, of course, brought snowshoes.

Pretending to be unconscious until he could get his iron chain around the barbegazi had been easy.

Preventing it from starving to death was turning out to be difficult.

But even if the services of a taxidermist would be required, the discovery and capture of a barbegazi was a breakthrough for science. A crowning end to his career. The means to restoring his professional reputation and making his colleagues across Europe envious. He sneered, imagining the astounded faces of the old guard, all those who usually sniggered behind his back at zoological conferences, convinced elves were as extinct as the dinosaurs.

He alone had been certain they were still alive. When the institute stopped funding his barbegazi research a decade ago, he continued the hunt. And every year he spent time in locations with barbegazi rumours: skiing in St Anton over Christmas and in Chamonix during Easter, and crossing the Swiss Alps on glacier hiking trails every weekend in summer and autumn.

After sitting down at the desk, he opened the drawer and extracted his black fountain pen. Unfortunately, he had no need of the red pen today. He only wanted to mark a few new crevices without barbegazi traces on the map. The map. Bahne flipped through the stashed papers twice, without finding it.

He struck the desk with a white-knuckled fist, saying aloud, "They are all liars."

Someone had been in his room and taken his map. Mrs Berger had been lying. Just like old Willy Berger had lied when he denied being rescued by a barbegazi. Even mentioning it in *Habits & Habitats* had not brought the stubborn mountain man to his senses.

Bahne stood up abruptly. The chair snagged on the carpet and crashed to the floor. He picked up his notebook and strode out of the room, letting the door slam.

Maybe from the armchair in the breakfast room, he might overhear something that could lead him to the map thief.

—30—

Icy pellets of hail attacked them on their way home. A bang rang out, nearby. Blurry green sparkles lit up the dark sky—an impatient child setting off early New Year's fireworks.

"Let's hope Bahne isn't here yet," Tessa said. She planned to wait for him in the ski room. "And for lots of snow and avalanches."

Felix punched in the code by the back door. "You *are* loony," he said, with a hint of admiration.

Yells warned them of the mayhem inside. A frantic mum unbuckled the tiny ski boots on her wailing toddler and wiped goo from its nose at the same time. Two drenched boys in ski boots fought, using poles as swords.

Luckily, it only took them a second to find Bahne's white ski boots on the boot heater. Unluckily, that meant he was already home, and Tessa needed to revise her plan.

Upstairs, Bahne was sipping a cup of tea in front of the fire in the breakfast room, a notebook in his lap. Unable to believe her luck, Tessa made straight for him, but was intercepted by Aunt Annie, who pulled her into the kitchen and shut the door.

"What on earth do you think you're doing?"

"I just want to ask Bahne—"

"Professor Bahne. Don't bother him. Can't you see he's working?" She sighed. "Wouldn't it be wonderful if he wrote his next book here by my fire?"

"But—"

Aunt Annie cut her off. "No buts. He's a valued guest. Not like them. Bless the poor mother." She nodded towards the noisy ski room. "Professor Bahne is a distinguished gentleman who doesn't want to be disturbed. Especially not by children." She shooed Tessa back into the hallway.

Over her shoulder, Tessa saw Bahne vacate the chair by the fire and walk up the stairs to the guest rooms. No wonder, with the racket from the ski room.

Later, she sat on Felix's floor, pulling her knitted thermal top over her knees. She'd just talked to Mum, who had tried to convince Tessa that her sniffling was only due to a cold.

"They might operate tomorrow." Mum sniffed and fake-sneezed. "Or Monday. I'm so glad you're at Annie's, so I don't need to fret about you."

Only about Oma. Tessa heard the unspoken words. She'd forgotten to ask if Oma had solved her puzzle, before Mum ended the call.

Felix stood by his desk, straightening the row of trophies. "What now?" he asked.

Tessa wiped her eyes. She'd have to concentrate on saving Maeg, and let Mum worry about Oma. She wound and unwound the hem of her top round her index finger.

After a while, she said, "I'll just knock on his door."

"Really? Sure you don't want me to come?"

"No. It's better if I go alone." Before she could change her mind, Tessa rose, and grabbed Opa's book and a pen from Felix's desk. "Just keep Aunt Annie down in the kitchen."

As she crept up the stairs, she heard Felix in the kitchen, saying, "Mum, can you wash my lucky ski socks? I need them for the race."

It wouldn't surprise her if he really did have lucky socks, and it didn't surprise her at all that he couldn't just wash them himself.

Walking along the corridor, music and the sound of splashing water emerged from behind one room door. From another, wails of the toddler from earlier, mixed with the older boys' laughter.

No sounds reached her from Bahne's room. Tessa stood outside it, taking deep breaths, and staring at the black book in her hand. Here goes, she thought, and knocked.

Folded paper stuck out in the middle of the book. The map. Tessa fumbled, trying to open the book while holding the pen. She'd used the map as a bookmark. Bahne's map.

On the other side of the door, heavy footsteps approached. Tessa's trembling hands dropped both pen and book. The map fell out. As the door opened, she bent low to collect everything, and stuffed the map up under her knitted top. She hoped she hadn't stretched her top too much with her knees earlier, or the map might slip out at the slightest movement.

"Yes?"

Tessa got up from the floor, her cheeks burning. Her heart beat fast and loud like helicopter rotor blades.

"Excuse me, Professor."

He narrowed his eyes, with no movement of the thin moustache.

"Ca... can I ask you to sign this?" She shielded her face, hiding behind the book.

Bahne's expression transformed. He raised both eyebrows. It relaxed his stern features. "*Habits & Habitats*. My first book!"

Tessa struggled to remember what she'd planned to say. That blasted map. She handed him the book.

"Please?"

In his hand, it naturally fell open by the most read page. Frowning, Bahne pulled at a pair of reading glasses which hung on a cord around his neck. But as he pulled the glasses up to his eyes, a chain, hidden inside his pristine shirt, got caught up and fell out of his collar. He slipped this chain back inside his shirt a moment later, but not before Tessa had seen its set of very interesting attachments—on the end dangled three keys.

Tessa gaped, then hurried to look down at the book, while she mentally ticked off this vital item in her plan.

"What is all this?" he said, surveying the sketches and scribbles in the margins.

"My grandfather's notes. I inherited the book from him, you see. He's mentioned right there." Tessa pointed at the paragraph about Opa.

When she looked up again, Bahne was studying her.

"I'm afraid he didn't tell you the truth," she said, her heart rate speeding up again, "Because there *are* barbegazi in Schöngraben."

"He told you?"

"Yes. And I've seen them."

A gleam appeared in Bahne's eyes. "And you know where they live?"

"Well, no." She smiled inwardly at Bahne's look of disappointment. "But they come to play when I whistle." Was it too far-fetched for him to believe? She'd discussed it with Felix. But there might not be enough new snow tomorrow for avalanches.

"Play?" Bahne's eyes narrowed again.

"One of them is very funny and talks like they do in films about the Napoleonic Wars."

"It talks to you?"

"Oh yes. He's told me how his family sleep through the summer." She grasped for something from the book, something Bahne knew already, so he would believe her. Perhaps... "And how they escaped from that zoo in Vienna."

"Could you take me to meet them?" Bahne asked. "I would be very grateful. I will even mention you in my next book."

Her wish come true. How ironic.

"What's your name?" he asked her eagerly.

"Tessa. Tessa Gilbert." She bit her lip and pretended to think hard. "It's actually a secret. I promised not to tell anyone about the barbegazi," she whispered.

"You're not betraying any secrets. I already know everything about them."

Like how to make them suffer, she wanted to say, while fighting to keep her face blank. The boiling anger inside her made it difficult to speak. "Oh. Okay."

"Tomorrow morning?" he asked casually, while he opened the book at the cover and signed his name under the printed title.

"No. I have a ski race. And they don't come out until the lifts close. Do you know Kapall, Professor?" she asked, knowing that he did. It was the first place she'd ever seen him.

He nodded.

"Meet me outside the mountain hut on Kapall at half past four."

"Very well."

Tessa snatched her book away, mumbled, "Bye," and made for the stairs. As she walked, the map slipped out from under her top and fluttered to the floor. Picking it up, she glanced behind her, but Bahne was gone. She sighed with relief. Step one of the plan had worked. Now she just needed everything else to fall into place.

Only about a million things could go wrong.

—31—

When the mountain transporters stopped, Papa came to inspect Gawion's work. He commented on the unevenness of the cave floor. "And the entrance tunnel is too short," he said, "Your ice block will melt."

"It is my cave." Gawion stamped on a pile of snow that had fallen from the wall, making a new, obvious bump on the floor.

Papa left without giving any further advice.

Maman brought him a handful of berries and marvelled at the cave's cosiness. To his surprise, she also admitted that Tessa had saved them from starvation, though she was still wary of the human.

"We are only afraid you will get disappointed," she said, caressing his beard. "Humans are so fickle, and as adults they forget the promises they made to themselves and others when they were children. At Schönbrunn, Francis Joseph visited our cage every day with an entourage of nursemaids, promising to free us upon becoming emperor, but it forgot too."

"Tessa's grandfather did not forget. Neither will Tessa."

"I dearly hope you are right." She parted her beard and removed something from it. "Give this to your human. It is a token of our indebtedness, and a promise to fulfil a wish."

Gawion stared at the precious gift in Maman's outstretched hand. "But that is fairy ma—"

"Hush. It is a snowflake charm as old as the glaciers."

"Did you make it from strands of your own beard, Maman?" he asked, unable to believe the sacrifice she had made for a human.

"The longest and strongest. True stamina."

"But your life will be shorter," he said, remembering the tales Maman had told them of the Fates spinning, measuring and cutting threads, determining lifespans. According to the myths, these goddesses of destiny gave the barbegazi their long full beards made of stamina, and therefore their long lives.

"Only by a few years..."

"Thank you, Maman."

She tucked the gift into the pocket in his beard and fastened it with two knots.

"I still have misgivings about your human," she said. "And I beg you to stay vigilant."

———

Papa returned when darkness had fallen and insisted on accompanying Gawion to the meeting with Tessa and Felix.

Why did Papa have to treat him like a child? Why could he not trust Gawion's judgement? Without him and his human friends, they would all be starving, and Maeg would be forever lost. Even if Maman remained sceptical of Tessa, she at least had faith in him. Papa trusted neither the humans nor Gawion.

As they made their way towards the village, a few strange lights lit up the gloom, followed by loud noise. Fireworks, ignited by humans. On one night each year, nine or ten nights after the winter solstice, the sky above the valley always erupted in a sea of coloured sparkles.

Was it that time already? He remembered the solstice, and his disappointment when there was no berry gift in the hole, as clearly as if it were yesterday. But so much had happened since he met Tessa three nights ago, that it felt like they had known each other for ever. Time was like snow, sometimes fluffy and spaced out, and sometimes compressed into glaciers.

Papa hid between the trees, near the human habitat.

"I am only a whistle away." His hand clutched Gawion's shoulder. "Are you sure it is safe, son?"

"Trust me, for once," Gawion snapped.

Under the pine tree, he found one of the ovals and threw it at Felix's bright see-through wall. It bounced back with a clink. Two faces appeared, their noses pressed against the glass.

A short while later, Tessa joined him under the tree. "Felix had to help his mum," it said, then inhaled deeply, as if preparing for a long-distance whistle. "We found Maeg. She's alive, but not well. And she's in an iron cage."

Gawion choked. The blunt words smothered him with the force of a wet snow avalanche.

Tessa squeezed his hand, saying, "Don't worry. I have a plan," and told him how and where it had found Maeg, while he gasped. Then it explained the elaborate scheme to rescue his sister.

When Tessa finished talking, Gawion stared at it, amazed that a human baby could conceive of something so ingenious. Liel would not understand half of it, and she was almost fifty. He closed his mouth, pleased that his beard had hidden his gaping.

"Very cunning," he said, "I shall do my part."

Tessa blew a long puff of warm air at him. "Thank you."

There was a loud control whistle from Papa, checking in, and Gawion whistled a short, "All good" signal back.

"My only concern is the shell on the elf hunter's head," he said. "How can I remove it?"

"Shell? Oh, you mean the helmet. Wait here, I'll show you." Tessa turned and sprinted back to the habitat.

It was far from his only concern, but it was the only one Tessa could help him solve. The plan was bold. Dangerous, even. And far from infallible.

Regardless of Tessa's suggestion, he would tell Maman and Papa nothing. With their lack of faith in humans—and in him—they would doubtless forbid his participation in such a risky scheme.

—32—

Tessa ran, hunchbacked, through the torrential sleet, trying to protect her ski helmet. Gawion was willing to do his part; another chunk of her plan was in place. But could he? He'd been so shocked when she told him Maeg was in an iron cage. Tessa had wanted to hug him—he'd reminded her of her favourite teddy bear. And a cuddly bear couldn't do what was required.

At least he wouldn't be alone. She'd asked him to get his parents to help. Did three cuddly barbegazi trump one evil professor?

She brushed wet branches aside and re-entered the tent-like space under the tree. Sitting on her knees, she showed

Gawion how to squeeze the clasp on both sides until it snapped open. Then she put the helmet on and leant forward. "Try. It's plastic."

Goose pimples chased chills all over her body, at his icy touch.

Gawion, having unbuckled her helmet for the third time with hesitant, clumsy fingers, shifted his focus to her eyes. "If we succeed–"

"When we succeed," she said, with a conviction she didn't feel. Watching him concentrate so hard on opening a clasp had not improved her confidence.

"We are already indebted to you for bringing the berries." He fiddled with his beard. "And I have something for you."

The "something" was a coin-sized tangle of hair.

In the low light, it was nearly invisible, blending in with the fur of Gawion's hand. After taking her gloves off, Tessa picked it up with thumb and forefinger, and brought it closer to her headlamp.

It wasn't a knot of hair. It was a thousand knots of hair, or the finest threads imaginable. Their intricate pattern formed a shimmering snowflake.

"Wow! It's beautiful," she whispered. In comparison, Aunt Annie's framed lace doilies were plain and lumpy.

"All snowflakes are unique wonders," Gawion said. "Maman has knotted this one of stamina."

"Stamina? Isn't that like strength or energy? How can you knot that into a snowflake?"

"Barbegazi only have little magic, but she has used strands like these." He lifted part of his beard. The pale hairs gleamed in the light. "And granted you a wish. The snowflake is a token of her promise." His nose turned the same shade of rosy pink as Mum's favourite lipstick, and he bent his head in a deep, formal bow.

"A wish? Really?" Tessa smiled despite her worries. "So, can I ask for anything? Like world peace?" she said, expecting a no. She had, after all, read lots of fairy tales.

"That is impossible," Gawion said.

"Can I visit your caves then?" She'd spent hours on the T-bar imagining cosy igloo-like domes under the snow.

"That requires Maman's permission, not magic."

"Okay, then my wish is for Maeg to be safe."

"You would do that?" Gawion frowned. "Use your wish to help us?"

She nodded.

"Thank you, but if a snowflake charm could save Maeg, Maman would have done it already."

"Let me think..." Tessa studied the knotted snowflake. If the barbegazi only had limited magic, she should wish for something smaller.

Felix knew the barbegazi existed, but she really wanted Lisa to know. Seeing Lisa's expression when she met Gawion would be priceless. Tessa could almost hear Lisa's "Oh my god", and see her cuddling the barbegazi. They'd be best friends again.

But part of her wanted to be the secret barbegazi protector. To only share the knowledge of their existence with Felix, until the time came for her own grandchild to take over the task of bringing berries.

Perhaps Lisa would like her more if she skied better in the competitions.

"Could I be the fastest tomorrow, and win the ski race?"

"Easily." Gawion grinned, showing layers of tiny pointed teeth. "You have the ability. You only lack belief in yourself. Is that your wish?"

"No. Wait. I haven't decided yet."

It would be cheating, a kind of fairy-doping. Still... Standing on the centre step of the podium, holding the biggest trophy high in the air... Swishing her hair, wavy after she'd taken it out of the plaits, and looking down at Lisa and Maria. Coach would slap her on the back, pleased with the points she'd gained for the team in the seasonal standings. And Mum, after being a nervous wreck while Tessa skied her run, would be so proud, and buy a winner's round of sodas for everyone.

But no, Mum wouldn't even be there. Mum might be a nervous wreck tomorrow, though not in St Anton. She'd be in Innsbruck, in the hospital with Oma.

Tessa's excitement drained away, leaving only worry.

"There is no need to decide now," Gawion said. "Think for a day, or a year, or a decade. The wish can be fulfilled at any time."

Tessa traced the fine outline of the snowflake and nodded. She'd save the wish for something that mattered. Right now, the only thing she wanted was for Oma's broken heart to mend, and fulfilling that wish was clearly beyond barbegazi magic. After wrapping the delicate snowflake in a paper tissue, she put it in the inside breast pocket of her jacket, right next to her own heart.

That night, she lay awake long after Felix had fallen asleep. She'd not shown him the snowflake. Perhaps she never would.

Under the duvet, in the light from her headlamp, she tried to follow the knotted paths of the shimmering strands. It might only be a token for a promised wish, but to her it was magical. The threads were much finer than fishing line, and much stronger. Gawion had said they were made of stamina. She still didn't understand how that was possible, but she believed him.

Clutching the snowflake, Tessa closed her eyes, and wished with all her heart that she could send some of its mysterious strength to Oma.

—33—

Bahne brushed his teeth until the sand ran through the hourglass. While he flossed, he considered his incredible luck.

This was it: his chance to capture another barbegazi. With two of the creatures in his possession, it would be easy to make them talk. Despite their animal nature, they presumably had enough human characteristics to protect each other. Chimpanzees did. When he stretched the feet of one barbegazi in the rack while the other watched, the watcher would spill all their secrets.

And two barbegazi of opposite sex could be the start of an acclaimed breeding programme. Science had come a long way since the middle of the nineteenth century, when the last incarcerated avalanche of barbegazi escaped, under puzzling circumstances.

He sneered, admiring the gleam on his sharp canines in the mirror.

It satisfied his need for order and patterns that his helper in finding the barbegazi was a descendant of someone who had caused him so much trouble. When he wrote *Habits & Habitats*, he was young and foolish, keen to pursue all possibilities. Now, with one sweep of his iron chain, he could overcome his regret of ever mentioning Mr Berger.

The only two other esteemed elf researchers in Europe still ridiculed him for believing Mr Berger's tale. Barbegazi couldn't thrive so far from the high Alps, they claimed. It was going to be an immense pleasure to prove them wrong.

His dental hygiene secured, Bahne strode to the desk. The pile of papers still lay there, and he returned them to the drawer, one by one, searching for his precious map. Its red circles indicated signs of barbegazi presence. Though most people mistook them for snowboard tracks, he never doubted when he saw their spoors.

He even suspected a barbegazi had once dug him out of an avalanche in Schöngraben. One moment he had been stuck under the white mass, the next he was inside a rescue helicopter, where a young doctor told him how lucky he was to end up on the surface of the snow. Whenever he tried to recall the location of the avalanche, however, his memory blurred, to the sound of awful music, like a ringing in the ears. So that spot was not marked on his map. His map that someone had stolen.

He slammed the drawer shut with a bang.

Was Berger's granddaughter somehow involved? If so, he might need to bring additional tools. He unlocked his suitcase and picked through the equipment inside, selecting with care.

The girl had said she kept the barbegazi a secret. That was good. Very good. If she truly saw them as her friends, she might not approve of his plans. A minor problem. After she had shown him to them, he would find a way to keep her quiet. The scientific insights to be gained were far too valuable to let such inconveniences stand in the way.

Children had accidents all the time, and the mountains were filled with dangers.

SATURDAY, 31ST DECEMBER

—34—

Race day began clear and bright and freezing cold. The blue never-ending sky and the glittering mountainsides promised sunshine, but no avalanches. It had stopped snowing before midnight.

Tessa stood with her teammates, sideways, canting her skis, on the steep World Cup piste, where the best skiers in the world sometimes competed.

Coach yelled instructions on how the run should be attacked.

"You wanna come at this blue gate from above. Then quickly shift your weight for the red. Like this." He moved his bulk with surprising lightness, and cut tracks in the snow, showing the ideal curve.

One at a time, Felix first, the group followed, slowly tracing his tracks. Above and below them, other ski teams from the region, in uniform outfits, mirrored their own coaches in slow motion. Of course, they couldn't ski as close to the gates as they would in the race, and their speed was turtle-like by comparison, but it was supposed to give them a sensory memory.

Tessa's memory didn't get it. Or maybe her brain was just too full. Plan details kept popping up in her head, when she wasn't thinking about Oma. The barbegazi snowflake was back inside her breast pocket. It was silly, but she almost thought she could feel its strength and energy, like heat radiating from a tiny flame.

"Wake up, Miss My-head's-in-the-clouds!" Coach yelled.

What had Coach said? Mimicking Lisa, she trailed the others.

The race began with the youngest age groups, and Tessa went inside to drink hot chocolate with Felix, who refused to discuss the plan before the race. Afterwards, in the ladies', she struggled to get her race suit up over her back protector and, in Mum's absence, had to ask a tourist for help.

When she returned to the start area, the U11 boys were already racing, and her own year group was getting ready. Some stood with their eyes closed, making slow, wavy motions with their hands, visualizing the course like World Cup skiers. Nerves bounced around, infecting everyone. Except her. Ambitious fathers shouted advice to their kids, sharpened skis, and argued over waxing techniques. Tessa's skis were in top condition—Uncle Harry had serviced them as thoroughly as Opa would've done.

Most of the mothers waited by the finish area, prepared to cheer or console. A sharp pang spasmed in her stomach. Today, Mum wasn't there to bundle her into a warm jacket and give her a hug.

Lisa made her way through the bustle. She belonged to the closed-eyes, visualizing group.

"Good luck," Tessa said.

Lisa's eyes widened.

"You too." Her mouth opened as if she wanted to say more, then closed as she gave Tessa's arm a squeeze.

"Does it help, the hand-waving thing?" Tessa asked.

Lisa shrugged. "Nah... but it makes Dad shut up." Lisa turned and wiggled out of her jacket. Her bib showed start number 113. With number 112, Tessa would be racing just ahead of her.

Uncle Harry shook her.

"Time for boots."

Tessa lifted her foot, like a horse having its hoof cleaned, and Uncle Harry scraped every single flake of snow off each boot, before he guided them into the freshly cleaned ski bindings.

Sliding her goggles on, Tessa entered the start box. Only one more minute, then she could focus on her planning. She'd never been less nervous about a race. Later today came the real challenge.

"Three push offs, Tessa! Watch the second blue. Knees!" Coach yelled. "Ready?" He held a lump of snow to the back of her bare neck. A shocking chill raced down her spine. "Steady. Go!"

Tessa pushed off, releasing the timer, and passed the first gate. In front of her, the red and blue gates made a pattern. A pattern she'd never really seen before. And suddenly it was like she was off-piste with Opa, him saying, "Look at the slope, Tessa. Decide your path." He used to drill her, forcing her to tell him her plans for a particular stretch, before they set off. Now she used the same method.

Shifting her focus from the gate immediately in front to the third gate out, made her mind concentrate on the path, not the movements. Skiing became effortless. She imagined Lisa overtaking her, even though Lisa wouldn't start until she was done. It spurred her on. The pattern continued until she passed the finish line.

Scattered cheers erupted, and a crackled voice from the loudspeaker shouted her time. She stood to the side, catching her breath. Less than a minute later, Lisa braked next to her, and the speaker's voice sounded. Both of them had times of 46 point something. The hundredths were inaudible.

"Race you to the board," Lisa said.

They clicked out of their skis and ran to the whiteboard where Karen wrote the recorded times. Tessa followed Lisa's finger to U12 girls. Their group began with number 106. Karen scribbled DNF by their last competitor with number 114. Did Not Finish. Tessa looked back at the course. Maria stood in the middle of the run with one ski in her hand, thwacking the ground with a pole.

Tessa's eyes scanned the list of numbers. Lisa had beaten her time by a mere 0.16 seconds. There were no other 46-second times, but some 47 and 48s, and a slow 53 point something. Number 108 had 45.86, and Karen circled the time with a red marker. The winner. Tessa was third. Unable to believe it, she stared at the rows of digits until Lisa congratulated her.

She'd be on the podium! Not at the very centre of the podium, but right next to it. And she'd get a trophy.

Tessa crossed her fingers, wishing her luck would last the whole day. She hoped she hadn't used it all up on something as unimportant as a ski race.

—35—

Three times, Gawion almost told Papa that Tessa had found Maeg. The certainty that Papa would never allow him to participate in Tessa's rescue plan held him back.

The first time was during the night, while he pretended to search for the elf hunter's vehicle with Papa. After persuading Papa that crossing the main road was too dangerous, they trudged along the mountain pass road. It was a waste of time and energy, and the only thing on Gawion's mind was Maeg. Maeg lying lifeless in an iron cage. Had she tried to protect herself by going into a deep sleep, or was it much worse?

If only they could free her now. But even if they broke the glass and entered the vehicle, they had no way of opening an iron cage. Tessa's plan was their only option. So he said nothing. And Papa was so distraught he did not notice Gawion's secret.

When the twinkling stars faded, again, he came close to telling Papa. With Papa's help, it would not take long to prepare what Tessa had envisioned. But explaining the plan and arguing with Papa might take all day. And he was running out of time.

"I feel queasy," he said. "Is that a side effect of long exposure to humans, Papa?"

As predicted, Papa sent him home at once. Guilt ate away at Gawion while he dug and scooped and scraped, preparing everything Tessa wanted.

The third time he almost told Papa was after noon. The quiet morning, resting and working in his own cave, had given him time to think. He might need his parents' help. Tessa expected them to help. The elf hunter was dangerous.

So when Papa entered his cave, he had decided to involve them. But Papa ruined everything. First, he told Gawion how he had done the floor-smoothing wrong, then he said, "No wonder your cave is a mess. You never pause to consider how to do things right."

Gawion clenched his teeth. He would show Papa about doing things right. Just wait until he rescued Maeg by himself... with a little help from his "untrustworthy" human friends.

Later, Maman came into his cave, trying to smooth over everything but the floor.

"Please come into the main cave and talk to your father," she said.

"I want to finish my room," he answered.

The moment she was out of sight, he popped halfway out of his own exit. The mechanical transporters were still emitting their metallic clanks. He waited, while the sun disappeared behind distant peaks and turned the clouds into a palette of berry colours. A pleasant wind rose, sending a refreshing mist of prickling snow across the mountainside. Before the transporter noise ceased, he took off. Alone.

It was not dark yet, but that did not worry him. His fear of normal humans paled at the thought of his looming confrontation with the elf hunter.

—36—

Tessa arrived on Kapall among rattling, unoccupied chairlifts, half an hour before her meeting with Bahne. An icy wind whirled loose snow down the deserted piste and round the corner of the mountain hut. Seats of abandoned deckchairs fluttered.

After the prize-giving ceremony—Felix had of course won his race—both she and Felix had been busy getting everything organized. Luckily, Aunt Annie had been occupied in the kitchen, making finger food for a small midnight celebration, and hadn't interfered with their preparations.

Mumbling, Tessa went over elements of the plan, convincing herself she hadn't overlooked anything. Still, there was plenty to worry about. What if Bahne didn't show? What if she couldn't find the right spot? What if the barbegazi couldn't do their part? The whole project suddenly seemed like a far-fetched idea with no possible happy end.

She shivered, and decided to wait inside. The empty bar greeted her with a lingering smell of frying oil. After taking off her helmet and gloves, she perched on a bar stool. The barmaid tidied rows of snacks and gave her a peppermint tea, although the till was closed. Tessa sipped the tea. The minutes on her phone changed at an unbearably slow pace. She slipped a hand into the breast pocket of her jacket, where her fingers pierced the paper tissue so she could touch the snowflake without taking it out. Staring at the photo Felix had sent, of her on the podium, she tried to remember that feeling of being lucky from this morning.

When she went outside, Bahne stood by her skis, looking towards Schöngraben. In profile, with his bulging backpack, he resembled a hunchbacked white giant on the prowl.

He nodded in greeting, without speaking. She nodded back, opened her ski jacket and made a show of turning on her Pieps. Unzipping his jacket using long leather zipper pulls, he showed her his own blinking avalanche transceiver. Two tick marks for the plan so far. Gawion would be able to open the pockets, and they might need Bahne's avalanche transceiver for their back-up plan.

Words weren't necessary, and all she really wanted to say was: Are you ready for the revenge of the barbegazi?

She led the way past the training area, speeding up when she saw he followed. He skied well for an old man, but lacked Opa's elegant lightness.

At the boundary of the prepared piste, she hesitated. She'd promised Mum not to ski off-piste without adult supervision. Bahne was an adult. Technically, she wasn't breaking any promises, but this, if she'd asked, would surely have been forbidden.

Without giving Bahne a chance to catch his breath, she let the wind push her over the edge. If she could exhaust him, it might help.

Before the landscape fell away on the steep slope, she paused. All contours vanished in the fading light. She knew the route, but she mustn't fall. After securing her headlamp, she adjusted the beam so it pointed at the ground.

"Clever girl," Bahne wheezed, when he caught up, "I didn't think to bring mine."

Her first whistle was inaudible. She licked her frozen lips, tasting salt, and whistled again. This time, a weak tone emerged.

Two high-pitched notes answered her.

"It's them," Bahne said.

"Yes. This way."

She took the steepest incline at a slower pace. Silhouettes of lonely trees gained colour when her light hit them. Her knees became springs, absorbing the bumps hidden under snowdrifts and layers of darkness.

Where the slope flattened came the tricky part: finding the exact spot. She stayed far right in the gorge, hoping the mountain stream was covered with hard snow, so that no one fell down before they were supposed to.

At the first glimpse of Gawion, she stopped. Where were his parents? She'd told him to bring them. Were they hiding? Afraid of her?

When Bahne reached her, she pointed with her pole.

Gawion waved at them.

"Hi, Tessa," he called, "Can we play?"

Bahne gasped.

"It's tame," he muttered.

"I brought someone who wants to play too." She hoped Bahne thought her voice shook because of the cold. "Go ahead, Professor."

Bahne rushed straight towards Gawion. His shadow blocked the light from Tessa's headlamp, and he glided right between the two forked twigs that stuck out of the snow and marked the hidden hollow. A moment later, as intended, the white surface collapsed under his weight. A half-choked scream preceded the sound of Bahne crashing against the ground at the bottom of the hole.

Tessa smiled and lifted both arms with ski poles over her head in triumph.

She heard a moan from the hole, before Gawion dived into a tunnel he'd already prepared. A deep clunk resonated in the hollow, as he walloped Bahne.

"Unconscious!" Gawion called. "Oh, good. It's a silver chain."

"Look for a car key in his pockets too. Pull the leather straps on his clothes. It's probably a square, black plastic thing," she called, not daring to move closer to the trap.

Moments later, Gawion appeared out of the snow next to Tessa, and handed her a car key and the silver chain. Of the three keys on the chain, one was old fashioned and heavy, with a rusted wavy pattern around the large hole. The other two looked like normal padlock keys. After she dropped all of them into her pocket, she zipped it, and double checked that it was closed. Under no circumstances could she lose these keys.

So far, everything had gone as planned. She had the keys to the cage. Bahne lay unconscious in the hole. Gawion was in control of him.

Dad always said "Fortune favours the bold". With such a bold plan, perhaps she'd stay lucky.

—37—

After Tessa left, Gawion walloped the elf hunter again, as a safety precaution.

It half-sat, leaning against the thing on its back, with its head drooping to the side. He opened the buckle under its beardless chin and removed the shell. By pulling on the plastic handles, he wiggled the sticks away from its hands. The wooden feet lay disconnected from the human. He avoided touching them. If only he did not have to touch the foul creature. Its faint whiff of thawing spring snow had disappeared. Now it only reeked of iron.

Standing over the human, Gawion rehearsed the memory alteration, mumbling, "Cover the eyes with my beard, touch the temples with all six fingertips, erase memories by speaking the charm three times, then say it backwards to seed replacement memories."

Although Papa had taught him the charm decades ago, he still lacked understanding of that last bit. It replaced the original memories with snippets of the awful noise that blasted from human dens on the mountain every afternoon. Somehow, this particular kind of noise matched the befuddled state of the humans just after they had been charmed. When he had told Tessa, it laughed and said "That's why I felt so funny, and kept hearing après-ski songs in my head".

He had nodded as if the explanation made sense.

Gawion had altered memories several times on his own, but he had never tried to erase such a long period of time: six days and five nights. And his last memory charm was a disaster—Tessa had remembered him asking about the berry gift. Perhaps he should have listened and involved his parents. If he failed to remove all six days' memories, the elf hunter remained a threat. The elf hunter! Its stench alone made him sick.

He hated what it had done to his sister. How it had made her suffer. Her time in captivity would torment Maeg for the rest of her long life, while this evil creature would remember nothing.

Ice-cold rage filled him. His fingers tingled. Tiny icicles grew at the end of his claws, and ice crystals appeared on the elf hunter's hair and eyebrows and wispy moustache.

Altering its memory, making it forget everything, was not enough. He wanted the human to know that everything it had achieved—the fulfilment of its lifelong dream of capturing a barbegazi—had been taken away. Of course, it would remember nothing after Gawion's charm. But at least in that one moment, when it realized everything was lost, it would suffer.

So he did not alter its memory right away. Instead, he sat down and waited for the human to gain consciousness.

At its first moan, Gawion stood. He paced along the circular wall until it stirred, then he said, "Elf hunter!"

"Mmmm... hmmm... yes?"

"My dear sister, whom you have captured, is being freed."

"Mmmm... How?" Its head rolled forward. A hand rose to its neck, searching for the chain. "The clever girl," it said very slowly.

"Oh, yes. My friend is very clever." Gawion continued his walk of the perimeter. He felt invincible, with the elf hunter in his power. "While we wait, I shall be a real fairy and grant you answers to three questions."

"Three questions?" The elf hunter raised its head, looking for him in the gloom. "But barbegazi are not fairies."

"Fairy, elf, or human—why does everyone focus on our differences?" he grumbled. Perhaps he had overplayed his role. Been too nice. He would speak in a tone it could understand.

"Yes, three questions. And that was the answer to your first question. You have two left."

"Sustenance. What do you need?" it asked without hesitation, sitting upright.

"That is an easy one. We thrive on frozen forest berries. They contain all the nutrients we need. As they discovered in Vienna..." Gawion threw this last comment to the elf hunter, like a fisher-human throws a line and hook. He had seen that once, when he was little. The desperate screams of the impaled trout still haunted him in daymares.

"The zookeeper's daughter..." the human said. "That wasn't a question."

Gawion flexed his fingers. Toying with the elf hunter gave him no satisfaction. Even though it was still weak, he should probably wallop it again.

"If you really are part of the Vienna avalanche of barbegazi, why stop here, when you are more than halfway to the high Alps and their expansive glaciers?"

"My mother was too pregnant to continue," he said, not bothering with a more detailed answer. "Are you happy, now you know everything?"

The human squirmed, but stayed silent.

"In a few moments, you will know nothing." Gawion arched his soles and bounced lightly on his heels. He stood three barbegazi feet from the human's head. The exact distance for a perfect leap.

The elf hunter's eyes roamed, searching for him. But to human eyes, in this weak light and standing in front of a snow wall, Gawion was almost invisible.

"I am going to alter your memory. Afterwards, you will not remember having seen either me or my sister, and the clever girl will be just another irritating human child."

The elf hunter still did not speak.

Gawion searched for signs of suffering or remorse in its stern features. To his disappointment, he found none.

With a hard rebound of his heels, he leapt with his arm outstretched. But the elf hunter pulled something out from behind itself, and swung it upwards. It connected with

Gawion's arm. A metallic *plink* sounded. Gawion screamed. He landed on the wooden feet, burning his hip. Fire spread down his leg and up to his ribs. His walloping arm felt heavy and numb.

The elf hunter swung its long animal-skin strap with the metal buckle again. With immense effort, Gawion pushed off with his uninjured hand and rolled away until he hit the wall of snow.

The human dislodged the pack from its back and scrambled up. While it continued to swing the strap, it rummaged in the pack.

Gawion had just sprung to his feet, when it withdrew a long, rattling chain. The foul smell of iron invaded his nostrils.

Brandishing the iron chain in one hand, and swinging the strap in circles with the other, the elf hunter advanced towards him.

Gawion pressed himself against the wall, unsure which way to move. Left or right? Could he jump over this tall human?

The elf hunter sneered.

"Did you think I would come unprepared? Without iron?"

—38—

Seconds after Tessa flashed her headlamp towards Felix's window, he came running out of the house, in his ski jacket, with normal boots for her and Mum's big rucksack, to carry Maeg in. Between gasps of breath, while she changed boots, she told him what had happened. She left her skiing stuff under the large pine tree, before they set off on their mountain bikes.

Despite the scattered gravel, they skidded on frozen puddles in every turn of the narrow village roads. Tessa kept one foot on the ground and glided more than she pedalled. She was grateful to be wearing her ski helmet and back protector.

By the hiking trail, they dismounted and abandoned the bikes. As they jogged up to the sawmill, the lights from their headlamps bounced on the stacked timber like glow-in-the-dark rubber balls.

The deep-frozen van still stood behind the shed. Tessa made a mental tick mark. She listened. Blood pounded in her ears. She heard nothing else. No long-distance barbegazi whistle yet. It worried her. Gawion had promised to signal when it was done, and he'd assured her the sound would be audible throughout the valley. Had he overestimated his own abilities?

After she extracted the keys from her pocket, she unlocked the van, wincing at the high beep it made.

"Give me the berries."

"Berries!" Felix hit his forehead, making his light disappear. "I forgot. Sorry, Tessa."

"Never mind. We'll stop and get some from Oma's freezer." Her house keys clanked, reassuring her, when she patted her pocket.

Inside, she crawled across the seats to the back, calling to Maeg. The bundle of fur didn't stir. A terrible thought struck her.

Could Maeg be dead?

Tessa crouched by the cage, her head bent to stay clear of the ceiling. Her hands shook, and she dropped the set of keys twice, before she managed to open the two padlocks with the modern keys. Clanking against the bars of the cage, the iron chains slithered down.

The keyhole of the lock on the cage door was rusty, and the big old-fashioned key wouldn't turn. Water dripped onto her fingers—a mixture of melting snow, sweat and tears of frustration.

"Help me, Felix," she screeched.

He pushed her aside and bent down there for a while, wiggling and jiggling the mechanism until something clicked, and the key turned. After he opened the hatch, Tessa crawled into the small space. She shook Maeg gently and searched for a pulse. Not even the slightest vibration quivered in the barbegazi's lifeless body.

Iron bars on the floor cut into Tessa's knees. Maeg had lain on them all week. No wonder she was paralysed.

"Is she hibernating?" Tessa asked, but of course she knew barbegazi slept during the summer.

Carefully, she scooped the limp body up and backed out of the iron cage. Maeg's lightness surprised her—she weighed less than Lisa's cat. Felix stood outside, and she handed Maeg to him, before she jumped to the ground.

"Let's get her in the rucksack." Felix handled the fur bundle like Oma handled the china she'd inherited from her own grandmother.

They quickly discovered, however, that they couldn't get Maeg into the rucksack without her sinking to the bottom, where she wouldn't be able to breathe. If she still needed to breathe.

But if they carried her in their arms, they'd be walking through the village with a barbegazi in plain sight! And they'd be moving much slower than on their bikes. If only they could get a ride in a car. If only—

"Come on, Tessa. We have to go."

"One sec. I have to think." She closed her eyes. The sound

of a passing car on the main road could be heard above the noise from the river. No whistles.

There was something she'd overlooked. It was something about a car. Mum's car? Uncle Harry's car? No. The professor's car... His van, right here in the deserted sawmill.

Suddenly she realized there was a hole in her plan.

"If Gawion succeeds..." At the twinge of doubt, she crossed her fingers for luck. "Bahne's memory will be wiped of everything that has happened this week. He'll not remember where he parked."

"Can't we just tell him? Or call the police about a stolen vehicle, like in the back-up plan?"

"No. We don't want him to be suspicious. I broke through Gawion's memory charm. In a dream. Without trying to." Gawion had told her the barbegazi only had little magic. He still hadn't whistled. What if, while they freed Maeg, Bahne captured her family?

How could she have ever imagined this plan would work? Her brilliant plan had a gaping hole, and that hole was growing into an abyss.

Tessa's luck had run out.

"What do we do?" she said, not even trying to hide her panic.

—39—

The iron chain and the metal buckle swung towards him. Gawion's eyes followed them as the elf hunter drew nearer. Left or right? Over or under? Forward or—

He swirled and dived backwards into the wall of snow. His enormous, long feet paddled in the air like parallel wings. They propelled him deep into crusty snow. He had escaped.

"Ow!" A hard slap, followed by a stinging, burning pain, travelled the length of his left foot and up his leg. He thrashed with his right foot, digging and sending a spray of icy crystals backwards. But no matter how much he kicked, he could not move forward. Something was holding him back. And he felt weaker.

He continued spraying snow behind him while he enlarged the tunnel with his uninjured hand. And then, looking back, he saw the iron chain. Looped round his left foot, it bit deep into his fur. Even worse, it must be digging into the sensitive skin of his soles. The taut chain stretched out of the tunnel into a pair of human hands, just visible in the hole.

He tried to wiggle out of the chain—it was not fastened—but his foot did not respond. His whole leg was now as sore as his walloping arm. If he used his good hand to remove the chain, he would be left with only one functioning limb. But if he made the chain go slack, it might loosen the hold on his foot. As much as he hated the idea, he had to move back, towards the elf hunter.

Gawion kicked violently with his right leg, pushing a load of icy snow at the human. Then he shifted the angle of his left leg and paddled backwards. He slapped the elf hunter's head with his good foot before he pulled himself back into the tunnel. Had it worked? His left foot remained senseless, but he kept going, unsure of his success until his hand met the hard crust immediately below the surface.

Not completely on purpose, he had dug a zigzagging tunnel—controlling direction with one leg was difficult. When he emerged above the snow, he lay for a while, massaging his left foot with lumps of icy flakes. His walloping arm throbbed and prickled, like the time he had fallen over a cliff into a cluster of snow-dusted brambles. If only he had some blackberries to restore his energy.

"Barbegazi!" the elf hunter called from the hole nearby.

"If you help me out of here, I will not harm you. And I will let your sister go."

As if it had any bargaining power! Gawion stood up on his good leg. His injured foot still burned. When he set it down on the snow, it prickled worse than those thorns from the brambles, and the leg collapsed under his weight. Somehow he stayed standing.

Perhaps he could imitate the strange one-wooden-footed humans he had seen surfing sideways on the slopes.

"Tessa has freed my sister," he said. Had Tessa freed Maeg? Was it waiting for his signal? He could whistle now. That was bound to bring Papa. But his task was not done yet, and if he could manage to complete it without Papa's help... His walloping arm did feel a lot better.

Hopping around on one foot exposed him, so he let himself fall forward. On his stomach, he wiggled to the hole and peeked over the rim.

The metal buckle, with its animal-skin tail, whizzed past his ear.

"Try again, elf hunter!" he called, hoping to goad it into hurling the iron chain.

The human swung the chain. Gawion clambered back. The chain dug into the overhanging snow, tearing fluffy chunks down over the human.

Unfortunately, it was not foolish enough to let go of the chain.

He crept back to the rim. The human stood in the centre—swinging the chain, turning slowly, staring at the top of the walls—prepared for an attack.

Gawion retreated and dug a short tunnel that stopped

just before breaking into the hole. After he returned to the surface, he watched the human make five turns, while he counted in his head.

The elf hunter made one fatal mistake: it kept the speed and direction of its turning constant.

Gawion, still counting, dived into the prepared tunnel and out through the thin snow barrier. With a forceful swipe of his recovered arm, he walloped the elf hunter from behind.

This time he proceeded without hesitation. While he spoke the charm, his fingertips pushed against its temples and his beard hid its stunned expression. A pleasant tingle travelled up his arms, as the elf hunter's recent memories evaporated.

FROM *HABITS & HABITATS: A HISTORIC ACCOUNT OF ALPINE ELVES* BY PROFESSOR, DR EBERHART LUDWIG FRITZ BAHNE

The only known instance of barbegazi surviving more than a few weeks in captivity is recorded by a zookeeper's daughter in Vienna's Tiergarten Schönbrunn.

In a diary entry from January 1862, the girl, Anne, mentions that the avalanche of barbegazi, which had been in the zoological gardens since shortly after the opening of the imperial menagerie in 1752, had escaped during a blizzard.

No one understood how their barred iron cage had been opened. I, of course, revealed nothing, she writes, leading to a belief that she had a hand in their escape.

A February entry strengthens suspicions of a conspiracy. *As I promised Aeglosben, I have destroyed the barbegazi notebooks my father inherited from his predecessors.*

This blatant disregard for unique scientific insight explains why no accounts have been found of where the barbegazi were kept during the summer months, or their dietary needs.

—40—

"I'll get Dad to tell the professor where he parked," Felix said. "We'll invent a reason. Just come on, Tessa."

The adrenaline that had surged through her body all day was used up. The light bundle in her arms had become as heavy as her tired legs. She couldn't face running all the way back to the main road and uphill through the village to Felix's house. And what if the sight that met them there was a sneering elf hunter, with a chain around an avalanche of barbegazi?

"Now." Felix pulled at her sleeve.

They really had to go. She took two tentative steps.

Just then, a piercing whistle reverberated in the valley.

She looked up at Felix.

It was Gawion's whistle. He had succeeded!

The shrill sound roused her. In seconds, her brain filled the gaping hole in her plan with possible solutions. One of them just might work.

Words tumbled out of her mouth: "You have that racing-car computer game, right? And you help your grandfather with the harvest. You can drive a tractor, can't you?"

"What're you getting at?" Felix looked back at the van. "No way. If I scratch it... Oh, man..." Holding his hands up, he took rapid breaths. "Okay, I'll try, okay? But no one can see us."

"They won't. Tinted windows, remember?"

They sprinted to the van. Its engine roared when Felix pressed a button. He adjusted the seat and surveyed the knobs and levers. His hands gripped the steering wheel, the strain visible on his white knuckles, in the light from the instrument panel. Tessa relaxed her own grip on the cold body she was holding, and cradled Maeg in her arms.

"Here goes," Felix muttered. The vehicle sprang forward and rolled along the track out of the old sawmill. Where the track ended, he hesitated before he slowly drove up the main road, staring straight ahead. A car behind them honked. When they turned onto the steep curving road to the village, it didn't follow.

"We need to get the berries from my house," Tessa said.

"No, Tessa. I'm sure Mum has—"

"And you're going to march in and take them?"

Felix didn't answer, but drove down Tessa's street.

"Be quick," he said, as she opened the door.

Leaving Maeg on her seat, she ran to the house, pulling the keys from her pocket. She entered, and, without closing the door, without turning on the lights, ran downstairs in her boots and grabbed a bag of mixed forest berries.

It was only after she had closed the freezer that she noticed the absolute silence. The ticks from the grandfather clock had stopped. No one had been winding it, that was all—surely it meant nothing else. Her fingers found the hole in the paper tissue and touched the snowflake, then she took a deep breath, willing the wave of fear away.

Outside, Felix had turned the vehicle around, and she'd just reached it when someone called, "Tes-sa!"

By the first house on Tessa's street, stood Lisa. With Maria. "We wanted to ask if you—"

"I don't have time now," Tessa shouted. She jumped inside while Felix lifted Maeg. "Go. Just go," she said, taking the fur bundle and hugging it to her chest.

"Hey! Isn't that the van..." The rest of what Lisa was saying was drowned out as Felix accelerated up the street.

Without scratching anything, Felix parked behind his house, by the large pine tree. Gawion wasn't there yet. They sat in silence for a moment, the lifeless bundle warm in Tessa's arms. The few times Gawion had touched her, the icy shock had given her goose pimples.

"She's not cold," Tessa screamed. She sprang out of the van, placed Maeg on the white ground underneath the tree, and began scooping snow over her. They had to cool her down if they were going to find a spark of life and revive her.

If there was life.

"Let me do that," Felix said. "Give her some berries."

Tessa pushed Maeg's beard aside and tried to squeeze a berry into her mouth. A tiny blueberry made it through her clenched lips.

Nothing happened.

Frantically, Felix packed more snow around the small creature. Tessa spilled berries out onto the ground, in her haste to find another miniature one.

"Why's nothing happening? We're too late, Felix!" she said, sinking back on her heels.

Maeg's eyelids fluttered.

They watched, holding their breath, as she swallowed the blueberry.

Tessa exhaled. Maeg was alive.

The little mouth opened and closed, like a baby's searching for milk, and Tessa fed berries into it.

"Maeg," she whispered. "Don't be afraid. Gawion will be here soon."

Maeg blinked. In the gloomy light her dark eyes darted back and forth between Tessa and Felix. Faster than Tessa could feed her, she devoured the berries.

Close by, they heard running footsteps and Lisa calling out.

"Tes-sa! Where are you? Are you okay?" She had stopped by the van in a spot where the twigs didn't quite cover their hiding place.

They scrambled to sit in front of the barbegazi, and the sucking noises she'd made ceased. Tessa got up by putting a hand on Felix's shoulder. She pushed him slightly backwards, and hoped he understood that he had to stay and shield Maeg. Careful to block the opening to their shelter, she pushed through the branches out to Lisa.

"Where's Maria?"

"Waiting for me by the bus stop. What're you doing in there?" Lisa craned her neck to peek behind Tessa.

Could she trust her? She'd so wanted for Lisa to believe her. It would be amazing if they could share the secret of the barbegazi and become best friends again.

But Gawion trusted her. And she trusted herself, now that she knew the barbegazi existed. Perhaps that was enough. Perhaps that was why Opa had never cared if people laughed at him behind his back. Because it was enough that he knew.

"It's nothing," she said. "Just a little surprise for a guest."

Lisa pointed.

"And the van—"

"Has been found," Tessa interrupted. "Thanks for looking for it. Anyway—"

"D'you want to come to my house? We can watch the fireworks together."

"What? Now?" Lisa couldn't have picked a worse time. Why now? Was it because she'd been on the podium? "I have to finish this, erm..."

"Or tomorrow. Whenever you want. I'll even help you look for those elves."

"Maybe. Thanks." It would be so easy to show Maeg to Lisa.

"Bye then..." Lisa's hand rested on Tessa's arm, before she turned and walked away.

Tessa looked after her until she rounded the corner.

As soon as Lisa was gone, a low whistle sounded nearby.

From underneath the tree, Maeg whistled in answer.

Felix crawled out into the open, gasping, and the strangest thing Tessa had ever seen came into view, behind him. Gawion and another barbegazi carried the professor on their shoulders, as if he were a decaying log. They also threw him on the ground like a log, and Bahne rolled twice before coming to a stop by his van's back wheels.

"Out of my sight, elf hunter," said a voice much deeper than Gawion's. The stocky barbegazi cast a fleeting glance at them before he ducked under the branches of the pine tree.

"Papa," Maeg peeped.

Gawion smiled. "The elf hunter's heavy," he said, nodding towards the white heap. "Good thing Papa came when I whistled my long-distance signal."

A bark announced the arrival of Brownie. Gawion answered with barks of his own.

"Good dog." Felix rubbed the big dog's pleated neck.

Brownie and Gawion barked some short laughter-like coughs, and Felix stared open-mouthed from one to the other.

When Gawion barked again, Brownie sped off.

"What did you tell him? I've never seen him run so fast," Tessa said.

"I wanted to present him to my father. But Papa is fearful of dogs, and I might have confused the barks for scared and scary." Gawion shook his head. "The local Dog dialect is tricky..."

Bahne moaned.

"We'd better get him away from here," Felix said. "Help me, Tessa."

Somehow they got the professor upright. He was humming a tune. Tessa sneaked the chain over his head, and Felix put the car key back in his pocket, while they supported him to the front door.

"*Take me home,*" Bahne sang out, and hiccuped. "*Country roooaaads.*"

At the top of the steps, they let go, and he slumped, then slid down onto the bottom step. Felix rang the doorbell until Aunt Annie appeared.

"What's this racket?" She saw Bahne and frowned.

He leant against the steps and bent his head back until he could see her upside-down, then he broke out in song again. "*Mu-mu-mummy... take me home.*"

"Mr Bahne," Aunt Annie said, her cheeks flushing a deep red. "I had not expected this kind of behaviour from you." She marched down and tugged hard on his arm. "Felix, let's get this drunk to his room."

Tessa watched them hobble up the stairs. Aunt Annie was ranting about alcohol, and skis being stolen if you left them outside bars, and proper behaviour. Bahne kept humming and singing "*Take me home*". His voice wasn't bad.

Just as she started back towards Gawion from the front steps, a car pulled up next to her. Mum jumped out and hugged her, laughing and crying at the same time.

"It's a miracle," she squealed. "Oma's so much better. She might not even need the surgery." Mum held Tessa in her outstretched arms and smiled. "Your little crossword puzzle cheered her up immensely! Perhaps you can make her another?"

Tessa nodded and wiped a tear away. In her mind, she began laying Scrabble tiles for *barbegazi, rescue, snowflake, stamina*, and all the other things she wanted Oma to know. Fitting everything into one secret message was going to be difficult.

"Then you can give it to her when she comes home on Monday."

"On Monday?" Tessa felt a smile growing across her face. She hugged Mum tight.

Gawion was waving to Tessa, from where he stood by the pine. He waved her closer. Behind Mum's back, Tessa made hand signals, trying to gauge whether Mum was allowed to see him. He nodded.

"Come," Mum said, taking Tessa's hand, "Let's go inside and give Annie the good news."

"I'll be right there, Mum. I just have to say goodbye to the barbegazi."

Mum's face fell.

"Tessa, no. Don't start that again."

Tessa swung Mum around, so she faced Gawion.

Mum just stared at him.

"Another miracle," she mumbled.

Tessa ran over to Gawion, crouched and embraced him.

"Thank you," she said, trying to cram all her happiness into those two words.

"Thank you, Tessa. Papa said I can bring you to see our caves." Gawion clung to her, making her shiver with cold. "If you had not found us, Maeg would not have survived."

She drew back, new anxiety rising inside her.

"But what if other humans find you?"

"Just bring them to me. I am getting quite adept at memory charms."

Tessa giggled. Part of being a secret barbegazi protector meant she'd become a specialized mountain guide. The kind who arranged covert excursions for people who knew about the barbegazi. Until suddenly they didn't.

Above them, the sky exploded in red sparkles. The year was ending, but not the winter. Tomorrow she'd visit their caves, and, before the snow melted and the barbegazi hid away to aestivate, surely she'd see Gawion surf on an avalanche.

ACKNOWLEDGEMENTS

I'm immensely grateful to Sarah Odedina for her encouragement and high expectations during the last couple of years, and for helping me find and shape the heart of this story. To Tilda Johnson for her thoughtful line and copy edits. And to the wonderful team at Pushkin Press for transforming my barbegazi tale into a beautiful book.

Massive thanks to my friends in SCBWI, Cafe Schreiber in Zurich and The Singapore Writers' Group for helping me learn and grow as a writer. I'm especially indebted to my early readers and those who listened to my endless barbegazi monologues: Jo Furniss, Sherida Deeprose, Helena Ryan, Rebecca Foreman, Catherine Carvell, Emma Nicholson, Annette Woschek and Dorte Sidelmann Rossen. A special thanks to the Asian Festival of Children's Content for creating inspiring conferences and providing brilliant opportunities for writers and illustrators, such as the one that connected me with Sarah Odedina.

An avalanche of hugs to the dedicated ski coaches, enthusiastic parents and tireless ski-club kids from my time in Trainingsgemeinschaft Stanzertal and all my other friends in St Anton. This book would not exist if I had not spent hours on the Schöngraben T-bar lift, watching my sons at race practice and gazing at the white wilderness (without binoculars), daydreaming about encounters with fantastical creatures. Any resemblance to real people and buildings is purely coincidental, but I have tried to stay faithful to the wondrous landscape on Arlberg, with the minor addition of a small glacier in the vicinity.

Last, but not least, infinite thanks to my father, who raised me to believe I could do anything, and my mother, who fed me fairy tales and passed her love of books on to me. To Marcus, who heard about this story first, for his suggestions, and August, who read it first, for his ski racing insights. Finally, to Claus, my teammate in life, who listens to all my implausible plans and supports most of them. Even when I had doubts, he always believed in my dream of becoming an author.

PUSHKIN CHILDREN'S BOOKS

We created Pushkin Children's Books to share tales from different languages and cultures with younger readers, and to open the door to the wide, colourful worlds these stories offer.

From picture books and adventure stories to fairy tales and classics, and from fifty-year-old bestsellers to current huge successes abroad, the books on the Pushkin Children's list reflect the very best stories from around the world, for our most discerning readers of all: children.